AF173853

BANDI
A LIFE IN CHAINS
JEEVAN

BANDI JEEVAN
A LIFE IN CHAINS

Sachindra Nath Sanyal

Introduced by

Sanjeev Sanyal

RUPA

Published by
Rupa Publications India Pvt. Ltd 2023
7/16, Ansari Road, Daryaganj
New Delhi 110002

Sales centres:
Bengaluru Chennai Hyderabad
Jaipur Kathmandu Kolkata
Mumbai Prayagraj

Translation credit: Maneesha Taneja

P-ISBN: 978-93-5702-563-8
E-ISBN: 978-93-5702-565-2

First impression 2023

10 9 8 7 6 5 4 3 2 1

Printed in India

CONTENTS

Part 3

The Revolutionary Movement in India after 1920

INTRODUCTION

This is the first time that Sachindra Nath Sanyal's famous autobiography *Bandi Jeevan* (*A Life in Chains* or *A Life in Captivity*) has been translated into English. The book is interesting not merely as the personal testimony of a key leader of the armed resistance to British colonial rule in India, but it is notable as it played an influential role in inspiring subsequent generations of revolutionaries across the country. Indeed, it provides a direct insight into the ideas and personality of a freedom fighter who inspired and mentored the likes of Bhagat Singh, Rajendra Lahiri, Chandrashekhar Azad, Ram Prasad Bismil, Ashfaqullah Khan and many others.

An important motivation for Sanyal to write this autobiography was to leave behind a first-hand account so that future generations would be able to know the truth about the revolutionaries, their activities and their motivations. In the preface to the first edition, Sanyal writes: 'I am leaving behind my testimony in this book so that these chapters of Indian history can be truthfully written in future.'

It appears that Sanyal had a premonition that the history of the revolutionaries would not be properly told or perhaps be suppressed. As it turned out, the role of armed resistance in India's freedom struggle would be deliberately diminished in the official histories written after Independence.* Until

---

*Sanyal, Sanjeev, *Revolutionaries: The Other Story of How India Won Its Freedom*, HarperCollins, Gurugram, 2023.

interest in the revolutionary movement revived in recent years, the story of the freedom struggle came to be told exclusively from the perspective of the non-violent movement led by the 'moderate' wing of the Indian National Congress. It is extraordinary that the revolutionaries in 1920s had a hunch that this would happen.

A more immediate motivation for writing the book was Sanyal's observation that there was a severe paucity of writings at that time that expressed an indigenous view of India's history and of its place in the world. Most of the narrative was dominated by a European worldview or by 'moderate' Indians who carefully toed the official line. Thus, he wanted to create an ecosystem of literature that would inspire a more militant resistance to British colonial occupation. Interestingly, a century later, a very similar line of thought would lead me to take up the study of Indian history. Exasperated by the persistent monopoly of western, colonial and Marxist narratives, I, too, would explore India's long civilizational history and try to encourage many young writers to do the same. It is extraordinary how the ideas of a grand-uncle, whom I have never met, subliminally moulded so much of my own thinking.

The first version of the book was originally written by Sanyal in the early 1920s after he returned from his first stint in the infamous Cellular Jail in Port Blair. This early version was mostly about his activities during the Ghadarite phase of the revolutionary movement (c. 1910–15) and his subsequent imprisonment in the Cellular Jail. However, Sanyal would later expand the book to include events of the 1920s—his efforts to rebuild the revolutionary movement, his marriage, the formation of the Hindustan Republican Association (HRA) and so on. This translation is of the fourth edition, which was expanded in 1938 after he returned to the mainland, having spent 10 years in the Andamans on his second stint. It does not, therefore, include the final phase of his revolutionary activities (1937–42) when he worked with Netaji Subhas Chandra Bose and Rashbehari Bose even as the clouds of World War II were gathering on the horizon. Oddly, it also says little about his second stint in the Cellular Jail.

The book was originally written in Bengali, although a Hindi translation was produced under Sanyal's personal supervision (as a Varanasi-based Bengali, his Hindi was quite good). It is also known to have been translated into several Indian languages by his followers as a part of the revolutionary literature circulating in pre-Independence India, but, as far as we know, there is no extant English translation of the full document. (We do know from British intelligence reports that Sanyal was trying to get one published, but he seems to have been thwarted.) Therefore, this translation is an important addition to the corpus available in English related to India's struggle for freedom.

As a primary eyewitness account from an important protagonist, the translation has been done as close as possible to the original. There is no attempt to 'correct' the narrative for possible inconsistencies or for opinions that may be today considered politically incorrect. This is an artefact of history and should be treated as such. Nonetheless, the reader should be aware of a number of issues when reading this book.

First, Sachindra Nath Sanyal wrote about events that had occurred from memory, often years after the events had taken place. As a person who was either in prison or on the run for much of his life, he did not have the luxury of detailed notes. He was also functioning under the fog of war and may not have been fully aware of many things. Therefore, there are instances in the book that may not exactly match other accounts of the same events. To be fair, the same can be said of those other accounts as well. Thus, *Bandi Jeevan* should be treated as the account of a participant in the middle of historic events rather than the post facto narration of a historian.

Second, the book was written while India was still under British rule and Sanyal was still an active revolutionary leader. Thus, there are many places where he deliberately leaves out names and events that may incriminate individuals and get them in trouble with British authorities. It is interesting, therefore, to triangulate Sanyal's descriptions of events with accounts written by surviving revolutionaries after Independence (see for instance, Jogesh Chandra Chatterjee's *In Search of Freedom**).

Third, the original *Bandi Jeevan* was expanded at different times, and did not have the benefit of professional editing (after all, it was underground revolutionary literature). Therefore, the language is not always tight, and there are meanderings that would not have been allowed by a modern editor. Nonetheless, these shortcomings do provide the text with a 'raw' quality that adds to its authenticity. No attempt has been made to 'improve' the text.

Fourth, there are many instances where Sanyal assumes knowledge of people and places that were well known in his time but may be unclear to today's reader. An attempt has been made here to provide a clarification where required, but there are some references that cannot be easily identified. These have just been translated as stated. Readers are welcome to provide feedback if they feel something is incorrect. Subsequent editions of the translation will try to incorporate the changes.

---

*Chatterjee, Jogesh Chandra, *In Search of Freedom*, Paresh Chandra Chatterjee, 1958.

In spite of the above caveats, *Bandi Jeevan* is a wonderfully readable autobiography of a remarkable man on a mission. In order to understand him, it is useful to have some background about his family as well as the socio-political milieu that shaped him.

Sachindra Nath Sanyal came from a family of Bengali scholars who were renowned for their knowledge of the Rig Veda and the Nyaya school of Hindu philosophy. The Sanyal clan had originated from a belt loosely known as Barendrabhumi in north-central Bengal, comprising Dinajpur, Rajshahi, Natore and Pabna, and the adjoining areas of Nadia and Kushtia. Most of this area is now in Bangladesh. Since medieval times, the Sanyals had a reputation for being scholars as well as participating in armed rebellions. The clan was said to have resisted the Turkic, Afghan and Mughal occupations of Bengal continuously over generations using the riverine landscape of the region for guerrilla warfare. At the same time, the Sanyals had been ardent followers of Shakta Hinduism (that is, dedicated to the worship of warrior goddesses such as Durga and Kali) and had played an important role in reviving the Nyaya (that is, rationalist) school of Hindu philosophy. This combination of activities provides an interesting context for ideas presented in *Bandi Jeevan*. In 'Foreword to the Fourth Edition', Sanyal reflected on all these influences when he wrote about his fascination for Chhatrapati Shivaji's guerrilla resistance, the strong attachments to Indian philosophical traditions and the importance of a modern, rationalist impulse to revive India's civilizational energy.

In the late eighteenth century, Sanyal's ancestors Lakshmi Kanta Siddhanta and his son Ramkumar Nyayalankar, both well-known scholars, moved from Belur in Bengal to Varanasi.

This was a time when the sacred city was being rebuilt, after centuries of persecution and destruction under Turkic and Mughal rulers, with the generous support of Maratha nobility, most notably Ahilyabai Holkar. Less remembered are the contributions of wealthy Bengalis, such as Rani Bhabani of Natore, and later Rani Rashmoni, who also supported the building of temples and Vedic schools in the city. The Sanyal family's move to Varanasi was part of this Bengali contribution to rebuilding the sacred city.

The Sanyal family settled in the Madanpura area in Varanasi, near the Shava Shiva Kali temple established in 1789. The family would go on to become the core of a significant Bengali community that came to settle in the neighbourhood. Ramkumar Nyayalankar, his son Devnarayan Vachaspati and his grandson Ishwar Chandra Vidyalankar* were among the most respected Vedic scholars of the early nineteenth century. They ran a traditional school (called a '*tola*'). Thus, the neighbourhood came to be known as Bengali Tola. The Sanyals, over time, would inter-marry other Bengali settlers such as the Lahiri family. In this way, the narrow lanes of Bengali Tola came to house an intricate web of family and friends by the mid-nineteenth century.

The early nineteenth century had been a troubled time for India. Having felled the Maratha Empire, the British had emerged as the dominant power in the country. This had led to economic exploitation as well as cultural domination by the British. Although resistance simmered till the Revolt of 1857, by the 1840s, it would have been clear to most Indians that they were dealing with a European industrial power that had technological and economic capabilities far in excess of what they possessed. It was soon accompanied by growing

*Also called Ishwar Chandra Nyayaratna

Christian missionary activity. This elicited different responses from the Indians.

The response in Bengal ranged from that of the westernising Brahmos led by Ram Mohan Roy to that of the ultra-orthodox. In this spectrum, the Sanyal clan's response was that of modernizing revivalism. They agreed with the need for rapid social reforms and adoption of modern ideas (which included learning English), but, at the same time, also emphasized the need to preserve ancient religious traditions. The modernist, revivalist stream in Bengal was supported by Rani Rashmoni, a wealthy businesswoman who provided large sums to this project and built the Dakshineshwar temple near Kolkata. This particular response to British domination eventually led to the emergence of thinkers such as Swami Vivekananda and Sri Aurobindo.

Although the Sanyal clan lived in faraway Varanasi, it was very much part of the intellectual developments taking place in nineteenth-century Bengal. One of the major concerns had been the acquisition of modern education without being beholden to Christian missionaries. In 1854, the Sanyals helped establish a school in Varanasi called Bengali Tola Intercollege, where modern science and English were taught. It was among the first 'modern' schools in North India and continues to function to this day.

It is also in this context that we must consider the contributions of Shyama Charan Lahiri, widely regarded as a saint by his myriad followers. He lived in Bengali Tola in the mid-nineteenth century and was married to Ishwar Chandra's sister (hence, he was Sachindra Nath Sanyal's grand-uncle). Lahiri gave Kriya Yoga its modern form and openly popularized it; it was earlier an esoteric practice. This, too, was part of the cultural response to colonial domination. This long history of cultural resistance explains the strong civilizational pride and unapologetic assertion of a Hindu worldview that is reflected in *Bandi Jeevan*.

Ishwar Chandra Vidyalankar had four sons: Umesh, Vishnu, Harikeshab and Harinath. Sachindra Nath Sanyal, born in 1893, was the eldest of Harinath's four sons. The other sons—Rabindra Nath, Jitendra Nath and Bhupendra Nath—would also participate actively in the revolutionary movement. So would many other members of the wider Sanyal clan, including the women, who contributed in keeping alive the effort over half a century by carrying secret messages, fighting court cases and providing shelter and financial support. The British would try to break this web of support by forcibly evicting the Sanyal family from Bengali Tola in 1927 following the Kakori case. The family would shift to Prayagraj (then called Allahabad) and Gorakhpur, where they continued to engage in revolutionary activities.

Sachindra Nath Sanyal's foray into the world of revolutionaries began in 1908, when, at 15, he set up a gymnasium for physical training called *akhada*, inspired by the Anushilan Samiti. The akhada was an open area with few trees and a platform where young men gathered to practise wrestling and other martial arts. Note, however, that he was also perpetuating the other old family profession. There was a small room containing religious books and revolutionary writings. After many twists and turns, one of the old Sanyal family akhadas survives as the Central Physical Institute, established in 1944, in the lanes of Bengali Tola. The only other reminders of the Sanyal family are Bengali Tola Intercollege and the home of Shyama Charan Lahiri that continues to be a shrine to the yogi. His is the only house that the British did not confiscate in 1927.

This introduction is not meant to summarize *Bandi Jeevan*.

The book narrates the exciting sequence of events during the attempted Ghadarite revolt planned by Rashbehari Bose; the first round of incarceration in the Cellular Jail; the return to the mainland; his struggles while rebuilding the revolutionary network; and the establishment of the HRA. This phase ended with Sanyal being sent back to Cellular Jail for another ten years.

What make the book especially interesting to read are his vivid descriptions of certain events—the furtive meetings with potential rebels in the British Indian Army in 1914–15; his journey on a small country boat through raging monsoon floods to a secret gathering of top revolutionary leaders in Mymensingh in 1923; his inner struggles, especially his guilt for having left behind his young wife and small children in the pursuit of a national cause. The book also provides a live testimony of someone witnessing various political and social changes of that time. Sanyal expresses his indignation at the casual attitude of certain Congress leaders towards the fate of incarcerated revolutionaries. Similarly, he is genuinely surprised that the same Sikh community who had imbibed Ghadarite ideas of rebellion were also simultaneously susceptible to British attempts to separate the Sikh identity from the Hindus. More generally, he wonders how Punjab had produced both the most passionate freedom fighters and the most treacherous collaborators. Thus, *Bandi Jeevan* provides a good sense of the messiness of history from the perspective of an important participant who is still engaged with the uncertainties of his times.

When the foreword to the fourth edition of the autobiography was written in 1938, he had just returned from his second stint in the Andamans. At that time, Sanyal was very concerned about the spread of Marxism, an ideology that he instinctively disliked. This is quite remarkable because this was before the economic costs of communism and the human cost of Stalinist purges was well known. Although he was sympathetic to some of the egalitarian objectives of the ideology, it appears that Sanyal disapproved of the dry materialism of Marxism and was not convinced of dialectic materialism as an explanation of history: 'There were other principles of Marxism that I do not agree with—among them the view that the manifestation of history is driven purely by economic factors, and this explains the origin of every kind of civilization in the world. I could not accept this.'

What worried him was that several of his followers seemed to have adopted some shade of Marxist thinking during his long absence. This was not just an ideological problem. The Indian communist movement of the 1930s was controlled by British and Russian proxies who were willing to sacrifice the goal of Indian Independence in favour of other objectives. Indeed, Indian communists would actively collaborate with the British during World War II against the nationalists.*

As this autobiography was last updated in 1938, it does not include Sanyal's activities in the run up to World War II; it does not even say much about his second stint in Cellular Jail from 1927 to 1937. Perhaps Sanyal would have added these to the story in a fifth edition or in a new book. Since these were live underground developments, it is understandable that he would have been reluctant to write them down at that time. As it turned out, he was arrested in 1940 when the British found out that he was in touch with the Japanese envoy and plotting something along with Netaji Subhas Chandra Bose and Rashbehari Bose.

---

*Sanyal, Sanjeev, *Revolutionaries: The Other Story of How India Won Its Freedom*, HarperCollins, Gurugram, 2023.

Although Sanyal was a senior leader who was eligible for an individual prison cell, the British deliberately placed him in a cell with a dying tuberculosis patient. As a result, Sanyal contracted the disease that was then considered incurable. He was not released even as his health rapidly deteriorated. Only when it was clear that he would not live much longer, he was allowed to go home. He died in Gorakhpur on 6 February 1942. Thus, he did not live to see the culmination of his life-long efforts—the formation of the Indian National Army in 1943 and, finally, the Naval Revolt of 1946 that directly led to India winning its independence.

Sachindra Nath Sanyal is one of the towering figures of the revolutionary strand of India's independence movement. He inspired and organized entire generations of Indian revolutionaries including Rajendra Lahiri, Ram Prasad Bismil, Ashfaqullah Khan, Bhagat Singh, Chandrashekhar Azad, Surya Sen and so on. Uniquely, he was a key part of virtually every generation of the movement from the early Anushilan Samiti phase, through the Ghadarite and HRA phases, and eventually to the revival during World War II. His networks extended from Lahore and Delhi in the northwest, to Varanasi, Prayagraj and Lucknow in the United Provinces, to Kolkata, Behrampur, Chattogram and Chandan Nagar (spelled in the translation as Chandernagore) in Bengal. Through associates like Rashbehari Bose in Japan, he was also in touch with the global network of Indian nationalists. Although he did not live to see the final Naval Uprising of 1946, Sanyal was the key thread that connected the movement both geographically and over time.

It is often forgotten that Sanyal was among the first to clearly articulate the vision that post-Independence India would be a democratic republic based on universal franchise. He stated this unambiguously in the constitution of the HRA in 1924, at a time when the Indian National Congress was still demanding limited freedoms under dominion status, and when few countries in the world allowed women to vote. Even a hundred years later, his ideas sound refreshingly contemporary.

Also important is the fact that Sanyal, one of the chief architects of armed resistance to the British Empire, was not an advocate of random anarchist violence. He makes this clear when he discusses his intellectual differences with another group in Bengal. Armed resistance had to be organized and targeted, as well as have a clear-end goal of triggering a large-scale rebellion. This distinction is important in case someone tries to interpret the revolutionaries as anarchists or proto-Naxalites. Sanyal was clear that a disciplined organization and clear ideals were needed to both win freedom and then build a democratic republic. This is why he created the HRA as an umbrella body and, despite his differences with the Gandhian faction, continued to engage with the Indian National Congress.

Let me conclude by saying that this translation would not have been possible without the support and encouragement of the Sanyal family, especially my father Jayanta Sanyal who had kept alive many family memories, my cousin Saurabh Sanyal who dug up valuable documents and photographs, and my uncle Surajit Sanyal, who helped clarify key points. I would also like to thank translator Maneesha Taneja, who diligently worked on the manuscript through the Covid years. These were difficult times, but she showed tremendous spirit by persevering through it. And finally, thanks to Yamini, Smita and Aurodeep, the ever-enthusiastic editors who pulled it all together.

Sanjeev Sanyal
July 2023

TRANSLATOR'S NOTE

Translation in all its forms is a great teacher, fostering a critical engagement with difference. In my journey of learning from this great teacher, and I must add, a most cherished one, I have lived with Sachindra Nath Sanyal's *Bandi Jeevan: A Life in Chains* for two years.

What does autobiographical translation entail? And how should it be handled differently from any other type of translation, if any differently at all? In relation to the translator, autobiographical translation necessitates preciseness. It should, however, also not be a word-for-word translation. Autobiographical translation involves a sort of translator's pact, in which the translator has a duty to present events faithfully through expressing the source text faithfully and, at the same time, make these original events comprehensible to their audience.

As for the readers, what are they receiving when they read the translation of an autobiographical text? They simply obtain a re-imaged copy of source text, which is accurate due to the translator's code of ethics. In opposition to forms of fiction, biography and autobiography are referential texts—they claim to convey information about a 'reality' that is external to the text and, hence, subject to the test of verification. History has many versions, and it is important we read all to understand our past.

It was a difficult work to translate, mainly because I was working from a text that had been originally written in

Bengali, and the language of the Hindi translation was dated and Sanskritized in a way that I found difficult to understand and decode. The handicap was a result of a generation gap between languages and not having access to the original to cross check with.

At many places in the text, the religious affiliation of people is highlighted as a descriptor, as was common at that time. Today, however, this would be considered politically incorrect except where it was necessary; so it was time to take a call on its use in the translation. It didn't always serve any purpose and could be easily removed in the translation. But what right did I have to edit and remove references that the original writer had put in? It also reflects the times he was talking about and a long history of religious markers. As a translator, I kept in mind these political and social histories and decided to leave the religious markers in the translation.

I do not know Bengali, and the one difficulty I had was figuring out names. That is when I wished for the original, so that some of them would seem clearer. It appears that in the Hindi version of the text, the Bengali names have been domesticated to Hindi usage and, therefore, to understand the original references required hard research! For example, it took me a while to figure out that Rabi Babu was Rabindranath Tagore! Additionally, while translating, I realized that 'Arvind' referred to Aurobindo, and have thus retained the original Bengali name.

At many instances, there were references to people participating in the freedom movement by just their first names. It seemed lazy to not find out their proper identities and put full names there so as to give them their due and importance. This was rather a tough job and meant a lot of reading on the freedom movement/struggle to identify and find all these people. I was rather proud of having done this and felt it was my little tribute to people who never got the fame and name that they deserved. I learnt about Pratul Ganguly, Jaichandra Vidyalankar, Sardar Gurmukh Singh, Barindra Ghosh, Upendra Nath Bandyopadhyay and Hem Chandra Kanungo.

There were many references to events, which seemed vague as there were no dates mentioned. For example, at one place he mentions 'the earlier revolution'. I could not put a date to it as, despite a lot of research, I could not figure out what he was specifically referring to! There are many quotes which one is not sure where they are taken from … Some of them we could find the source and give citations, the others we just accepted at face value!

At the level of cultural references, should I turn the 'Shri' into 'Mr' or let it be 'Shri'? What do I do with the 'ji' suffixed to names for respect? Do I use 'ahimsa' or 'non-violence' in English? These are some of the challenges that I faced as a translator. I could go on and talk about so many things but then my note will be as long as the book itself! I leave it you my reader to judge my efforts.

Suffice it to say that translation makes the strange familiar. The utmost satisfaction lies in finding a voice that walks alongside the original and manages to keep in step with it. There is joy in finding the right words, phrases and sentences.

I have translated many writers between Hindi, Spanish and English, and my fervent hope is that each of them has a distinct voice in the translated works—and that none of those voices is mine. I hope I have been able to bring across Sachindra Nath Sanyal's voice to the people he fought for and gave his life to.

I would like to acknowledge here the tremendous support extended to me and the confidence reposed in me by Sanjeev

Sanyal to take on a task he holds dear. I am grateful for his help through the translation.

I wish to extend a word of thanks to all those who made this possible. Thank you, Minakshi Thakur, for trusting me to do the most difficult translations! My family has always been the wind beneath my wings. My mom Dipali Taneja is my sounding board for all literary activities. She reads all that I write and translate and always has valuable suggestions. My dad Vinod Taneja asked everyday about how much I still had left to work on. Suveesha and Aman did their all to make life easy and keep me supplied with goodies to eat and drink. Anand helped me with any poetic references and material that I came across. Sukanti relieved me of housekeeping chores. My dog Chhotu passed away when I was working on the translation after diligently keeping me company in his bed plonked next to my desk. I missed him while I finished the work. Poco Loco and Billo have provided the required circus.

Ashutosh, as always, has been my biggest cheerleader. He explained all historical references that I had missed and helped me make sense of Hindi where it seemed incomprehensible. All my love and huge thanks.

I hope this book reaches a wide audience and is a reminder of what it took to achieve our freedom, the struggle that it was and the sacrifices that it entailed. May we cherish that freedom and never undermine it or squander it.

FOREWORD TO THE FOURTH EDITION

(Written in 1938 after Sachindra Nath Sanyal returned from his second stint in the Cellular Jail)

I started writing *Bandi Jeevan: A Life in Chains* 16 years ago. In the foreword to the first edition, I had written, 'I think the book will have three volumes, but I don't know with my involvement in complicated matters how much of the book I will be able to write. The reason being that for some reason I have never been able to complete any task that I have undertaken.' I wrote these sentences in Calcutta on 25 August 1922. Strange are the ways of destiny! Before I had been able to complete two volumes of the book, I was once again dragged off to prison. Today, 16 years later, I am editing the book.

I returned from the Andamans in February 1920. After I came back, I got involved in a brick kiln business on the insistence of my mother and brothers. Only someone who has truly suffered will understand what it is to be stuck in a business. It was during this difficult time that I started writing *Bandi Jeevan: A Life in Chains*. Sometime later, I left the business and, in 1921, I went to Jamshedpur to work with the Labour Association.

I wanted to write the book slowly and take my time publishing it. But a friend of mine, Mr Hemant Kumar Sarkar, took a handwritten draft of the manuscript to a magazine. At the time, Hemant Kumar was a trusted aide of

Deshbandhu C.R. Das. In those days, Mr Das was the editor of a monthly magazine called *Narayan*. Hemant Kumar oversaw the publication of this magazine. I was not sure my work was worth publishing. However, Hemant Kumar had convinced me that it was and that he would get it published in *Narayan*. That is how I started to write *Bandi Jeevan: A Life in Chains*.

Meanwhile, I had to contribute regularly to a monthly magazine. I was also busy with my work for the Labour Association. Therefore, I could not write my book regularly.

Today, as I sit down to edit the book once again, my mind is flooded with a thousand different thoughts and feelings. India is changing rapidly with the times, and with the clash of emerging principles, the nation faces new problems today. When I started my work in politics, there were many obstacles to surmount. But I overcame those problems, and today, I am faced with a fresh set of difficulties. I cannot describe my present situation without clarifying the difference between the problems of the past and the present. And I cannot write the foreword to this book without referring to the clash of principles in this modern era.

Although I do not wish to write about personal matters, I will nonetheless have to mention some details of my private life to talk about my state of mind here.

When I was a small boy, for various reasons, I had resolved that India had to be liberated and that I would dedicate my entire life to this endeavour. There is a story to how I came to feel this way, but I will speak of it elsewhere. Around the time I started working with an organization with revolutionary ideas in Banaras, I befriended a young man who was the same age as me. As I write this today, this man is in Calcutta. It is a stroke of luck and a mystery how such friendships come about. A friend just appears beside you who will stand next to you for life. The moment you meet, you share a feeling of warmth. One haggles and buys many things in life, but what is priceless and most cherished comes to you serendipitously. I had found one such friend, but soon, we had strong differences of opinion.

I had already made a resolution to rid India of foreign rule, and for that, I knew I had to secretly marshal arms and people. I used to think of Shivaji as the ideal man. When Father would ask me what I wished to do in life, I used to say that I wanted to be like Shivaji or that I wanted to lead a life like Napoleon's. But my friend's outlook on life had now confused me. We must have been about 15 or 16 years old then. But he had chosen the life of an ascetic—to live alone, meditating, shunning any contact with society. For me, it was impossible to dissociate from social work. My friend tried to convince me that the ultimate aim of human life is to be one with God. How can one work for the welfare of one's society, he argued, without having encountered God? How can we choose the right path without experiencing truth? Only when we encounter God can we understand what is truth, and what is untruth, or what is good and what is evil. Social work sans communion with God is like the blind trying to lead the blind. Our work in society will be useful once we take God's blessings and directions. While arguing his points, my friend mentioned the autobiographies of Swami Vivekananda and Ramakrishna Paramhans.

I was at crossroads in life. I couldn't abandon society and I didn't want to leave my friend, but my friend was not willing to walk my path and I wasn't willing to walk his. We wrestled with this conundrum for six months. Teenage friendships have a strange charm. We were not able to renounce the friendship, nor were we able to reconcile our differences. Today, my friend is still an ascetic, a *sanyasi*, and I am still doing what I have always wanted to do.

On my friend's recommendation, I read the biographies of Swami Vivekananda and Ramakrishna Paramhans. I thought about their philosophies seriously. I read them again and again with the help of translations of the Gita and the Upanishads. I spent time with ascetics of all persuasions. I tried my best to understand the Hindu tradition of living. There is no doubt that I benefitted greatly from the company of sages and saints, but it did not give me the satisfaction that I sought. I didn't understand why these great men of our society did not participate in social life. Why weren't they active in social work? In the company of saints and sanyasis, I realized that they only pray and are not willing to do anything else. In fact, they don't even want to transcribe their experience of prayer in a book and share it with people. They are imbued with the spirit of sacrifice, and they are industrious, determined and dedicated, but they do not want to be involved in social life.

If our ancestors, too, had been like them, I thought to myself, we would not have had Panini's grammar, neither the Vedas nor the Upanishads, neither astronomy nor mathematics nor Ayurveda! However noble-minded these *sadhus* were, I suspected that they didn't have the brilliance or the thorough vision of the ancients who had laid the foundation in our country of a flourishing civilization. No, I was not satisfied. The Gita's lesson of 'karma' comforted me, as did the Upanishads. In Vivekananda, I found voice for the life of an ascetic who was also a '*karmayogi*', but I did not get any substantial proof that the only way to truth was through karma.

Over time, I concluded that this meant that we could choose our path according to our nature and ability, and no path was better or worse, longer or shorter. The path we chose for ourselves would be the right path and all the others would be wrong. Walking other paths would surely bring some misfortune or the other. The question now was: how do I determine my nature and which path is best suited to it? Through my association with sadhus and study of the scriptures, I understood that there were three ways to determine this—one, using one's intellect and powers of reasoning and reflection; two, with the help of a true guru or guide; and three, the scriptures. The three must come together. Merely reading the scriptures wouldn't do. For one thing, there are so many scriptures that one would first have to choose amongst them. Besides, the scriptures, too, were based on the individual perception of various great men who had experienced truth by walking different paths. Therefore, in addition to the scriptures, I needed a teacher, a guide. But finding a guru would not be enough. If the disciple wasn't good, what could the teacher do? Also, would I have to decide who my teacher would be? In the end, I told myself that perhaps what mattered most was one's ability to think.

Yet I could not do anything contrary to my nature. In the Indian tradition, the first requirement of searching for truth is to make oneself objective. It is not possible to achieve ultimate enlightenment without being completely dispassionate. In reality, it is almost impossible to be so. In order to attain this state of objectivity, one must be completely selfless and alienated from passion. To be dispassionate is not to be without passion for anything but to reach a state where one controls the passions rather than being controlled by them. One should, therefore, be free of all worldly attachments and obligations while embarking on the search for truth. That is the essence of asceticism in the Indian tradition. I have reached this conclusion after interacting with sadhus and sages and reading ancient literature.

My friend and I chose different paths after six months of severe conflict. Later, I saw that millions of our brothers, invoking such Indian principles and using 'spiritual' excuses, but in reality motivated by their selfishness and enslavement to their meaner instincts, chose not to participate in the Indian freedom struggle. For such spiritualists, there was no barrier to having a home life—they are happy; they eat and drink, shop, marry, have children and work to earn a living. What I mean to say is that they live a full, normal life in this material world, but when it comes to participating in politics, they cite the call of spirituality and hide their cowardice under its guise.

Let me talk of my first mental conflict in political life. My heartfelt desire for my country was for a great man to be born who would unite the characteristics of Shivaji and Guru Ram Das, someone who was both enlightened and a dedicated worker for the cause. I was fixated on the idea that what the nationalist struggle lacked was the spirit of true dedication and that the country could only progress when work life would be suffused with esoteric knowledge. But I had not found my ideal leader in real life. If a person like Swami Vivekananda or Swami Ram Teertha became a leader in the Indian revolutionary movement, I would have been happy indeed. In Mr Aurobindo Ghosh, I found the shadow of my illusory great man. I went to Pondicherry in 1911 to meet him, but unfortunately, the meeting did not take place. I will talk about this elsewhere. Ultimately, I ended up in a revolutionary group, the leaders of which were strongly influenced by Aurobindo's philosophy. There has not been a greater satisfaction in life for me.

Without this background to my inner conflict, my readers

may not understand certain portions of *Bandi Jeevan: A Life in Chains*. It was with this mental conditioning and thought process that I worked in the revolutionary movement, went to prison, then to the Cellular Jail, and came back.

In 1920, when I came back from the Andamans, Mahatma Gandhi had already made his appearance in national politics. The Indian revolutionary movement faced a great many obstacles due to Gandhi's policy of ahimsa, and his towering personality and active participation in the freedom movement. The Mahatma preached that the Indian revolutionary movement was not in sync with ancient Indian thought. This was tantamount to saying that Shri Krishna's saying in the Gita and the Mahabharata were not a part of the Indian philosophical tradition! Teachers and students of Sanskrit schools, too, like Mahatma Gandhi, spoke against the Indian revolutionary movement in the name of ancient Indian philosophy. This was the backdrop to my second mental conflict—with ideas of violence and non-violence—although it was less severe than the first. I wrote a letter to Gandhi to refute the charges that he had levelled against the revolutionaries in the Belgaum Congress session. This letter was published verbatim in *Young India* on 12 February 1925. The Mahatma wrote a reply to the letter in the same issue.

I was first introduced to the communist ideology in 1923, after my return from the Andamans. This was a new political ideology and, at the time, nobody in the revolutionary movement was familiar with it. Before I was imprisoned again in 1925, I gained considerable understanding of communist thought by reading a lot of books, debating with communists and exchanging ideas with them. During this period, I was deeply involved in the revolutionary movement and was also editing the second volume of *Bandi Jeevan: A Life in Chains*.

I did incorporate some aspects of the communist ideology into my political thought, but there are parts of this worldview that I have not been able to accept even today. I accept some of the economic arguments of communism, but I don't believe in most of the principles of materialism that have been forcibly connected to these economic principles. Many young men in our country are influenced and inspired by the success of the Russian Revolution. The materialists believe that modern science has eradicated subjective modes of knowledge, but that is not true at all. I still believe in Divinity, and I am of the strong opinion that modern science is increasingly reaffirming the contributions of Indian philosophy. Ironically, many people in our country are today paranoid and dismiss these worldviews as subjective, making fun of those who hold such beliefs.

The truth, though, is that our thought process and our beliefs are formed by our interests, our ambience and the company we keep. It rarely happens that human beings accept a principle or an ideology just by thinking deeply about it. It is also true that the influence of those who are leading the national movement today in the spirit of sacrifice and bravery will be strong.

If we objectively criticize modern science, it is evident that science only researches that which is perceptible. But how can we assume that the imperceptible does not exist? We have enhanced our sensory perception using machines and can see that things which were not perceptible before have become so. Today, thanks to advances in science, we realize that apart from the light rays that we see, there are many kinds of rays and emissions that are a lot more powerful than the ones we can perceive through our senses. We are learning that beyond the world that we know, beyond the perceptible and tangible world, there is a world that is more extensive and miraculous still. We humans occupy the expanding threshold between the known world and realm of the unknown. And even without machines, a human being can acquire the power to unravel some aspects of this mysterious universe.

With the latest developments in the biological sciences, not to mention psychology, even scientists now feel that materialism is merely a superstition or at best a tenet. The well-known biologist J.N. Holden went so far as to say that if people didn't have blind belief in scientists, they would have detested those who believed in materialism. [See *Materialism* by J.S. Haldane C.H., M.D., F.R.S. Hon. L.L.D. (Birmingham and Edinburgh) Hon. D. Sc. (Cambridge, Leeds, and Witwatersrand) Fellow of New College, Oxford and Honorary Professor Birmingham University- p. 39.[1]] Dr Carrel, a Nobel laureate and a renowned biologist, who is a researcher at the famous Rockefeller Institute, opines that the materialist worldview is a subjective belief-system and has no scientific basis. In short, science now seems to be going against materialism. [See *Man the Unknown* written by Carrel.[2]] Bertrand Russell has also said that barring Russian political scientists and some scientists in America, most of the philosophers and scientists in the world did not believe in materialism. This way of thinking rose as a reaction to the pervasive influence of religion and specifically of the Christian worldview in Russia and America. [See *History of Materialism* by Lange, English Translation—Introduction by Bertrand Russell, written in 1925.[3]]

I would need to write another book to do justice to this discussion and prove my point. Hence, I will not go into much more detail here. However, I would like to clarify my statements by mentioning one last thing. On the one hand, physical science has reached the conclusion that all matter is a form of electrical power. On the other hand, it is being demonstrated that electrical power is produced in mental activity. It just remains to be proved that thoughts are produced as a result of the electrical charge in the mind. Let us not forget that until very recently, we were unaware that matter can change form, but today, it is a proven fact. Therefore, one day soon, it will be proven that all beings—all forms of life and consciousness embodied in matter in this world—are different forms of the same thing. The renowned Calcutta High Court judge and scholar, Sir John Woodroffe, had the courage to say that the development of modern science was beginning to converge towards the principles ofVedanta, and not the reverse.

There were other principles of Marxism that I do not agree with—*among them the view* that the manifestation of history is driven purely by economic factors, and this explains the origin of every kind of civilization in the world. I could not accept this.

According to Marx, the growth of factories and businesses would give rise to unrest among workers the world over and their anger would know no bounds. In the ensuing struggle between the two classes, the capitalists would lose and the workers would win. But today, in Germany, France, England, Italy, America and Japan, we are seeing capitalism prosper and reach new heights. However, there has been no workers' revolution in these countries. On the other hand, the communists have worked to set up vast regimes in Russia and China, although these political changes were not motivated by economic reasons alone.

An objective study of all this is essential but not possible in this foreword. I wish to write such a critique somewhere, some other time.

I wish to record here, using the methods of modern

science and historical research, a bona fide history of the Indian revolutionary movement. Therefore, no major changes have been made in this edition of my book *Bandi Jeevan: A Life in Chains*. I have not written the book in Hindi but in Bengali. However, I have started to write in Hindi after my release from jail this time. I hope that I will be able to write the next volume directly in Hindi and not resort to a translation. I apologize to my readers for the errors in this volume.

Sachindra Nath Sanyal
Lucknow
13 December 1938

AUTHOR'S PREFACE TO FIRST EDITION

Today, I am writing the past. Just as that period of time seems infinite, so does its grandeur. The passage of time seems to beautify that which wasn't; it glorifies that which wasn't glorious. Time has the magnificent power to romanticize memory. The memory of time past is very sweet; like the string of the veena, it produces a melodious sound, but the string must be shaken.

Memory makes small things bigger and big things smaller. Some memories just disappear and are difficult to dig out. Other memories are painful; there seems to be peace even in that pain. It has the capacity to open the most vulnerable part of our mind, as if we are having a secret conversation with ourselves.

Hope and hopelessness, joy and sadness—*these emotions* seem often to be playing a game with us, but none of them stay for long. They come for a couple of days, pay us a visit, make us cry or laugh and then depart, leaving only memories.

On 26 June 1915, I was arrested on charges of involvement in the Banaras Conspiracy. On 14 February 1916, I was sentenced to the Cellular Jail in the Andamans for life and my property was ordered to be seized. After some months in the prison in Kashi, I was sent off to the Andamans. I entered the Cellular Jail on 18 August 1916. Thanks to the will of the Almighty, I was released by royal decree in February 1920.

The years 1915–20 were the first instalment of my life

in captivity. I would like to begin by telling you why I was arrested. After all, I am leaving behind my testimony in this book so that these chapters of Indian history can be truthfully written in future.

India's destiny is moving forward to the juncture of two great epochs. The fierce revolution that rages in India, within and without, moving on its ordained path with God's blessings, is forming a powerful vortex that grows larger and larger. It was into this vortex that I, too, was drawn by the will of the Almighty.

Many young men like me, overcome by their deepest instincts, knowingly or unknowingly, came together to fulfil destiny's wish. For a long time, I have wanted to write a brief history of the innermost core of that group that had got lost in the great maelstrom of this revolution. I am trying to fulfil that wish today.

We tend to look at the past in perspective and give importance to big events. But we don't understand that behind each incident, however small it may be, lies the power of the Almighty. That is what makes an incident valuable. We always desire success. Even when the mind denies it, doubts it, we are unable to separate ourselves from the desire for success. But the small things in life are no less important than the big events. Everything that happens begins at the level of thought.

If one keeps this in mind, one realizes that the criticism of a particular individual is not a personal attack. The totality of events in the past cannot be understood without talking about certain persons. That is why personal criticism is important.

In writing this, the foibles of a lot of people in the movement and from my group will be laid bare. Is there any reason to unnecessarily try and hide the weakness and faults that have paralysed us, damaged us? Such an effort will be pointless because truth shall always prevail and trying to hide it only makes one weaker. History has upheld the maxim '*Satyam bruyatpriyambruyat. Na bruyatsatyamapriyam. Priyam cha nanruthambruyat*'. [Truth, if spoken correctly, is always soft and soothing, while fabrication and lies, spoken anyhow, always end in unsettling ways.]

Sachindra Nath Sanyal

Part 1

Chapter 1

THE YOGA OF SELF-REALIZATION

There was a small two-storeyed house with a tiled roof in the Raja Bazaar area in Calcutta. A house suitable for the poor. People of the ilk of tram conductors lived there. One room upstairs was occupied by a young man whose name was Shashank Mohan Hazra. When he was arrested, a bomb sheath and some articles on yoga practices were found. No one thought these essays on yoga were important during the trial; it was said that their purpose was to defraud or mislead people. But I know that this is not the truth. This practice (yoga) was an integral part of our lives. We didn't just mouth the fact that the Divine was in everything; in fact, we believed in it with all our heart and soul. We did not drag the Divine into our selfish desires and requirements, but we spent many a day and night debating the Universe's supremacy.

This great movement began and is continuing in the heart of India by God's mercy and will; that is what we all strongly believe. The sheer thought that drives it—an infinite inspiration that has driven thousands of young men in India to willingly face death and suffer insurmountable difficulties with dignity and honour, to endure agony and contempt—cannot be merely human in origin. It must have a cosmic source. Can any individual awaken and sustain such emotions—both passion and stability?

When I was just a child, the desire and determination to be of service to my country was ever-present in my heart. I have spoken about this to my younger brothers since boyhood. Nobody taught me to feel this way. So, who instilled this passion in every nerve of my body at such a young age? The Swadeshi Movement had not yet made its appearance. Yet I was not the only one who felt this way. When I grew up, met and spoke to other people, I realized that there were many who thought like I did across the entire country. I feel that, through us, God has been preparing the ground to have his desires fulfilled.

We, the young men of this movement, achieved a kind of spiritual realization that can be summed up as a capitulation to the higher being. This has a close relationship with the tradition of bhakti yoga, which is aimed at self-realization. I love God; I love him so much that apart from him, there is nothing that is truly mine. Whenever I do something, in reality, it is not me who is doing it. I am merely the tool. God is fulfilling his purpose through these tasks performed by me. Theology, too, speaks of one supreme power that actuates everything that happens in the universe. Hence, one does not see the world as an illusion but as God's creation. We tried to see the manifestation of that divine purpose in our private lives, in the country and in the world.

Chapter 2

THE TIDE OF REVOLUTION

The wave of revolution sweeping Bengal in 1906–7 did not stop at the borders of the province. Many centres of revolt sprang up in various parts of India, some mimicking, or inspired by, the movement in Bengal. The revolutionary outfits in Kashi, Delhi and Lahore were a result of this.

My story begins after the Delhi Conspiracy Case. In those days, the common people were largely unaware of the efforts of the revolutionaries outside of Bengal. Lala Har Dayal was in America at the time but Rashbehari[4] stayed on in India till 1915, even in dire circumstances. He was the leader of the group of revolutionaries operating outside Bengal. We used to call him *dada* (elder brother) or Rashuda.

∽

Rashbehari had fled and gone into hiding just before the prosecution of the Delhi Conspiracy Case began. His photograph was posted on the walls of every major railway station in the country. The reward announced for his capture was 7,500 rupees. But despite all its efforts, the government could not apprehend him.

After a lot of thinking and on my advice, Rashbehari decided to stay in Kashi. He stayed with me for a year. I can never forget the pleasure his company brought me. I don't think I ever saw him unhappy or despondent during that time. But yes, I did see him cry in solitude the day the judgement in the Delhi Conspiracy Case was announced, and four people were sentenced to death by hanging.

During his stay in Kashi, he was actively involved in setting up centres of revolt in the United Provinces (Uttar Pradesh) and in Punjab. As a result, our group became so powerful that when the World War started, we were able to work in full force.

The year 1915 will always be an unforgettable one for India. It is doubtful that the preparations that were made for a revolution at that time had ever been organized at that scale anywhere in the country, except in the Kuka revolt in Punjab after the mutiny of 1857. The Defense of India Act was enacted after the arrest of this group of conspirators. The then home member Sir Craddock,[5] in his statement asking for the law to be passed, said, 'We had anarchism for a long time in Bengal but the situation in Punjab was serious; in Bengal it was less so.' The situation in India at the time was indeed delicate. And Sir Craddock was not familiar with Bengal's situation at that time. A few days later, the gentleman accepted that the government's opinion about the rebel groups in Punjab and Bengal had changed.

Many things have been said in reference to the cases connected to the revolts in northern India. Many people think that these accounts are exaggerated. In fact, many have said to me, 'The police have constructed false cases and nothing like this has happened in the country.' Listening to such speeches broke my heart; I would be so angry that I could not say a word, and this would distress me further.[6] It grieves me to think that my countrymen have lost their self-confidence to such an extent that they did not have faith that their compatriots were capable of such acts.

Meanwhile, the sparks ignited in the Sikh community when the news of the Indian passengers of the Japanese ship *Komagata Maru* were not allowed to set foot on Canadian soil, had spread like wildfire. Back in India, we were eagerly awaiting their return. Our companions in Punjab had been instructed to immediately recruit the passengers of the *Komagata Maru* to our group the moment they arrived in the country. But the moment the passengers stepped on Indian soil, there was a disaster. However, that only strengthened our resolve. Before we knew it, groups of Sikhs from Canada and California started making their way to India. On their way here, they planned to get off at every Indian port and ignite the fire of revolution in the hearts of the Sikhs in the police force and the army. They had been outside the country for a long time and were unaware that rebellion should be stoked in secrecy in these times.

The result was that when the ships reached India and Sikh groups began disembarking at various ports, the government became alert and started detaining them. A group of nearly 300 Sikhs was sent straight to Multan jail. Many of them had donated all their wealth to the Jugantar Ashram in California before sailing to India. Many others were carrying large sums of money as they had brought their savings from working in America for so many years. One of them had 30,000 rupees. Sardar Jwala Singh was his name, and he had made his fortune from farming in California. The government confiscated the hard-earned savings of these men. Their poor family members, who had been hoping to lead a decent life for some time with the money, were left empty-handed.

The groups that managed to elude capture reached Punjab and started banding together there. The gurudwara is the Sikh place of worship. Their priests live in these holy places.

The Sikh word for priest is *granthiji.* There is one granthiji in every gurudwara. The gurudwaras became the meeting points for the rebel Sikh groups. I was sitting at one such meeting place when a Sikh gentleman came and said that he had met so-and-so while coming into the gurudwara, and in no time, every important person from that community had reached the gurudwara.

As soon as the topic of money came up, they put the large gold discs that were the currency in America at the time in front of me. They were worth many thousands of rupees. Every Sikh group made generous contributions from their life savings. Bengal did not have the good fortune of seeing anything like this—the way these people donated their hard-earned money to the cause of mutiny. However, such generosity was seen only in the Sikhs who had been to America. And it is also a fact that natives of Punjab, although close to the Pathan and Sikh soldiers, had little sympathy for the rebels. Nonetheless, the empathy and compassion that the Sikh community has for its own is unseen elsewhere.

Most of the Sikhs who had come back from America had worked as porters there. Many of their relatives were in the Indian Army. They started making secret pacts with the soldiers the moment they arrived in India. It was during this time that Bengal and Punjab connected and became allies in the revolutionary movement. Despite their many strong points, the people of Punjab did not have the organizational skills of the Bengalis. Once an alliance was formed with Bengal, things became smoother. Soon, our people were regularly going in and out of the cantonments of North India. From Bannu in the northwest to Danapur, no cantonment was left untouched.

The soldiers refused to initiate anything but promised to join the rebels once the mutiny had started. Only the regiments of Lahore and Ferozepur had agreed to take the first step. In the beginning, the government did not realize that the secret conspirators were laying such a strong and wide foundation; hence, the whole operation proceeded rather smoothly. However, a Muslim deputy superintendent of police in Punjab had managed to insert a spy into a rebel group. In the end that gentleman, Kripal Singh, exposed it all.

Chapter 3

MY INTRODUCTION TO THE SIKH GROUP

How Kripal Singh came to be a part of this conspiracy and how he sabotaged the whole operation will be disclosed in good time, but first, I would like to try and introduce the Sikh group.

This was not a small group. About 6,000–7,000 Sikhs had come back to the country from America and Canada. The patriotic sentiments with which these men had returned to their motherland changed soon for many after getting here. Thousands of homecoming Sikhs got sucked into their family lives, but an unspecified number continued to participate in rebellious activities. However, many had been sent to jail under the Ingress Ordinance Act of 1914, and several others were under house arrest. The latter (those who were not permitted to leave their villages) could not contribute much to the rebellion.

They had to be present in their homes between sunrise and sunset—who knew what time the police would land up to check on them! Even after sundown, they could not leave their villages. No person from another village was allowed to meet them. Later, when our work began, some of these detainees who were very keen on serving the country managed to slip away from the police. This meant that neither the police, nor their families or friends had any news of them.

The majority of those who came from America, with the exception of a handful (about 25 or 30), were Sikh. They were mostly adults, above the age of 40 and had wives and children. In fact, some were elderly. Bhai Nidhan Singh, Bhai Sohan Singh, Bhai Kaal Singh and Bhai Kehar Singh—*even* some of those arrested in the Delhi Conspiracy, such as Amir Chand and Avadh Behari—were on the wrong side of 50.

The Bengal group of rebels was composed largely of students—boys and young men. Most of them had no experience of the world, being between the ages of 16 and 20. In Bengal, it is customary for men, after crossing the age of 30, to lose all enthusiasm and drive and concentrate only on family life. Hence, it seemed as if all our hope and faith was invested in the youth in schools and colleges. But those who were working for the movement here, despite their young age and their inexperience in worldly affairs, demonstrated a single-minded resolve that was not seen anywhere outside Bengal.

Whatever the people of Bengal have undertaken, they have done so without a care for their lives. I find that during the Buddha's time, for instance, no one else had embraced Buddhism with the intensity of the Bengalis. Later, when the other regions parted ways with Buddhism, they looked at Bengal with scepticism because it refused to give up its affinity to the faith. Then during the British rule, Bengal took to Western education and ways of living, giving up its own prevalent systems like no other province in the country. Consider it positive or negative, but what Bengal accepts, it makes its own in thought and deed. Today, when the Bengalis resolve to work for the country, they ignore everything else. They don't get married and set up homes or accumulate worldly possessions. They leave their homes and come out to fight.

I felt the pulse of inspiration in these youngsters. It was not merely to create chaos that they were involved in the struggle—serving the motherland was a vow they seemed to undertake and adhere to with sincerity and integrity. They also seemed to be looking for an answer to a deeper question: how can we be more humane? How do we build a character?

I did not find this sentiment in the others, save for a couple of Sikhs. In my association with the rebels of the region that was then the United Provinces, I realized that they had not been able to internalize the cause as the Bengalis had done. When these questions came up, they only had a disbelieving smile on their faces.

The Sikhs had ample valour and enthusiasm, and they could withstand a lot of torment. Their large bodies and broad chests attracted many an eyeball. Even their tormentors' hearts would melt seeing the resolve on their bearded faces. They seemed to walk with the weight firmly on both their feet and radiated an attitude of patriotic courage, but the high-minded idealism of the beardless Bengali youth was out of their reach. I am writing this with no malice, for I have a very high regard for the few Sikhs that I know personally. I will say more about this when I talk of the Andamans and Kaalapani.

None of those who returned from America were educated by our definition of formal education. Most of them had decided to travel abroad from Punjab to seek their fortunes as they were not satisfied with the little that they managed to make here—unlike people from other parts of the country, who tended to make do with whatever they earned, however meagre it was. It started with the Punjabi exodus to Singapore, Penang, Siam, the Malay Peninsula and China. Soon, they reached the shores of the USA and Canada. In Singapore, Penang and Hong Kong, large numbers of Sikhs joined the

British Army and the military police. Many others worked as coolies in Siam, the Malay Peninsula and China. Some of them became contractors or were self-employed in similar ways.

But in America and Canada, they were mainly coolies. Some of the factories favoured Sikh labourers over Americans because they worked harder. As a result, they would often get into fights with the American workers. I heard from them that in one city, the bad blood was so strong that it turned into constant friction. On the one side were the Sikh labourers and on the other, a city full of white American workers. There was a lot of violence, but there was no negative action against the Sikhs on the part of the government. Had this occurred in India, God knows how it would have ended!

Despite their lack of education, the America-returned Sikhs could read their holy book in their mother tongue. They were enthused about the education of the Sikh community in their villages. To this end, they had collected and donated large sums of money while they were working abroad, to the tune of nearly 15,000 at a time. They had developed a lot of self-esteem and confidence after having lived and earned their fortunes in a free America. They had not given up their religion or traditional garb during their stay abroad in America. Many of them used to cook and eat Indian food. When they arrived in America, they did not know a word of English, but in time, they managed to speak a certain kind of broken English. It was wonderful to hear them speak this dialect and to think that they communicated with this broken English in America. Evidently, it did not pose any obstacle to their work or interfere with their earnings.

But the most significant thing is that they did not break their connection with the motherland after establishing themselves in America. They were always eager to know what was happening back home. The wave of the renaissance in Bengal at that time had swept the other parts of the country and had reached the hearts of Indians in far-off America too. Likewise, the sparks of the revolution had spread across the subcontinent and ignited Indian hearts, both at home and abroad. It was during this time that a young man by the name of Bhai Kartar Singh became a member of the Sikh group. He had gone to America after graduating from Ravenshaw College in Orissa with a first-class degree. Although he was very young, I saw that many Sikhs, much older than him, were working under his leadership. He decided to publish a newsletter with the help of a couple of like-minded people.

It was around this time that the patriot Har Dayal Singh, a well-known rebel from Punjab, had lost all hope that the rebellion would succeed and was trying to establish contact with the American communists. Kartar Singh and his friends got in touch with him at this very juncture with a proposal for a newsletter. Har Dayal Singh was waiting for such an opportunity. He happily took on the task. This is how the well-known newspaper *Ghadar* (meaning 'mutiny' or 'rebellion') came to be published and eventually its founders went on to establish the Ghadar Party. These events took place in the Jugantar Ashram in California.

Before the beginning of the First World War (1914–1919), the Indian revolutionaries did not realize the immediacy of the British–German confrontation. As a result, they were organizing and planning their revolution as though they had 10–15 years before it would take place. It is for this reason that the rebels were caught totally unawares when war broke out. Furthermore, none of them had any contacts worth mentioning with revolutionary groups outside the country. Consequently, when groups of revolutionaries started arriving from America, the rebels here found it difficult to assimilate them into the movement. Had they been able to work together, India's destiny would have been very different.

The revolutionaries among the Indian diaspora in America did not realize that Britain's war against Germany was imminent and hence their preparations would have to be of a different kind. They believed that they could rely on help from external powers and had planned their operations accordingly. Unfortunately for them, the War in Europe broke out at the worst possible time, and their plan failed before they could even launch it. They then decided that groups of Ghadar Party[7] cadres would travel to the homeland with the purpose of recruiting Indian soldiers to their ideology.

This was the only strategy that was decided on for the revolution. Thousands of Sikhs packed their bags and returned to the motherland.

Meanwhile, the British government in India had discovered many things about the Party because its members had been talking about a revolution in India in open assemblies in the USA. The newsletter *Ghadar* was also already in print. The government had a keen eye and kept close watch on Lala Har Dayal especially, so much so that many times, they managed to get hold of his personal diary! However, when the plan to arrest him was taking shape, an American warned him of the same. At this juncture, Lala Har Dayal and his comrades thought it better to leave America.

In many places and on several occasions, German envoys used to help those who were desirous of a revolution in India in various ways. Hence, the rebel groups that were returning from America did not miss a chance to meet and greet them. For this reason, some went to Europe to garner support for the movement while others decided to press on to India. On the way, these people would talk of their cause wherever possible.

One such group reached a Japanese port. Here they met a lanky young man by the name of Parmanand. He was a native of Bundelkhand. In the Andamans, we used to address him as 'Chhote Parmanand' (junior Parmanand) because there was also Bhai Parmanand ji, a former teacher at DAV College, Lahore. The senior Parmanand, too, was sentenced to life imprisonment at the Cellular Jail for his part in the Lahore Conspiracy. Back in the days when Sikhism was on the rise in Punjab and fearless patriots would sacrifice their lives rather than their religion or their land in the face of Muslim atrocities, when they would willingly have their heads cut off but not give up, a forebear of Bhai Parmanand had been the epitome of sacrifice. He had been sawed in half by the Muslims. From then on, this family of Sikhs had earned the sobriquet of 'Bhai' (meaning brother). Over time, it became a title accorded for respect in Sikhism. That is why we used to address our Sikh companions as 'bhai' along with their names.

Bhai Bhagwan Singh was a fervent Sikh leader. Countless Sikhs left their jobs abroad and came back to India to take part in the revolution after hearing his speeches. These people had not joined the revolutionary movement on a whim—they were true patriots. Often, when I spoke to Sikhs who had come back to the homeland for this purpose, I realized that they felt the affront of subjugation with every heartbeat and in every pore of their being. Some had been employed in the Military Police in Penang, some had worked as guards in Hong Kong and others were businessmen. In Hong Kong, there used to be a Sikh regiment at this time. These people had established their supremacy in the regiment as well. Many people in the groups that came back to India had served as soldiers in the British Army. Most of them had served for eight, 10 or even 11 years. Nobody had less than three years' experience, as this was the minimum duration of military service. Several of them had worked in the artillery unit and knew how to operate machine guns.

On their way to India, when the police had asked them why they were coming back to Hindustan, some had said to get married and others had said that it had been a long time since they had visited their homes and families. Later, when they were questioned in court during the trial, they would give similar reasons. Only one man had given a proper answer. The judge asked the accused, 'Why did you come back to the country?' He answered, 'Because it is my motherland.' The man was Jagat Ram, a Punjabi brahmin. He worked in the editorial department of the *Ghadar* newsletter.

There was a lot of enthusiasm in the Sikhs that came from America, but they were disorganized and their work ethic left much to be desired. They had neither a central office nor any branches. About 20-odd people would be under the direction of one man. He was known as their *sardaar* (commander). These commanders would get together once in a while and there were phases during which they would not meet for days at a time. The truth is that they did not have the wherewithal to work efficiently together, the main reason being that they did not have a headquarters that served as a base for their operations. Nobody knew how many people were involved in the uprising in this haphazard manner. Those who were incarcerated in the Muslim jail would say that riots were imminent and that would mean an early release from prison. The result was that they were sent off to different jails and, consequently, deprived even of the comfort of staying with people of the same religion and culture.

The Sikh rebels had started to seek out the secret

revolutionary groups of Bengal the moment they arrived in India. But before getting in touch with anybody or thinking about anything, they started speaking openly of a revolt. I remember that at that time, even in the by-lanes of Calcutta, there was talk about preparations for a revolution in Punjab. Lord Harding cited the unrest among the Sikhs when he framed the Defense of India Act.

Meanwhile, Kartar Singh[8] had arrived in India and soon met with a renowned and popular leader of the revolutionary movement in Bengal. The latter advised Kartar Singh to carry on his work for the uprising in Punjab and to the best of their ability the Bengalis would come to their aid at the right time. There is no need to hide the fact that this person was Sir Surendra Nath Banerjee.[9]

The need of the hour was for arms and ammunition. The soldiers of the Sikh groups were the main support of this revolution, and a need was felt to arm every worker or volunteer with revolvers and other weapons. To this end, Mr Jagat Ram was sent off to Kabul with some money, and it was with this mission that the agonies of imprisonment began for him. Poor Jagat Ram was arrested in Peshawar, and I later met him in the Andamans. Chhote Parmanand, too, had been sent to Bengal on the same mission, but he, too, came back empty-handed.

Chapter 4

THE PUNJAB VISIT

In Kashi, there were special houses to accommodate outsiders engaged in preparations for the revolution. People who came for meetings from Punjab would first go to these houses. When the news of their arrival in the city was received, the visitor would be identified surreptitiously from afar. When there was no longer a doubt about their identity, the visitor would then be met. I was in Kashi the day a member of the Punjab group brought news of the rebellion that was underway in Punjab. When he told us that 2,000–3,000 Sikhs were preparing themselves for an uprising, our joy knew no bounds. The Punjab functionaries had sent word with the emissary that they needed Rashbehari Bose there. At that time, he was absconding after the Delhi Conspiracy Case, and his fame had spread as far as America. It was there that these people had heard of him.

For certain reasons, Rashbehari could not make the trip to Punjab. Therefore, it was decided that I should go, see the conditions in Punjab for myself and bring back detailed reports so that the future course of action could be decided.

It had been decided beforehand that I would go to Jalandhar and meet the Sikh leaders there. It was almost the end of November. Winter was setting in. When the train reached Ludhiana on a cold morning, we found a young man who was known to my friend waiting for us at the station. My friend introduced me to him. This was Kartar Singh. He got onto the train and accompanied us to Jalandhar. We chatted a bit on the way. At that very moment, he told us, 200–300 people had gathered in Ludhiana, and they would be sent out in different directions for various tasks. They had gathered there under the guise of meditating in the gurudwara.

I remember that day vividly. There were many people in the coach, but everyone had varied thoughts. We spoke briefly and intermittently, but there was much more going on in the mind. All through, I kept wondering what the Sikh group of volunteers would be like—their education, their behaviour, their attitude. I had already heard that several of them were at least 30 years old if not older, and I wondered how they would perceive me, for I was a mere 22-year-old then. Would me going there be of any use, how could we harness the mass fervour that was building up in Punjab for realizing our desired goal—many such questions plagued me the entire way.

There was also a warm feeling, albeit unconscious, that the dream of a lifetime would soon be realized and that the darkness that had plagued us for aeons was now going to be lifted. But then I would be pricked with doubts when I thought of how underdeveloped Bengal was now—it was so far from this amazing land! The dark smear that has ravaged Bengal for centuries seemed like an open wound that throbs and pains me infinitely. That is why I desperately wanted to go and work there. Anyway, let that be.

Ludhiana was soon left behind. We reached another station. Kartar Singh bought a newspaper called *Bulletin*. We read that there had been a bomb blast in the Muslim Pada lane in Calcutta. It was reported that two or three bombs had been hurled at the house of Mr Basant Chatterjee, the deputy superintendent of the secret police. A head constable had his leg blown off, a few people had been injured, a portion of the wall and a lamp post had collapsed, and a lot of decorative items inside the house had landed up on the road. But Basant Sahib had escaped unhurt. I understood a lot of things when I read that news report. After I have given an account of what was happening in Punjab, I want to write about Bengal and the state of affairs there at the time.

These bomb blasts seem to have triggered an awakening of patriots all over the country. A lot of people perceived that these events were visible signs of the preparations for a massive revolt, and they now wanted to be part of revolutionary organizations like ours. Kartar Singh was thrilled by the report. We spoke to each other through our eyes, conveying our joy. And so we reached Jalandhar. Many of Kartar Singh's student-companions were waiting here. After saying what needed to be said to this group, we crossed the tracks and went to a park nearby.

Several leaders of this group had gathered there. I was relieved to see that there was nobody significantly older than me. My friend introduced me to these people. I didn't ask them their names to begin with, as too many questions were seen with suspicion in groups like these. But as the conversation took off, I got to know their names. Among them were Prithvi Singh, Amar Singh and Ram Rakha. Kartar Singh must have been about 19 or 20 years old at the time. Amar Singh and Prithvi Singh, both Rajputs who had been living in Punjab for ages, must also have been of the same age. The young men had been waiting to meet Rashbehari. My friend introduced me by saying that although Rashbehari had not been able to come due to unavoidable circumstances, he had sent his right-hand man. Kartar Singh insisted that they would deal only with Rashbehari. I then explained that he wanted a full report on the situation there before coming to Punjab, and, moreover, his situation was such that he would not be able to make the journey anytime soon.

To gauge the situation in Punjab, I asked them how many of them were there, how they managed their meetings, who the actual leader was and so on. I said, 'I would like to meet and get to know your true leader.' Amar Singh said, 'Actually, we lack a true leader, and that is why we need Rashbehari. None of us has the experience to lead, and that is why our work doesn't progress. We really need Bengal's assistance. You people have been working in Bengal for a long time and have considerable experience.' Although Kartar Singh agreed with this, he said to Amar Singh, 'Why do you lose hope, brother? Wait and watch—when things move many hidden gems will appear amongst us.'

From what he said, it was clear that their resolve was firm and that they had put their heart and soul in the cause. All they were looking for was some support from the outside. I also understood that the one who was the most committed and competent was Kartar Singh. He had the confidence and self-assurance, without which nothing great could be achieved. Others lacked such qualities, and they were very arrogant. Confidence and arrogance are two very different traits; arrogance hurts others, but true confidence is that which lights in oneself the fire to achieve great ends.

Anyway, moving on, I learnt a lot about the situation in Punjab from these people. I have already spoken about most of it. Among other things, I got to know that the success of the revolution they were planning hinged mainly on the support of the Sikh troops. Kartar Singh told us that these people were part of those who had come from America and had been preparing for an uprising since September.

Now Kartar Singh asked me, 'Can Bengal help us with arms and ammunition? How many thousands of guns does Bengal have?'

I asked him, 'What do you think? How much ammunition would Bengal have?'

'I think Bengal has amassed a lot of arms as it has been preparing for the revolution for a really long time. One of our group members, Parmanand, has been promised 500 guns by a Bengali friend of his. That is why he has gone to Bengal,' said Kartar Singh.

'Whosoever made this promise to Parmanand is a complete fraud because Bengal will not be able to provide you with 500 revolvers. Your friend's Bengali friend was a barefaced liar,' I replied.

'Then how can Bengal help us?' asked Kartar Singh. 'How many people are working with you in Bengal?'

We normally did not allow such questions, and in situations where someone did manage to pose them, our replies were, 'What will you do with this information? Suppose we were to say that there is no preparation, would you still like to be part of our group? You will have to start from scratch; would you still like to join us?', and so on. Of course, there were people in Bengal who exaggerated the scale of the preparations for the revolution and boasted about them to all and sundry. This was their way of trying to recruit people to the cause. However, when Kartar Singh posed his questions, it did not seem right to sidestep his queries.

I said, 'If, in Bengal, we had the opportunity to join the army as you do here in Punjab, there would have been a massive revolution already. The Bengal group is mostly made up of students and youngsters, and we admit people only after strict and vigilant scrutiny—recruiting only those who are willing to lay down their lives at any point. And that is why we don't have too many people, maybe a thousand or two at the maximum. But we firmly believe that the day the revolution begins in earnest, thousands will join us. And you may rest assured that when there is a revolt in Punjab, Bengal will not sit and watch from the sidelines. The British will face such a situation of dissent in Bengal that the government, distracted, will not be able to concentrate its might on Punjab.' I added, 'Even now the revolutionaries in Bengal can loot the treasury or attack the police barracks, but then what? What will happen after that? It is because we thought, "What after that?" that Bengal has not taken such a step.'

I told them in no uncertain terms, 'Do not take any step suddenly without consulting us. We need to work with extreme caution so that the energy is not wasted and misused in just creating a scene.' I advised them to tell most of their people to go and stay in their villages. It would be best if only the leader of the group and his close associates stayed in constant touch. Members should be divided into small groups and each group assigned a leader, so that they could be called upon as and when required. If such small sections were not constituted, there would be a constant danger of arrest for everyone. Finally, I said to Kartar Singh, 'One of you can come with me, and I will take you to where Rashbehari is. You can consult him in detail on these matters.' They liked this idea. It was decided that we would meet Prithvi Singh in Lahore once again and take him to meet Rashbehari.

Kartar Singh asked for help in procuring some revolvers and other small arms. They needed these weapons for self-defence and to raid small government reserves. They had brought some guns from abroad when they had come back to India. Despite the intense scrutiny of the British, these arms had managed to make their way into the country. Some of the weapons were smuggled in, hidden under a wooden or tin plate fixed on the bottom of buckets, but very soon, the authorities had caught on to this method. Sometimes, before reaching an Indian port, the weapons would be handed over to the Khalasis (a group of people traditionally employed at ports and dockyards; '*khalasi*' is an Arabic word that means dockyard worker or sailor, 'lascars' as they are called). Later, when the occasion allowed, the travellers would go back and collect them. That is how they managed to secure some revolvers, but more were needed. I had brought some revolvers and bullets with me from Kashi. I handed them over to Kartar Singh, saying that those were handy when I was leaving, and so I had brought them with me. I said that I would bring more, but I also impressed upon them that we did not have any great reserves of arms and ammunition, and, therefore, they should not have too many expectations of us in that regard.

With reference to bombs, I told them that Bengalis had some expertise in bomb-making and would provide them whenever required. The Punjabis too used some kinds of bombs at the time. For instance, a kind of inkpot made of lead and brass served as the outer covering of the bombs that they made. These were small bottles made in India and were readily available in the markets of Punjab. The explosive material inside was the same as that used in firecrackers—sulphuric acid, sugar and so on. The mouth of the bottle had a screw on top and as a result the cover closed tightly. Once filled with acid, closed and put inside the bomb, it would break at the slightest nudge. When the bottle broke, the potash would react with the sugar and the bomb would explode, scattering shrapnel from the inkpot. These bombs were not deadly and often did not explode when they were hurled. And even if they did, the explosion was not powerful enough to kill a man.

I told Kartar Singh and the others that the bombs made in Bengal were formidable. I informed them that some of our bombs were already stashed at some places in Punjab and could be used if the need arose. When they agreed to take them, I asked where I could meet them again. They replied, 'We don't have a fixed place to stay.' I asked them, 'Do you not have a central office where one can get all the information required?' The answer was a 'no'. It was revealed that the practice was to take off for their different tasks, and once those had been accomplished, they would meet up at a pre-decided location. If for some reason they could not meet at the appointed place and time, the only remedy was to look for information at the gurudwara. There was no other way. I was very surprised to hear this. At that time, I thought that maybe they weren't willing to reveal all their secrets to me. And, therefore, in keeping with our practice, I did not ask too many questions, nor did I offer any advice.

Later, when our relationship deepened and we got to know each other, I realized that this was truly their modus operandi, and I found a solution as well. During the conversation in the park, it was clear to me that they did not have a dedicated meeting place in Jalandhar. Yet all the people present belonged to Jalandhar and had come for the meeting. They did not even know of a place where I could go and rest. And they had wanted to invite Rashbehari, for whose arrest a bounty of 7,500 rupees had been announced, into such a chaotic and unsafe situation! Anyway, after all had been said and heard, I asked Kartar Singh to meet me at a designated spot the next day, and he agreed. It was decided that I would wait for him at the railway station, take him to a place where some bombs were stashed and hand them over.

Soon, everyone decided to be on their way. It was time for their train. My friend and I went to a hotel. There, I came to know that my dear friend did not eat non-vegetarian food, so I also had to make do with vegetarian fare. However, the *tandoori roti* and *daal* served in Punjab are fantastic.

I, too, had avoided non-vegetarian food earlier. I can't even count the number of times I turned vegetarian only to revert to eating meat. Once, I had come from Haridwar to meet Rashuda[10] at Laksar Junction. He was to reach by the afternoon train. There was a good refreshment room at the station. After washing up, I went there and asked for roti and curry. The rotis were well-made, but I was served meat with them! I did not know then that, for people in Punjab, curry was meat, whereas, for me, it meant vegetables. I was in a quandary. I did not know how to return it, for what would these people think of me? I wrestled with the dilemma and finally decided to eat it. Then later in the afternoon, when Rashuda sat down to eat, he asked for roti with meat. Then he looked at me and whispered, 'Oh, but you will not eat meat!' He was about to change his order when I told him to let it be and not change it. Then I told him about the incident in the morning and said that to have eaten then but to not eat now would be hypocritical. But Rashuda said, 'Make sure you don't feel guilty later.' That was the day I started eating meat once again. But readers, despite relishing meat and being a maker of bombs, I am no savage!

Anyhow, after eating my fill of tandoori roti and wonderful daal, I left to pick up the bombs for Kartar Singh, and my dear friend left for Lahore. I went to our hideout, the secret place where our weapons were stashed. I did not mention meeting the young revolutionaries of Jalandhar to our companion there, only that I needed some bombs and that a Sikh gentleman would be picking them up. The moment he heard the word 'Sikh', he became alert and told me to be careful while meeting Sikhs as the government was keeping a close eye on them. In fact, he warned, it was better to stay away from them. This was a difficult situation, I thought to myself. I felt that this man could not be trusted, and it was better to not have any further association with him. I pretended that I agreed with him and left, reaching the station at the decided hour.

The train was on time, but Kartar Singh was nowhere to be seen. I looked for him on the next train that came in, that too in vain. I searched every corner of the station and stared at every face but did not find that of Kartar Singh. Finally, I gave up and went back to where we were staying. I did not know where I could find the man, but the interesting thing was that no one from his group knew either! The bombs remained where they were and I went back to Lahore. But first I met some old acquaintances in the city and tried to find out more about the situation in Punjab from them. So, I have already told you all that I managed to glean from different people and places. One evening, Prithvi Singh met me in a public place near Lahore, and I mentioned Kartar Singh to him. He could not tell me his whereabouts either. It was decided that in three or four days he would leave for Kashi, arriving on 5 December by the Punjab Mail, and I would take him to meet Rashbehari. I had still not categorically told them where Rashbehari was.

I would like to talk a little bit about the old acquaintances that I met and spoke to before I went to Lahore. Many were not native Punjabis; they had earlier been living in various parts of the United Provinces. But if you didn't know their background, you would never suspect that they were not Punjabis! The character of the place had seeped into their being. Many Bengalis live outside Bengal these days, but they don't lose their regional characteristics so easily. In fact, for three to four generations or even beyond, Bengalis living in other parts of the country remain Bengalis and even set up mini-Bengals in those areas. But I have noticed that people from North India in such situations let go of their native culture and become one with the place they have chosen to live in.

Before I went back to Kashi, I got a glimpse of his narrow-mindedness, and I was very sad about it. In the course of a long conversation, he began to talk about the Delhi Conspiracy Case and said that whereas they had not received any financial help from Bengal, not only money but a barrister was also provided for the Assamese Basant Kumar in the same matter. I was not aware of all the facts of the case as I had joined the group shortly before the Delhi Conspiracy. Based on the little that I knew, I said that we had not provided assistance to anybody on behalf of the group—either in the form of money or of legal help. A friend of Basant Kumar had spent his own money and made arrangements for him. When questioned about the new Sikh group in Punjab, his answers were rather disingenuous, trying to project that he knew nothing, but some of his responses revealed that he was not unaware of the group. But he did not want me to know about it.

This was frustrating, for I had every right under the circumstances to make enquiries about the Sikh group. However, from my conversation with him, I could make out that the Sikh group was working according to its own principles and methods and did not expect anything from anybody else. Basically, their attitude was 'Why is Bengal the interfering busybody?' When I asked, 'Would it help if Rashbehari came to Punjab at this moment?', the answer was,

'Yes, if he wants, then he can come.' And I thought to myself, 'If he wants!' I realized that they were not really interested in inviting Rashbehari, although they had been acquainted with him for a long time. When I requested him to introduce me to some members of the Sikh group, he responded by saying he was not acquainted with such leaders. But he had said to me earlier, 'We have given these leaders 1,000 rupees collected from Lahore.' And I was smiling to myself at the way he was trying to hide the details of the group from me.

However hard we try to separate our ego and banish it, it manages to find a way to stick to us. In fact, no one should conclude from his narrow-mindedness that all Punjabis are like this. The truth is that the really dedicated workers in the movement were, in fact, fonder of Bengalis than people from other regions. In my experience, the Sikhs were more fond of Bengalis as compared to other Punjabis as well! I feel that people who are good for nothing are good at criticism. However, I had felt that it was important for me to approach everyone I knew there to understand the real situation in Punjab at this moment. This acquaintance of mine would help us well enough in our work, I realized, but he preferred to maintain a distance from us and, therefore, we would also do the same. In any case, we had enough trust in him to know that he would not give away our secrets in a difficult situation; this had proven true once before when he had been caught.

Anyway, I left, thinking that a new chapter had begun in our preparations for a revolution. I was impatient to reach Kashi and report everything to Rashuda.

After having seen for myself the situation in Punjab, I was convinced that if this new energy was not coordinated and consolidated, it was possible that the Sikhs would end up doing something ill-timed, which would dissipate and disperse all the energy and effort. Who was to know then that, even though we were vigilant, the uprising[11] would turn out to be a damp squib? Is anything wasted in this life? I spent the journey mulling over such thoughts. But we are not going to dwell on that question here. I decided that as soon as possible, Dada should make a trip to Punjab and work should immediately begin in the cantonments. I will speak later about why we had not paid attention to this aspect so far. I resolved to send Rashuda to Punjab and go to Bengal myself. I had long been desirous of going and working in Bengal. I had spoken to Dada about this many times and expressed my wish, but so far, he had not given me permission to go.

The train pulled into the United Provinces, leaving Punjab behind. It was evening by then. There weren't many passengers in my bogie; in fact, there were only three or four other people. I don't think there was any place in the world at that time where conversations about the twentieth century's Kurukshetra (an Indian metaphor for the World War) did not take place. We introduced ourselves and, immediately, the conversation shifted to Europe's catastrophe. I asked one of the travellers, 'What kinds of people are being recruited in your village?' The answer was, 'It is very difficult to get youngsters for the army, although there is no dearth of pleading and cajoling and luring with promises and prizes. Magistrates and other officials travel to the villages for recruitments. People are told that they will get decent pay and that one month's salary will be paid in advance. The officials who manage to recruit people for the army are paid a special commission. But despite all this, they do not find many recruits. In fact, those who are eligible to be recruited run away to other villages to avoid it.' I asked the man I was speaking to, 'So they don't find young men like you to recruit?' He replied, 'Those who are absolutely witless get lured into the army by greed. But when they are faced with the reality of being a soldier and are unable to leave the job despite trying very hard, they often run away from the cantonment, and then they are pursued and tormented by the police.'

I realized one thing categorically—whether it was the train, the road or the market, everywhere amongst the uneducated people, there was an increasing bitterness against the British. In Kashi, one day, just outside the colony, we were sitting on a wellhead and talking about our work. A farmer was cutting grass nearby. After some time, he moved closer to us and, smiling as he worked, asked us, 'Will the British reign end or go on?' We asked him, 'What do you think?' And the answer was, 'They can't stay on in Hindustan now, Babu. Their end is nigh. When will the Germans come?' We then explained to him that we would not benefit in any way from the arrival of the Germans, but he said, 'No Sir, these English are not fair anymore. It is better that they leave.' Our answer to this was what it should have been. It is not necessary to mention it here. I realized that when people like us agree with them, they tend to distrust us.

Chapter 5

RELATIONS WITH THE POLICE IN KASHI

The Punjab Mail reached Kashi at three o'clock. The police had a special interest in me and kept a keen eye on my activities. From early morning until about nine or ten at night, they would be parked either at my front door or somewhere close by. So, if I stayed at home, it was not convenient or safe for those who wanted to meet me. And the moment I stepped out, the police would shadow me wherever I went. In those days, it was almost a crime for people to meet a person like me, even if it was a casual meeting. But, despite the strict police surveillance, I managed to do the work that I did. I would transport bombs, revolvers and other weapons from Bengal to Kashi, and from there I would take them to different parts of Punjab—all this under the very nose of my watchers. However, it was no big deal for us to fool the police. Before I write about other things, I will speak of certain incidents and episodes that show how we would dodge the police.

The best thing to do, we realized, was to fool them and dodge them just as we stepped out of the house. But on the days we couldn't do this, we neither did any Party work nor did we meet anybody from the Party.[12] So, either we went to a classmate's house and spent time there or we went to the market and bought groceries for the house, prompting the family to exclaim, 'Today Sachindra is really paying attention to the house!' Otherwise, one went to the Carmichael Library and read various newspapers and magazines leisurely before returning home. And lastly, if it was summer, one would go to the ghats, have a light massage and then cool off in the holy waters of the Ganga, giving the policeman the rest of the day off. This was an act of kindness because these poor men often had to go through hell while following us around.

I did not have anything against these policemen personally. If our eyes met, I would smile. Sometimes I would open my third-floor window furtively to see what the policeman on watch was up to, and coincidentally, he would look up at the same time as well. I would then just throw open the window. More often than not, the gentleman would then look away and walk away from the house smiling. It was fun to dodge these guards, and the failure to dodge them on occasion has proved the source of many an interesting and funny anecdote. I will recount these later. But sometimes, their sharp eye posed a hindrance to our tasks and this would make us very angry. Occasionally, we would tell them, 'Brother, just manage to keep your job somehow. What kind of misplaced noble-mindedness is this—to stand outside someone's door? What will your family and the people around you say? If the government believes we are carrying out God knows what kind of dangerous activities, it is the government's fault. Be that as it may, you carry on with your job, but please don't trouble us thus!'

There were many good men amongst these spies. They were so polite and considerate that we did not ever feel angry or irritated with them; in fact, we would often feel sympathetic towards them. Having no choice but to do their job, they would come around to the house in the morning, afternoon or evening, and then they would go and rest in a nearby street or sit and chat with people in some shop. All they did was to ascertain, once a day, that I had not left Kashi. But if they saw us leaving, they would not let go of the opportunity to follow us. Some of them were so persistent that I felt like we were enemies for a lifetime. It was fun to tease them and disappear. Sometimes we would walk around aimlessly from one street to the other, then suddenly melt into the crowd and, thus, lose them. In case a secret police constable spotted us without a tail, then we would take extra pleasure in dodging the guard who was thereafter made to tail us.

This constant game of hide and seek with the police had given us the ability to recognize spies at a single glance. Everything is out in the open now and it is apparent that we were never fooled by the police. They were unable to find out information about any new person involved in the movement by following us around. Under the strictest possible vigil, we managed to transport bombs and revolvers to various places in Kashi; we moved weapons in and out of the city too. One morning, I was on my way home. I ran into a constable of the secret service right outside the house. He had a lackey with him. The moment he saw me, he approached and began speaking to me. I replied good-naturedly. 'Coming back from a morning walk?' he asked me. I played along. 'Yes Sir, I just went for a walk.' He pointed to the small notebook I had in my pocket and asked, 'What is this?' I immediately took it out and handed it to the constable. In the notebook were a few quotes from Napoleon and anecdotes from the lives of such famous people. He examined it from cover to cover and returned it to me. And we went our separate ways happily. That day—in fact at that very moment—the lower pockets of my coat were filled with guncotton (this material is used to make fuses in bombs) and other such dangerous substances.

As I have mentioned, we could spot a policeman from far away at a glance. We could recognize small-time guards just by their shoes. As for the rest, most of them were given away by their caps or their manner of walking or holding their stick, thus saving us a lot of trouble. Sometimes these people were recognized because of their companions. We had developed a habit while walking on the road, which stayed with us for a long time even after coming out of jail. When we were outdoors, we would suddenly stop on reaching the turn of a road and start chatting with someone while looking around carefully to ensure that no one was following us. These habits of vigilance tend to amuse others. But I could not walk down the length of a street without stopping midway, sometimes at a shop on the pretext of buying something, and casting a look around.

I was aware that even the tiniest carelessness on my part could cause grave harm to the Party. Hence, I never looked back without pretending to stop for some other reason. If I sighted a face a couple of times or more, I would immediately become suspicious, and to confirm my suspicion, I would walk into a deserted lane. This way, he would either be detected and exposed as a spy or give up the chase. Once we identified the tail, the first thing to do was to try and lose them. In such a scenario, the most characteristic thing to do was to go down a desolate lane and then suddenly get into a crowded space, pulling off a disappearing act. Other than this, I was always extremely cautious when I stepped out of the house. And on the days that I had important work, I would make sure I left early in the morning. When I got back, I would find the guards entrusted with following me sitting around the house as if I was still inside!

Such was our relationship with the police. Such was the

scenario when, returning from Punjab, I reached Kashi at three in the afternoon. I reached home, avoiding detection by the police, and went from there to Dada's camping grounds. Rashbehari was in Kashi at that time. But the police did not, in their wildest dreams, have any information about our activities.

After consultations with Dada, it was decided that word about the revolution should be spread amongst the soldiers of the United Provinces too, and Bengal should very soon be informed of the rebellion in Punjab. The wait for 5 December began, for that was when I was to go to Bengal. This had been decided after speaking to Prithvi Singh. Now I was on the lookout for ways to infiltrate the barracks in the Kashi cantonment. A couple of days later, I read in the newspaper that a group of Sikhs, newly returned from the USA, were going to a village in a tonga and had been apprehended by the police. They were carrying revolvers and other weapons. When the police tried to arrest them, they opened fire and one policeman was wounded. It later came to light that the men had gone to loot a treasure somewhere. One can only 'appreciate' the 'intelligence' of the police who had suspected them at a single glance.

It is important to note that the villagers had helped the police in this instance. However, they had thought that the police were after ordinary thieves and criminals, and it was because of this misconception that they had helped them. A few days later, there was another incident. It had come to light that a revolution was being planned. Punjab was reeling from the police's efforts to nab the rebels. The police were trying to catch a Sikh youth called Bhai Pyara Singh. One day it so happened that a mounted policeman was in hot pursuit of a young man. The youth ran for about three miles. He was just about to give the horseman the slip when some villagers came and blocked his way. In a matter of minutes, the policeman rode up on his horse and arrested the man.

When the villagers realized that the person they had helped to apprehend was from their village and was in fact the beloved Bhai Pyara Singh, they were extremely repentant. Those who may have met Bhai Pyara Singh were invariably impressed by his sweet nature and will agree that his name 'Pyara' (beloved) is very apt. He was a gentle young man and his personality radiated an aura of peace and humility. Truth be told, the villagers were genuinely very fond of him, but look at the games destiny plays—those very people ended up helping the police to apprehend him.

We were very upset after reading the news about the arrests in Punjab because we were constantly worried that a golden opportunity would be wasted by a small careless mistake. At this time, we had concentrated on convincing the soldiers to join us and done nothing else. One day, I went to the barracks with a Maharashtrian friend of mine. We did not go straight to the barracks but went first to the cantonment station. This was to ensure that anyone following us would be misled about our destination. By walking along the long platform of the station, we could ascertain clearly if we were being followed. There was nothing to suggest that we had a tail. We started walking along the tracks. The railway track goes on through the Grand Trunk Road, passing by the barracks. When we reached the turning on the Grand Trunk Road, we saw two Sikh youth leaving the barracks. They were probably going to the market, but they stopped when they saw us.

I put forth many questions to them. Some of them were, 'Where are you going? What is your platoon called? Who is your sergeant? How many soldiers are there in the platoon? Where were you all before coming here? Are you going to be transferred from here soon? How many soldiers are there in the English platoon? How long have you been in this cantonment?', and so on. After replying to all our questions, they smiled and said, 'Why are you asking all these questions? You aren't going to attack us, we hope?' We laughed with them so that they would not suspect us of malafide intentions. They went their way, and we resumed our slow walk along the tracks, close to the barracks. We could not muster up the courage to enter the barracks. Soon, we saw another Sikh youth coming towards us. When we asked him where the sergeant was, he pointed to a section of the barracks and told us to go there. Thus, we understood that there were no restrictions on outsiders entering the barracks. Nonetheless, we did not have the courage to go in without knowing somebody there who could give us a modicum of an introduction at least.

We found out some things about the English and the Indian army that day and came back home. I was very excited to see a Sikh platoon in Kashi because, in Punjab, I had seen how easy it was to motivate the Sikhs. I also decided that if the platoon was to stay on for some more time in Kashi, Sikh leaders from Punjab could be invited to talk to the soldiers and work with them. In those days, no platoon or brigade of the army stayed very long in one place. This platoon, too, had visited various cantonments in a short time, and there was no saying when they would be sent off to the battlefield.

The fifth of December arrived. I reached the railway station, and the Punjab Mail arrived at the designated hour. There was a thrill running through me. It felt as if the engine had a close relationship with our revolution, and seeing it thunder into the station made me feel that it had come in frenzy, carrying news of the uprising from Punjab. Now the spark from Punjab would spread in these parts of the country too! But Prithvi Singh was not on the train. I looked hard but did not find him. I was angry with the Punjabis' utter lack of respect for time. What was I to do now? Already I knew that it was not easy to find these people. I could only guess that Prithvi Singh was unable to make it that day for some reason, and so I went to the station the next day but in vain. I did not find him on the third day either.

Chapter 6

SENTIMENT AND DEED

After conferring with Dada, I left for Bengal. Dada was in fact the leader of the entire revolution cult in the north, although, according to the old scheme of things in the Party, he had to share his position with two or three other members. Earlier, Rashbehari, too, was an ordinary worker of the Party, but slowly, with his extraordinary organizational abilities, he started taking on more and more work, and eventually took the lead. However, I will not start talking about Bengal before I finish talking about Punjab.

At this time, our party was spreading its wings from the eastern border of Bengal all the way to Punjab. I was sent to Bengal to inform our party chief and some leaders of the East Bengal wing about the developments in Punjab. I did not find anyone from East Bengal in Calcutta, so I left a note in an appropriate place, communicating that a comrade from East Bengal should come to Kashi as soon as possible. Then I went to the leaders in Calcutta and apprised them of the situation in Punjab in detail. I did detect a certain thrill in them, but they did not seem to believe all that I told them. We kept talking late into the night. What if there was a rebellion for real, and if the situation turned out to be such that instead of engaging in a face-to-face fight, we were forced to retreat? Where would we find asylum? Where would we find provisions and how would we keep the communication lines secure?

There is no point in talking about all the things we discussed that night. At the time, many Sikhs from the groups which were coming to India from various countries would rest in Bengal for a few days before making their way onward to Punjab. I told the leaders to try and establish a rapport with these people who were returning from foreign lands. We also spoke about the fact that, now, more bombs would be required and that we had to start making preparations for their manufacture right away. In the end, the discussion veered to the very old but still relevant subject of the yoga of self-realization.

Once this topic would come up, the discussion would carry on endlessly. Although the path was the same and everyone was inspired by the same principles, the sentiment of patriotism gave rise to such different thought processes in different people. One song can give rise to different emotions in five different listeners! Therefore, even amongst us, despite travelling the same route and venerating the same ideals, there were many disagreements. There has been a lot of accord, but the discord too has not been any less. The beliefs that inspired us and controlled our life and desires—personal and collective—manifested differently for each of us. We spent many a night arguing about small things related to these ideals but often failed to reach any consensus.

It was only when the eyes would droop with sleep that we would realize how exhausted we were. Yet, when one person would leave after having understood a bit about where the other was coming from, the sunrise would spread its beauty like a flowering bud on the horizon. We had to vacate the shelters before daybreak, and often during the day, amidst the many tasks that had to be undertaken, it was as if the night's argument was looking for an opportunity to make its way into a conversation. And sometimes, while we were busy with the urgent work of the day, the sentiment of yoga would once again creep up on us and overtake us. Our life was, thus, spent in a strange frenzy of sentiment and deed.

Chapter 7

IN THE ARMY BARRACKS

When I got back to Kashi, Dada told me that work was progressing well. He said, 'This afternoon, a soldier is coming to Amuk Bagh. You should go there.' I also heard that the platoon had left Kashi and there was a new platoon in its place. I reached the Bagh (garden) later in the afternoon. A friend of mine took me there and, on the way, I asked him how the Party had got to know these people. He said, 'These people used to come to the market to buy groceries. Once, on the way to the cantonment, I saw them and we got talking. Then we ended up walking back to the city with them. There was a lot of talk about the war in Europe. We also spoke a lot about Hindu–Muslim relations. We reached the village while talking about the sad plight of Hindus today and their degeneration. And that was it. We asked them their names and told them that we wanted to discuss something important if they could spare some time another day. The next day, they came to the village to bathe in the Ganga. Then we told them about ourselves. In a long conversation, we explained to them that it was better to die for their own religion in their own country than to go abroad and sacrifice their lives for the benefit of heretics. This struck a chord with them. It was easy going. They are going to meet us today after having spoken to their companions in the platoon.'

We had been waiting for a while when we saw a man walking up to us with groceries in his arms. My friend said, 'This is him.' He was dressed in white from top to bottom, as if the purity of his soul was reflected outside in his clothes. I was very happy after speaking to him. It was as if the humility of the Hindu faith was incarnated in his body. I felt a sense of joy and eagerness in him that was untouched by impulsiveness or anxiety. That day, I went to the barracks with him and had a long conversation sitting on his charpoy. Midway, he went and made arrangements to get sweetmeats for us.

This was the first time I had stepped into the English barracks. Before this, God knows how many strange things I had made up in my head about this place. On that day, sitting there, it was as if my imagined secrets were all around me. It seemed as if a long-held dream had come true. The room was long, and charpoys were laid out in two rows at the centre. Somebody was reading a book on a charpoy, others were chatting, and some were coming and going on some errand or the other. We were talking to the soldiers that we were acquainted with, but somewhere deep down, there was fear, wonderment and a strange excitement. When they started to organize the sweetmeats for us, we tried to dissuade them, saying that was no need for it. But when they insisted, we had to quiet down. When the sweets were too long in coming, we became uncomfortable and began smelling a rat. Maybe a messenger had been sent to the officer to report on us?

Very soon, the soldiers gathered around to talk to us. We had declared ourselves Rajput kshatriyas[13] in the barracks. In Banaras, there was a school and a college exclusively for Rajputs. No one but Rajputs could study there or stay in the hostel. As discussed earlier with our soldier friends, we told this lot of soldiers that we were students of the Rajput college. When they asked us our names, we promptly said Amar Singh and Jagat Singh. But we were quaking inside for the fear of our real selves being discovered. It is unnecessary to state that we had not dressed like Bengalis when we went there. Our attire was that of people from the United Provinces. My friend had a turban on, and I wore a cap. For the life of me, I couldn't tie a turban.

The soldier that we had met earlier had promised to introduce us to a sergeant. He had already spoken to the sergeant about us, and the gentlemen seemed favourably inclined towards us. A little while later, we were introduced to the officer. His name was Dalla Singh. He spoke to us rather hesitatingly and left soon, saying that he had some work to do and would come back later. I did not take to Dalla Singh; he did not appear to be trustworthy. When he made the excuse and went away, I quietly asked our acquaintance, 'Can Dalla Singh be trusted implicitly? I hope there will not be a problem.' The soldier told us to not worry and that he was a good man. I had not hidden the fact, even then, that I did not find Dalla Singh trustworthy. Till the man came back, I kept saying to my friend, 'What do you think, where has he gone? Why isn't he back yet?' We looked at each other and kept wondering. Anyhow, our suspicions were laid to rest when he came back to the barracks that day. The talk went on, and before we knew it, it was evening. Dalla Singh walked out of the barracks with us and our soldier-acquaintance to speak to us privately. He accepted our proposal and said that he would speak to some other soldiers as well. The soldier stayed with us for a little while after the officer left. He told us to rest assured about Dalla Singh. We were happy to think that we had at least one sergeant in our group now. This is how we entered the barracks. Since then, we must have gone there at least a dozen times in a month. Some of these soldiers visited us in the city and we also served them various kinds of Bengali sweetmeats, especially rasagulla. In this manner, slowly, we got to know three or four sergeants and a few soldiers.

Apparently, there was no town in India that did not know about the Swadeshi movement and the bombs. We invited these soldiers to our home and showed them revolvers, bombs and Mauser pistols to convince them that we really were members of the Party. After a few meetings, they were told that preparations for a revolution were in full swing in the Punjab Army. We were aware of the catastrophe that could befall us if they revealed our secrets. If the government heard even a whisper of the preparations for the mutiny through them, it would spell doom for Punjab. But there was nothing to be gained by keeping things from them. When they were told, 'If you don't believe us, send an emissary to Punjab, and we will introduce him to the regiments which have accepted our proposal', they believed us.

We visited the barracks mostly in the evening or at nightfall, but a couple of times, we had to go during the day as well. On one occasion, my friend and I were waiting under the shade of the trees near the barracks while another companion of ours had gone to the barracks to summon a couple of soldiers. When he did not return for a long time, we became anxious and worried that some danger had befallen him. It did not seem safe even to wait there. But how could we leave our companion there and walk away? We started imagining the worst scenarios. We were used to fear; we felt it but it never incapacitated us. Despondency never touched us, not even with a barge pole. We had been to the barracks so many times, and each time, fear had accompanied us. Yet we had come away unscathed on every occasion. Each time we came back, we realized that another day had gone by smoothly.

On that day, when our companion had not returned after a long wait, we were convinced that something untoward had happened. We are Bengalis with a turban and a cap in our hands, we thought to ourselves, sitting under the shade of the trees near the barracks like innocent people. But the Grand Trunk Road passes near here, and if anyone were to see us sitting thus, what would they think? We were contemplating all this when we spied our companion approaching us, with two soldiers in tow. We heaved a great sigh of relief. After this, I visited the barracks a couple of times in the morning when the soldiers were practising their parade. On seeing a sergeant known to us taking part in the drill, it felt as if the whole regiment was ours and as if all this was in preparation for our success. A couple of English officers passed by on horseback, but nobody paid any attention to us. No one had any doubts or suspicions at all.

I remember one day very vividly. I had just returned from another trip to Punjab. The preparations for the revolt were almost complete. One day, sitting under those very same shady trees close to the British barracks, a secret plan was hatched to overthrow the British regime. There were three of us, and some soldiers, including three officers—sergeants and deputy sergeants—joined us under the trees that evening. On one side of these trees is the railway track and on the other is the Grand Trunk Road. Across the road and beyond a small field lie the barracks. Some of the soldiers stood guard behind the trees near the road so that they could warn us if they saw danger approaching. We were also sitting hidden by the trees, discussing the dates for the impending revolt and other such things. But we would often look around to ascertain that all was well.

That day, it felt as if mythical creatures of aeons past had been reincarnated and were dancing like shadows in front of our eyes. After the spark ignited by the mutiny of 1857, thoughts of fresh preparations for a war that would destroy the British could not but be pleasing to the mind and heart. There was affection in the voices of the soldiers as they spoke to us. However, if any one of them had gone to a senior officer and divulged our secrets, all of them would have been court-martialled. Hence, they were also cautious and alert. But in such situations, the nervousness of concealment is very visible and easily caught. This was why I opposed the idea of hiding in the trees that day, and told them to stop looking around continuously. Whenever we got together to plot and plan and talk, it was important to appear natural and not seem overly excited.

But when, despite my instructions, the soldiers continued to be alert and anxious, I realized that it was because they had come there innocently and with a sense of great eagerness, having put their heart and soul into the revolt. Although they knew that meeting us put their life in danger, they would go through with it now that they had committed themselves to the cause—in for a penny, in for a pound. And that is why they did not hesitate to come and meet us under the trees outside the barracks countless times.

On the one hand, we had managed to establish contact with the barracks, and on the other, with the coming of a young Maharashtrian from America, there was now a new way to deepen our ties with Punjab. This Marathi boy was called Pingle.[14] I can't recall his first name. While sailing back to India from the United States, he had decided that he would first find out about the revolutionary movement in Bengal and then go to Punjab. He met a lot of people from the

Party in Calcutta, and this was how news of preparations for a revolution in Punjab spread all over the city. Pingle also asked many people for bombs in Calcutta; at that time, our centre used to supply explosives to all of Bengal. And so, it was his quest for bombs that brought Pingle close to us. Moreover, some of his friends were known to members of our party, and as a result, the young man soon became a part of our group. He was sent off to Kashi soon after joining.

During this time, we were beginning to think that for us, at Kashi, it might be difficult to communicate with Punjab. Prithvi Singh was to come to Kashi on the fifth of December, but there was no sign of him, nor was there any news from Punjab. In such a situation, meeting Pingle seemed as if we had struck hidden treasure. We were reassured when he came. He was tall, well-built and fair, and his eyes and his face reflected intelligence. It is very difficult to judge people, but after seeing him and talking to him, we were convinced that he would accomplish a lot for us.

What should be the principles of a man's life? While talking to Pingle about this, we somehow ended up discussing the Gita. And when he recited a few verses from the Gita, we realized that he knew it verbatim. He said, 'When I was leading the life of an ascetic, I could recite all eighteen chapters.' This made us want to know more about his past and his life, and he told us in great detail, while he removed his coat and settled down, how he had become an ascetic and travelled to various parts of the country, and then how he had gone to America to study mechanical engineering and eventually joined the revolutionary party there.

Chapter 8

THE PUNJAB STORY

Now I don't recall very well all the stories about Pingle's early life. All I remember is that he roamed all over India as an ascetic and then he went to America to study engineering, where he had joined the revolutionary party. But I don't know why he became an ascetic; why he then decided to become an engineer; and how he came to join the Ghadar Party. Perhaps Pingle did not mention any of this.

The things that I want to talk about in this chapter have faded from memory, and so I might forget to pen some things down. It seems that remembering and forgetting are related strongly to our nature. So many incidents that are important, so much information that is crucial, takes on an insignificant hue, whereas smaller issues become bigger, and then there are so many things that we forget entirely. The reason for this seems to be that that which is in our nature and that which matches our attitude stays inked on our mind, whether it is an incident, a philosophical opinion, or anything else. But we tend to forget the things that are against our nature or remember them only so that we can refute them and then we mould the memories in such a way that they help us to do so.

I remember that one day, while on the Andaman Islands, such serious thoughts had occupied my mind on reading Ramendra Babu's book *Vichitra Prasang* (Unusual Episode), and

I had recorded them in my notebook. I used to show these notes to Upendra Dada (Upendra Nath Banerjee, the editor of *Jugantar* who was serving his sentence at the Cellular Jail in connection with the Alipore case), and it was very satisfying when he praised my writing. When I speak of the Andamans, I will mention how this notebook of mine was later destroyed.

We sent Pingle off to Punjab after two days in Kashi. The mission was to get a bona fide ground report on the situation there. On arrival, he requested that we send him a large number of bombs, and he was told that we could send some. Each bomb cost about 16 rupees to make and so it would be impossible to send so many without some financial support. Pingle was instructed to arrange for some money and to also make contact with Prithvi Singh and Kartar Singh. He had the addresses for some of his contacts. Within a week, he was back in Kashi. There was nothing to stop Rashbehari from going to Punjab now, but before his visit, I managed to go to Punjab once more with Pingle.

It was a cold December when I reached Amritsar with Pingle. I was dressed like an average Indian. I could not speak Punjabi, but Pingle could. We stayed in a gurudwara. Here, Pingle introduced me to a Punjabi leader. His name was Moola Singh. This man had worked in the police department in Shanghai, and, once, he had led the policemen there on a strike. I also met some men who had worked in Penang. They were rural folk, mostly farmers or labourers, who were all very keen to do something for the motherland. The Sikh community is raised amidst such values. Most of them were tall and well-built.

This time I explained very clearly to Moola Singh the need to set up a centre for the Party, and he accepted the charge to set up the headquarters and lead the revolutionaries.

In hindsight, we know it would have been better had he not become the head of the centre.

Several of the men who had come from different parts of Punjab were complaining that there was no livelihood for them in revolutionary work and were consumed by dissatisfaction and anxiety. Moola Singh had to take on this obligation as well. These people had abandoned their homes and work in distant villages to come and serve the motherland. None of them had businesses or any other means of earning a living. These poor people were living in the gurudwara and eating in a hotel nearby. It is but natural to not want to work for something that involves paying obeisance to a leader morning and evening in order to be able to eat two meals a day. In India, such issues have often stood in the way of people who want to do something for the country, and, at times, this has resulted in disaster as well. This makes me believe that one should not attempt to serve one's country or countrymen till one has enough money to afford two meals a day. But on the other hand, financial independence implies working to earn a living, and this means you cannot dedicate all your time and energy to the cause wholeheartedly, but then nothing can really be accomplished.

Many revolutionary groups have been destroyed because they had no work or sources of income. At that time in Punjab, many workers were sitting idle because there was no leader to give them direction and see to their basic needs. The entire country was suffering a crisis of unemployment, and those who were looking for work could not find any. Rashbehari was the only revolutionary leader of the time who managed to harness this discontent among the general public and organize it well. I too tried to manage the mess as best as I could.

During the visit to Punjab with Pingle, I came to know

from Moola Singh that many regiments had promised to side with the rebels in the event of a revolt. I made a list of all the platoons we had not yet sent emissaries to, and arranged for Punjabi workers to go to the barracks where they were stationed. After introducing me to Moola Singh, Pingle had gone off to the Muktsar Fair to look for other Sikh acquaintances of his. I must say a few words about this wonderful fair for the benefit of my dear readers.

Once, Guru Gobind Singh, along with his family and other followers, was surrounded in the Anandpur Fort by Aurangzeb's Muslim army. This siege lasted almost seven months. Both sides—those under siege inside the fort and those laying siege outside—became weary of conflict. The Mughals kept proposing that the Guru give up Anandpur and leave. But the Guru did not accept this proposal. When they saw that the Guru was not willing to budge at all, some of the Sikhs managed to convince the Guru's wife, Gujri, to persuade their leader to leave. But Guru Gobind Singh was not willing to listen to her either. Hunger was rampant inside the fort, making many of the Sikhs desperate, and they were ready to disobey the Guru. It was then that Guru Gobind Singh said, 'Till now you were under the refuge of the Guru, but hunger has made you restive, and you are going to go surrender to the enemy against the wishes of the Guru. The Guru is not answerable for this. Therefore, you can all sign a *bedaawaa* (memorandum) and leave if you wish to.'

So, 40 men signed the memorandum and left. In the end, Guru Gobind Singh was compelled to leave Anandpur and roam from one place to another seeking safety. When he reached the Madr kingdom, many of the Bedaawaa Sikhs came to meet the Guru.[15] They requested the Guru to sign a treaty and make peace with the enemy once again. Hearing this, Guru Gobind Singh said, 'If you want, you can write "I am not a Sikh" and leave.' The 40 men wrote these words, handed the document over to the Guru, and left. But they felt guilty and sorrowful about deserting their guru at a difficult time, and they regretted leaving.

Later, the enemy attacked Guru Gobind Singh again near the Khidrana Lake. In the intense fighting that ensued, the Guru saw a group appear suddenly and attack the enemy from the other side. Guru Gobind Singh could not fathom who had come to his aid in this difficult hour. Their attack weakened the Muslims, but they too fell. When a body felled by a Mughal spear was examined, it was found to be that of a woman. She was called Mai Bhago. It was she who had urged the Bedaawaa Sikhs to repent. Once the battle ended, the Guru went back to the battlefield and cleaned the face of every Sikh slain there as a father would do for his son. He realized that one of them was still alive. His name was Maha Singh. The Guru cradled his head on his lap and asked him, 'What do you want, Maha Singh?' Maha Singh's eyes filled up. He said, 'All I want is that you tear up the document on which we wrote "I am not a Sikh."' The Guru now understood clearly who had attacked the enemy suddenly. He saw that all 40 of those disciples had lain down their lives in the battlefield. He also saw women amongst the bodies lying there. The Guru tore up the documents. Soon, Maha Singh also entered eternal sleep.

Guru Gobind Singh addressed those present there and said, 'A Khalsa[16] that is so strong cannot be destroyed. Wherever a devotee sheds blood for the cause, that place is sacred. This place has seen the sacrifice of many devotees and will, henceforth, be known as *Muktsar* (the pool of liberation) and those that bathe in this lake will be liberated.' That is how the Muktsar Fair started. This is a huge occasion for the Sikhs, and more than 100,000 Sikhs gather here every year. All Sikh festivities have such contexts and history attached to them, and Sikhs are brought up on these stories, making them sterling human beings. In my opinion, the Sikh community is the bravest there is.

When Pingle came back from the Muktsar Fair, Kartar Singh and Amar Singh, too, were at the gurudwara. Kartar Singh was very happy to see me and asked, 'So, when is Rashbehari coming?' I replied, 'Now, that is the next thing. We just need to make some arrangements for his stay here and once your work is organized a little better, he will come.' I categorically explained to Kartar Singh the need for a centre and told him that Moola Singh had taken on the responsibility of setting it up. I told him to rent two houses each in Lahore and Amritsar for Rashbehari. Dada had already spoken to me about this; we should have access to various houses at the same time. And that is what was done. In fact, I chose the house in Amritsar. Someone else was sent to look at the house in Lahore. I was very hopeful when I heard Kartar Singh's reports on the actual situation in Punjab. I felt that this time the work being done was quite tangible.

Another group of Sikhs came into Amritsar from the USA, and I met with some of their leaders. One of them was so old that the wrinkles on his face seemed to weigh it down. I think it was this elderly gentleman who would later spend the last tenacious years of his life in the Andaman Islands, passing away in prison around the age of 70. Even at that age, he was involved in the strike at the Cellular Jail and never drew back. None of the members of this group had yet reached home. They had stopped over at Amritsar on their way back from America. They gave us 500 rupees of their hard-earned money.

In those days, Kartar Singh would go to the villages,

travelling about 40 to 50 miles on his bicycle every day. He visited village after village, never tiring of this hard work. The more he worked, the more energy he seemed to have. After having made a round of the villages, he started on the army platoons that had not yet been approached. The methods of the revolutionary groups in Punjab were so raw and they were so untrained that, soon, arrest warrants were issued for many of them. Once, the police surrounded a village in order to arrest Kartar Singh, who had been sighted in the area. When he got news of the police cordon, he got onto his cycle and went to the very same village. The police did not recognize him, and Kartar Singh was saved by sheer courage. Had he not done what he did, he would most probably have been caught on the way.

Expenditure had risen so much that the donations were no longer enough. So the revolutionaries in Punjab were forced to resort to dacoity. It later came to light that Moola Singh was not an honest person and that he had misappropriated party funds. Moreover, he had organized a dacoity in someone's house to settle some personal scores. We realized all this too late. However, a few days later, he was arrested in an inebriated condition.

In all great movements, along with the dedicated and hardworking, there are some rotten eggs too. The movement cannot be faulted for this; after all, it is a human endeavour. I think even Lenin said that for every honest Bolshevik, at least 39 thugs and 60 idiots had joined his party. And I had heard from the respected Saratchandra Bandyopadhyay that Deshbandhu Das had once said that although they had grown old practising law and seen the biggest crooks, they had never in their whole lives encountered as many crooks as they had come across in the Non-Cooperation Movement.

This time I stayed with the revolutionaries for about a week in Punjab and was able to observe their behaviour closely. They would wake up early even in the extreme cold, bathe and recite the Guru Granth Sahib every morning. Their food habits were not healthy as they would often eat in hotels. But they were very cordial with each other, always addressing their comrades with prefixes that were used to accord respect. It was around this time that I met Bhai Nidhan Singh. He was a 50-year-old Sikh who had lived abroad for about 30 to 35 years and had married a Chinese beauty during his sojourn there. I often saw him reading the scriptures. Once, I spotted him at the railway station, quietly sitting and reading a miniature copy of the Guru Granth Sahib. He did not do this just for show because I saw him do this in the Andamans as well. There was a kind of energy in him that I have not seen in youngsters.

The common perception in India about the sexual conduct of Punjabis is not good. The Sikhs have a particularly bad reputation in this regard. Maybe the reason for this is that the ratio of men to women is skewed; there are far fewer women in their community than men. Constant struggles against foreign invaders and contact with aggressive groups had weakened their culture. Despite these periods of degeneration, this extraordinary culture also has great potential for progress in better times. Even those who have gone astray have an immense capability to change for the good, which is not often seen in other people. Therefore, just as debauchery, brutality, depravity and a propensity for violence have besmirched the Sikh character, they are also capable of great austerity, magnanimity and forgiveness. And that is why, in the past, this 'degenerate' Sikh community had shown extraordinary valour and restraint in Nankana Sahib and Guru ka Bagh.

The women of this land are just as treacherous, but in the very same Punjab, there was an example of unparalleled honour and loyalty. Bhai Balmukund, Bhai Parmanand's paternal cousin and the son of a former teacher at DAV College, Lahore, was arrested in the Delhi Conspiracy Case. Motidas, an ancestor of Bhai Balmukund, had been sawed in half during the Sikh upsurge. Balmukund had got married only a year before his arrest. His wife Shrimati Ramrakhi was very beautiful and very young. The day her husband was arrested, she became very anxious and put her body through various sufferings. When Bhai Balmukund was sentenced to death by hanging, she went to meet him. She was crying so much that she could not even speak to him properly and to her heart's content. She came back home and went on existing, almost like a corpse. One day, she was in her room when she heard the sound of weeping outside. When she came out, she heard the news of her husband's death. After that she simply wasted away and passed on, thinking only of him. Where can you find such sacrifice and love? Just the thought of this sends shivers up one's spine, and the throat chokes with emotion. You are great, Balmukund's wife! Can there be such a husband without such a wife? Bharat is ill-fated indeed, as it could not see such a couple thrive!

Chapter 9

THE STORY OF THE KASHI CENTRE

Even though the trip to Punjab had been invigorating and I came back very hopeful, during my stay there I felt that I had been surrounded by malpractices and irregularity. I cannot even begin to explain how peaceful and pleasing Kashi is in comparison to the cities of Punjab. I can't say why this is so, but this time, on my return, Kashi seemed more salubrious than in all my years of living here. Just the touch of the breeze on one's body felt as if all the sins had been wiped off. One day in Kashi seemed to remove the accumulated guilt of many months. When Rashbehari came back after all the preparations for the revolt had failed, he too had the exact same feelings!

After returning to Kashi, I heard that yet another leader we were acquainted with had just been arrested. Even in the atmosphere of hope that prevailed in those days, news of the frequent arrests and jailing of many acquaintances caused me to despair. Whenever I had a bit of free time amidst all the work, my thoughts would turn there, and it would hurt to think that they were not there with us.

Mr Jatindra Nath Mukhopadhyay from Calcutta came to Kashi at this time. He was well-known and highly placed among the leaders of the revolt. History has shown that when a new movement rears its head against the established norms of society or nation, it cannot be successful if the people involved in it are not extraordinary. Such exceptional people do not wither under the wrath of the state or due to rejection by society. That is why, although such people are few in number, the impact of their life and work is deep. The history of the revolt has proven this to be true. Jatindra Babu was one such person, and his influence on the people he worked with as well as on society as a whole was strong and visible.

While working for the revolt, one must operate in great secrecy. Hence, though many different groups were formed all over the country for the revolt, they may not all be known to the public even today. These revolutionary groups could not be united into one huge organization due to the lack of a strong and influential central leadership. They remained separate despite the fact that the effort to integrate them into a big party had been made for a long time. No group wanted to merge with another and lose its independence. As for the leaders, they opposed the move as they did not want to lose power over their groups. It is difficult to say whether it was good or bad to have so many small groups. However, when a man is truly inspired by an ideal or has lofty ambitions, such egoistic and selfish feelings do not surface.

'Man does not want to defer to another naturally, but he does bow before a stronger person.'

Jatindra Babu's leadership was such that, under his influence, many small revolutionary groups in Bengal had merged. Although he was no renowned intellectual, many a scholar in the movement had acknowledged his leadership. He was as generous as he was valiant. All those who were associated with the revolt in Bengal were aware of the strength of his character. But even he was able to bring all these different groups together only when news of preparations for a revolt in Punjab provided the impetus and excitement. Nonetheless, the merger showcased Jatindra Babu's amazing capabilities. There were many groups consisting of people of diverse behaviour and extraordinary character. Therefore, to manage all of them was no mean feat.

At this time, in Bengal, there were two important groups working for the revolt. Jatindra Babu was one of the leaders of the first group. The other was divided into two sections—a group that worked in Bengal and one that operated outside it. Rashbehari had been given charge of all activity outside Bengal, but for the work that was being carried out inside Bengal, there was no single leader.

Jatindra Babu was asked to come to Kashi so that the movement across North India could be consolidated. From the border state of Punjab to East Bengal and Assam, the whole country was, in a way, ready for a revolt. The soldiers in Punjab were so impatient to get going that it was impossible to calm them down. It is difficult for me to say whether we did the right thing in holding them back. However, I do feel that had we not done so, something drastic would have taken place in Punjab at the time. Who can say whether the result would have been good or bad? We had hindered them because we wanted the whole country to rise up together in revolt and show its power.

I don't know if the government was aware of Jatindra Babu's visit to Kashi or of his purpose in coming here. I should clarify why I have mentioned this here. Whatever I have narrated here till now, I have not let out anything that is secret; I have only mentioned those things which have already come to light in connection with the conspiracy cases and been proved in court. I have, however, refrained from speaking about certain things that the government does not know clearly, lacking the requisite evidence to prove these incidents. Hence, the facts and details I talk about here cannot harm anybody, although the public has only a vague idea of them. The hearings for the conspiracy cases that were filed and prosecuted during the last war were held mostly in jails, and people knew very little about these proceedings because the government and judges did not want the details published, even though they had been proved in courts of law.

For that reason, the incidents I recount here must be unknown to many of my readers. All I want is that the people should know what the government knows. I want to speak unhesitatingly about all that happened in our country—concealing neither our strengths nor our weaknesses, and pointing out where we used poor judgement or were narrow minded. This will only help us; it will never harm our cause! There is no need to hide the extensive preparations that were carried out for a revolt. I want my countrymen to be aware of every little detail. Once my book is done, people will know that the revolt was not a mere thought in the minds of a few youngsters, and the preparations were nowhere as disorganized as the Rowlatt Report makes them out to be.

The Report was written with the aim of ensuring that the Indians lost their self-confidence; hence, it narrates the incidents in a manner that justifies the government's policy of oppression and subjugation. There are many exaggerations in the document, mostly about very inconsequential things. The purpose of it all is to ridicule the revolutionaries and make sure that they are the laughing stock of the entire country. Moreover, important information that could give hope to our countrymen has been suppressed. Reading the Rowlatt Report, no one can imagine the slow and careful process of collecting and organizing manpower—akin to putting together carefully polished gems on the string of a necklace—that went into choosing revolutionaries worthy of fighting for this country. It upsets me that I am not capable of presenting all the details and instances of this great endeavour, but, of course, I shall try and do the best that I can.

A lot of people believe that revealing all these secrets by writing about them in this manner (as if anything is secret any longer!) is providing the government with more ammunition and encouraging it to be more coercive. In answer to that, I will point out that the fire of revolt, which once simmered only in a part of Bengal, has spread all the way to Rawalpindi and Peshawar in 16–17 years, thanks to the government's coercive policies. Therefore, those who wish to eradicate these oppressive policies should be careful to not laugh at the preparations for the revolt in 1915 and not demean it or reject it entirely. Instead, they should tell the government in categorical terms that if the country's true desires are suppressed and a rightful movement for independence is not allowed to develop, then such secret activities are bound to flourish. An underground movement or revolution is no less legitimate than an open protest. The very fact that England allows protests and movements in the public sphere, however powerful the protests may be, ensures that there are not as many covert organizations and activities there as in France and other European countries. A society that is lifeless can be governed by coercion, but a society that wishes to progress cannot be controlled in the same way under any circumstances. Everyone should understand this—be it the government or the people of India.

Jatindra Babu is no longer with us, and that is why I am not hesitant today to share all this. Our countrymen probably do not know that we were working together in North India with only one purpose and with all our heart and soul. Even the revolutionary groups in Bengal may not be entirely aware of this. It was Jatindra Babu's explicit request that the day of the revolt be pushed back as much as possible so that he would get at least two months' time once he reached Bengal to arrange for some money. He kept reiterating that it would not be sensible to undertake such a massive uprising without enough funds at one's disposal. But his definition of 'enough' was rather huge. It was impossible to collect such an enormous amount of money in such a short period of time and under such duress. In the end, Jatindra Babu did accept this, but he could never understand it.

Meanwhile, the soldiers in Punjab were getting very impatient and restless. They lived in a constant state of indecisiveness, not knowing when they would be sent off to the battlefields of the Great War in the West. Moreover, even within India, the soldiers were regularly transferred from one end of the country to the other. If they were sent off to a station in the south, all their dreams would lie broken! For all these reasons, it was becoming increasingly difficult to manage the soldiers in Punjab. We, too, were constantly worried about all the soldiers ready for a revolt being sent off to some other place. That is why we could not accept Jatindra Babu's request. It felt as if we would be letting a golden opportunity slip out of our hands. On the one hand, we were trying to keep the soldiers calm, and on the other, we were amidst feverish preparations to show the country that we were capable of something. We were insistent that our project should not be needlessly delayed. All this was also explained to Jatindra Babu, and he had no choice but to agree and march on with us, however unwillingly.

For a long time, we believed that it was not a difficult task to provoke uneducated people to revolt. We also knew that our task could not be accomplished just by goading the people, and that is why we did not pay much attention to this aspect. We believed that a firm foundation for the revolution could be laid if we got the educated youth together first and built a strong nationwide organization, followed by efforts to spread our message among the Indian soldiers and to convince them to join us. But we did not endeavour to establish any contact with foreign organizations or movements, and that was a huge mistake on our part. Many times, the idea of making arrangements for better arms and ammunition was discussed, but the leaders were not too keen on this. They kept saying that there was still time. But when the time came, unfortunately, we had neither the means nor the contacts to procure these supplies. In Bengal and Punjab at least, if not in the entire country, there was extensive recruitment of the youth for the movement, but the kind of development and acceptance it saw in Bengal was unmatched by any other place in the subcontinent.

The strength of an organization, built on the strengths of the inherent nature of a person and the company he keeps over time, cannot be matched by any other. It is for this reason that the organization in Bengal was the strongest. In Punjab, it was compromised by the fact that all activities towards a revolution were carried out by Sikhs who had come back to India from America and other countries. To the people here, these foreign-returned Sikhs were outsiders. Moreover, the organization in Punjab was not consolidated with the kind of camaraderie that existed between people from diverse backgrounds in Bengal. Although, here too, the countrymen were a little unresponsive to the need of the hour, the people of Bengal were not indifferent to the Party. Above all, the stronger the aims and beliefs of the leadership, the stronger the organization.

When you look at things with this perspective, you understand why the movement was so powerful and cohesive in Bengal. There was a true nationalistic fervour in this region, whether it was in politics, literature or religion. Hence, the action and reaction of various principles and ideals that was seen in the Bengal groups was not visible outside it. When I talk about Bengal, I will describe how the nationalistic awakening in the country was reflected in the personal lives of the revolutionaries. I have not seen the same attitude or the kind of impact it had anywhere else. Here I am mainly referring to places outside Bengal, where we were preparing for the revolution.

If Bengal had the same ease that other regions had to join the army, then the revolt would have happened much sooner. But at this time, the preparations in Punjab were taking place at such a fast pace that we were left wondering if Bengal would be able to participate in the revolt at all. I felt very upset thinking about the taint on Bengal's reputation from earlier times, and that is why I wanted to work there. When Jatindra Babu and the others returned to Bengal to carry on their work there, I was eager to go with them. But Dada did not agree to this. He said that he would go to Punjab soon, and I was assigned the task of staying between these two states and coordinating things for everyone. I had no choice but to remain in Kashi.

It was around this time that the motor dacoities began in Bengal. In a short time, many dacoities were committed and a lot of money was accumulated. A few days before these incidents, about 50 Mauser pistols had been stolen from the Rodda Company. So far, the preparations for the revolution in Bengal were led by two main groups. Jatindra Babu was talented but did not take much initiative in the beginning.

As a result, the other groups were not productive either. This time when Jatindra Babu jumped into the thick of things and got completely involved in the preparations for the revolution, the work in Bengal picked up. Seeing his renewed vigour, we were all happily surprised.

Rashbehari also left for Punjab. A reward of 7,500 rupees had been announced for his arrest. The failure to arrest Dada was a stain on the efficacy of the government, which had left no stone unturned to apprehend him. On one side was this majestic British superpower that had endless money and power at its disposal, which was running this huge country from end to end with a superbly organized administration, and whose spy network was second maybe only to that of Russia in Asia. On the other side was our impecunious revolutionary group, so steeped in penury that one day Rashbehari suggested, 'Hand me over to the British and earn 7,500 rupees.' This group had the sympathy of our countrymen, it was too scared to help in any way. Moreover, the leaders of this group were not prominent men in society. All they had was complete faith and confidence in their aims and principles. To put it succinctly, these men were on their own, working for the cause without aid or heed by their own people.

In such a precarious position, the revolutionary group not only managed to defend itself but also led the British government on a merry chase. The main reason that the British with all their power and resources could not arrest Rashbehari was the extensive and well-organized arrangements we had as a group. It would have been impossible to save Rashbehari had we not had this network. Undoubtedly, Rashbehari's quick wit, adroitness and luck played a crucial role too. He would walk away unscathed from many a dangerous and difficult situation. I still get goosebumps when I think of those situations today.

What else can one call it but God's grace! I will describe all this in the second part of the book. Not only Rashbehari, but many other youngsters had succeeded in avoiding detection and arrest during this time and, in fact, managed to dodge the powerful enemy for three to four years. If the unknown stories of these people are ever written, Indian literature will be richer for it.

Rashbehari left by the night train that went to Punjab via Delhi. One of us would always stay with him. Up till Delhi, the journey was smooth and incident-free. Just as the train left Delhi, Rashbehari happened to spot a constable of the secret police whom he knew in his bogie. One can only imagine what Dada must have felt on making this discovery. Fortunately, he was wearing a cap that concealed his face and went unnoticed. At the next station, he quietly changed bogies and travelled on in the same train. That is how courageous he was. Rashbehari was the kind of person who jumped into the fire with his eyes wide open. Eventually, he reached Amritsar.

Meanwhile our people had started approaching the cantonments in United Provinces, Bihar and Bengal. In a few days, Kartar Singh and other Sikhs came to Kashi with news from Punjab. We now had information on the troops in the north, and what we understood was that the British soldiers were very few in number in these cantonments and most of them were fresh recruits. Looking at the thin, lanky youngsters in the provincial army, we wanted to seize the earliest chance to test our powers. In those days, there were only two or three big cantonments in all of India, and with the exception of the station closest to Kabul, there were no more than 300 British soldiers in each cantonment. In the other cantonments also, their number was not more than 1,000 or 2,000. One could easily carry on a war for at least a year with the arms and ammunition that they had. We had obtained information on every little detail that we could think of. For example, how many rifles did each regiment possess? How many cartridges did they have? How are the magazines guarded and by whom?

The Indian soldiers were mentally disturbed in those days. They constantly worried that they would be ordered to go to Europe at any time. Yet the soldiers would welcome our people warmly in the cantonments and listen to them with attention. Once, a young man who worked with us went to one of the cantonments, and a meeting of the soldiers took place there that very night. Both officers and soldiers were present, and they heard the foreign-returned youngster out with respect. In the end, although they did not offer to take the lead in this revolt, they gave their word that they would not fire at the rebels. And when the revolution began in earnest, they promised they would join in too.

I visited the Kashi regiment many more times. There were good men, apart from Dalla Singh, in this regiment. They were willing to participate in the revolution for the welfare of the country. One day, Dalla Singh asked us, 'Sir, once the country is free, will we get some land or a state pardon?' Another day, we took some guncotton with us to show him how it burnt to a crisp at the mere hint of a fire. The soldiers were surprised to see the magic; this is one of the ways we tried to influence Dalla Singh and his companions to side with us. I met some of the men from this regiment later, and they treated me with a lot of respect. One of the soldiers was more than 50 years of age. He said to me, 'Sir, none of my acquaintances are alive now. I am the only one surviving. My end too is near. I am no longer scared of death; you are my guru now for you have taught me to look at God and not at worldly possessions.'

Many of the regiments that we made contact with got transferred to other parts of the country. As a result of this, word of our work travelled across India. Apart from spreading the message and convincing the regiments, we also started going to the villages and trying to talk to people there. In the United Provinces, there are certain villages that are inhabited only by Thakurs.[17] Cadets of the British Army are chosen from such villages. The uneducated people from the United Provinces and Punjab are not like the illiterate in Bengal. One, unlike the Bengalis, they are physically strong and have a strong sense of what is theirs and what is not. They may be uneducated, but their political sense is finely tuned. As compared to even the most educated and refined people in Bengal, the people in these regions also have a very strong sense of belonging to their religion. These uneducated people, if given able leadership, can perform the most impossible of tasks.

We started interacting with them, and the response from them was promising. Rashbehari, too, was meeting soldiers in Punjab. However, none of the meetings took place in the house that he was staying in. There were two or three other houses that were designated for this purpose. He used to meet the soldiers in one such house. The story I heard about two soldiers from Lahore can never be forgotten. One of them was called Lachhman Singh. The other soldier was a Muslim, and I don't remember his name. Both were sergeants. Lachhman Singh had a strong influence on the other soldiers. I spoke to one of the soldiers from this regiment later in the Andamans. He told me that many years earlier Lachhman Singh had formed a small group in his regiment and they would meet often to read Sikh scriptures and talk of various issues. The English officers had ordered them to stop when they heard of it. But this group carried on intermittently over many years. The people in the regiment considered Lachhman Singh to be a man of very strong moral character, almost a saint.

When Lachhman Singh was sentenced to death, the government tried to entice the Muslim sergeant to reveal some secrets about his companion with the promise of sparing him the noose. He was also asked if he would like to be hanged with a *kafir* (infidel). This brave and patriotic Muslim sergeant had a wonderful answer. He said, 'I will be sent to heaven if I have the honour of being hanged along with Lachhman Singh.' He too was hanged.

As the day designated for the revolt drew closer, our hearts were plagued with doubt. Would we be able to make it through? Will we be able to take on such a big responsibility? We had left no stone unturned in our preparations for the revolt, but the thought of the day drawing closer was giving us goosebumps. Even Dada had admitted to feeling this way before he left for Punjab.

What we wanted was that one fine day, without warning, at exactly the same time, the British soldiers should be attacked across all the cantonments. And in the ensuing chaos, whosoever surrendered to us would be arrested. The revolt should begin in the night, the supply of electricity in the city should be cut off, the English volunteers and other strongmen should be incarcerated, the treasures looted and the prisoners freed from jail. Then the governance of the city should be handed over to one of our able companions, and all rebels should thereafter meet in Punjab. We did not take it for granted that we would win the war with the British. But we were sure that if the abovementioned strategy was followed, the revolt would result in a peculiar international situation. And if we could sustain this war for a year with help from some foreign countries which were enemies of the British, liberating our country would be difficult but not impossible.

One day, some men came from Punjab with the news that the date for the revolt had been finalized. The mutiny would begin on 21 February 1915. It would begin in the night. I got the news on a Sunday. My feelings were so strong that I was trembling in body and in spirit. I had never had this strange emotion ever before. It was neither pleasure nor apprehension.

There was just one week to go before the revolution began. All our centres were informed of the date for the revolt. Many of us felt an indescribable fear despite the ongoing preparations for the revolution; it was as if we couldn't believe that it was really happening. Centuries of humiliation and inferiority had robbed us of our self-confidence to such an extent that despite desiring freedom from our colonizers and working towards it with all our heart and soul, we could not believe that the flag of revolt was soon going to fly high. Just as a person who has seen too much unhappiness cannot believe that his fate will change one day and that he will be happy, just as a person who is always rejected and has always been cheated learns to live without hope and does not believe that he will one day be loved, I too had lost all hope of India's fate ever changing.

Chapter 10

BETRAYAL AND DISAPPOINTMENT

The preparations for the revolt carried on despite such thoughts. Shorts were stitched for the mutineers at different centres of the Party in Bengal. A national flag of India was made in Punjab. The Sikhs requested a specific colour, one that represented them, to be incorporated into the flag. In the end, the national flag was composed of four colours, to represent Hindu, Muslim, Sikh and other religions and communities of India. Arrangements for provisions were made; lists were drawn up of motor lorries that could ferry people. All the revolutionaries in North India were counting the days and looked towards Punjab with a lot of expectation, as if on one signal from Punjab, the volcano would erupt and spew hot ash. Apparently, Shri Mahaprabhu Jagadbandhu[18] had said that the day he stepped out of the cave after meditating for 12 years would be the day that India's era of freedom would commence. Maybe that is why he came out of his cave in February 1915. He had no inkling about the revolution. But when he came out, he signalled that there was still time and went back inside. One cannot always understand God's design.

Eventually, the huge edifice of the revolt crumbled to dust, as if a bud had been plucked and offered to God before it could bloom into a flower. I shall tell you why this happened.

A Muslim deputy superintendent of the secret police in

Punjab brought to the revolutionary group a Sikh called Kripal Singh.[19] He was a spy for the police. Kripal Singh managed to get in with our group because of his cousin who was a soldier in the British Army and also worked with us. But very soon, a lot of people began to suspect that he was spying on us. Some leaders suggested that he be kept under surveillance. Consequently, it was discovered that he met with police officers every day at a particular time. At this point, there were merely a couple of days to go before the revolution began. It was agreed that killing him could only result in complications that would obstruct our plans and, therefore, nothing was done to remove this thorn from our midst.

In a similar situation, the people from East Bengal would not have settled for anything other than relieving the spy of his life. Later, it was learnt that the police knew of the day designated for the revolt because Kripal Singh had informed them of it. It was then decided that Kripal Singh would not be allowed to leave the house where he was staying and the date for the revolt was advanced by two days. It would now take place on 19 February instead of 21 February. Unfortunately, or maybe it was meant to be, when the person entrusted with the job of conveying the message about the change of plans to the cantonment came back and told Rashbehari, 'I have informed the cantonment about the nineteenth of February', Kripal Singh happened to be sitting there. I think this happened on 18 February.

That day, after lunch, when everyone went their ways, Kripal Singh tried to sneak off. The guard who had been assigned to keep an eye on him stayed with him all day but did not use force on him. In fact, not everybody knew the truth about Kripal Singh. Finally, he managed to step out of the house. At that very moment, he saw a man from the secret police coming his way on a bicycle. Thus, the information about 19 February was passed onto the police, and a few hours later, the arrests had begun. There were seven or eight arrests from the house that Kripal Singh was living in. Some of them were leaders. Only a couple of them knew where Rashbehari was staying, as he was always careful to meet people in other houses. The arms were now being guarded by the British troops and not the Indian soldiers. The British volunteer army was readied and ordered to move to camps. It started patrolling or what in a war situation is known as 'picketing'. Armed British soldiers were prowling around the villages. This was happening everywhere—in Lahore, Delhi, Ferozepur.

People thought this heightened activity must be because of the War in Europe. The Indian soldiers who were part of the secret plan were nervous and because the date had been advanced a lot of the people from the villages could not reach the designated spots. Only Kartar Singh managed to reach the Ferozepur cantonment on time with 70 to 80 people. The situation there was the same as in Lahore—the arms and ammunition were now under the charge of the British soldiers who were guarding it vigilantly. But Kartar Singh did not get any news of the new developments in Lahore.

Despite the strict surveillance, Kartar Singh managed to meet the sergeant of the Kali platoon (During British rule, the Indian soldiers in the regiment were called the 'Kali paltan' [black army]) in the barracks. The sergeant told him that they would have to wait it out; doing anything right now would be inviting ruin. Kartar Singh understood that all was now lost. He knew what the situation would be if they let the next couple of days pass. He tried everything possible to convince the soldiers that this was their last chance and, if action was not taken that very day, nothing would happen. But the soldiers pointed to the English guards and said that it would be a foolhardy effort. How can one jump consciously into a raging fire or swallow the fly after seeing it float in your milk?

Had the Indians had sufficient arms and ammunitions that day, nobody could have stopped the revolt from taking place. Had educated youngsters with an understanding of and belief in the revolution joined the army, the preparations for the revolution would not have gone waste.

Kartar Singh went home dejected and empty-handed. The villagers went home too. When Kartar Singh reached Lahore, there had been a series of arrests in Punjab. Some of those who were apprehended would blurt out the names of other 10 or 15 companions, and the British Army would raid a village and arrest them all together. The Indian soldiers in cantonments across the north were restless. A Kali paltan in Rawalpindi was dismissed. There were home searches and arrests in Lahore. Even on a shadow of suspicion, Sikhs were carted off to jail. In this nab-and-arrest scenario, things got tense and shots were also fired at times. In a few days, the matter had become very serious. It was difficult to trust each other even inside the group.

Kartar Singh was an intelligent youngster. When he reached Lahore, he went straight to Rashbehari's place without making any other stops. Since very few people knew about it, it was the most secure location. Rashbehari was lying on his cot; all life had seeped out of him. He was dead with exhaustion. Both men were quiet. Their silence expressed their intense pain. How many of us must bear such heartbreak in life? The bigger your imagination, the deeper and more serious your thoughts, the more pain you suffer. Their biggest dream had just been torn to shreds. Their gigantic plan had turned to dust before it could materialize. In such a situation, even a languid mind can feel distress, and if fear is roused in the heart of a soldier, it is only natural. Both leaders had pinned their hopes on the opportunity provided by the upheaval in Europe and were devastated by the fact that despite so much preparation, the Party had accomplished nothing. Only God knew when such an opportunity would arise again!

However, despite this enormous failure, they pulled up their socks and got to work again. Their immense hope, it seemed, did not let their hearts despair. Holding on to their hope like a lamp underneath India's darkly clouded sky, they moved forward. They had suffered a huge loss but could not give up. How many of us can understand such mental strength? Can the Indians look at the revolutionary group as the British see them? Only the brave can respect the brave. Perhaps this is why Indians have always regarded the revolutionaries with contempt. This attitude weighs like a huge stone on the hearts of the revolutionaries. Nobody else has dishonoured the group thus. The people that the group expected the most empathy from are those who scorned them.

Nonetheless, the Party did not lose hope. It was as if its very heartbeat was fuelled by a dream that refused to die. The revolutionaries no longer trusted anybody but themselves, and the revolt did materialize, but it did not make sense to judge a movement by the success or failure of a single event. To analyse this movement, one must look at the ideals and imagination that inspired it as well as the innumerable people who risked and sacrificed their lives to achieve its goals. These should be the parameters for measuring the worth of a movement. In the next part of the book, I wish to look at the ideals that prompted Indian youngsters to commit their lives to the service of the country. I will also discuss the preparations made by the group before the start of the World War in Europe and the form the revolutionary party took after the failure of the revolt in Punjab.

Part 2

Chapter 1

AFTER THE FIRST FAILURE

The revolution in Punjab may have come to naught, but that did not quell the fire of rebellion in India. All the efforts of the revolutionaries seemed to have been in vain. Many were hanged, and thus sacrificed their lives for the motherland; many others suffered and died in jails. So many families were destroyed: countless mothers could not bear the sight of their sons suffering and lost their minds; countless fathers lost their jobs and whole families fell into poverty. These people went from one place to another, looking for a roof over their heads and some means of sustenance. Entire villages and communities were ravaged by the crackdown on the rebels but the revolutionaries themselves were undaunted. Why?

Throughout India's history, we have seen that under a strong and able leader, many times, our people have shown bravery that has brought glory to the country. Often, our countrymen have turned the impossible into the possible and surprised the world, but it is India's misfortune that in the absence of a strong leadership, the country has always fallen into despair—to such an extent that it is difficult to believe it is the same India that attained such heights of grandeur. The glory of the past seems but a mirage. For instance, we see that after Ranjit Singh, the Khalsa community lacked a strong leader and was weakened. Rajputana fell into decline after Rana Raj Singh, and after Maharaja Chhatrasal, the kingdom of Bundelkhand lost its voice. I believe that India has seen some illustrious leaders and rulers, and many a colossus have been born here. But that has never made any qualitative change in people's attitudes. (Many great men have come and gone but the people have not learnt much from them.)

But the novelty of this revolutionary movement was that we did not wait for anyone. When the well-known and respected leaders of the country were walking one path, this community of poor unknown youngsters—undeterred by thousands of disasters, holding on to hope and fervour in the face of innumerable difficulties and impediments—forged ahead against the wishes of these leaders and on the path that they had forbidden. Esteemed Tilak came out of prison, saw error in the old ideals, changed his opinions and even decided to leave the country and move to Germany. Wise Vipin Chandra, on his return from England, spent all his energy in convincing his countrymen that perhaps total freedom for India was not in its best interests. Rishi Aurobindo renounced politics, turned to God and meditation, and began to preach integral yoga. The central theme of this vision was the evolution of human life into a divine life. He believed in a spiritual realization that not only liberated but also transformed human nature, enabling a divine life on earth.

There were no other leaders worth mentioning in India at that time. These leaders had earlier advocated the struggle for complete independence. The vitality they brought to the soul of India runs through its veins even today and inspires the whole country. Yet, two of these great men renounced their principles and beliefs; the third acquiesced. There was nobody to lead the way and guide in the political sphere. But the spirit of India had been awakened, and it could not be denied now. Where there is life, the soul shows the way. The youngsters who had listened to their conscience, to their inner voice, had not swerved from the path. They had not become a part of the process after consulting the political leaders of the country, nor had they trusted the leaders implicitly on this journey. The latter had not done what the younger generation thought was necessary to achieve the ideals that they had espoused. Barring a couple of older leaders, even the most famous among them did not say the right things, and what was more, often did not do what they said. What I mean to say is that they lacked complete dedication and sincerity in their work for the cause.

But the same cannot be said of the young revolutionaries of India. The older generation of leaders in the country decided the best course of action based on what they felt they could do or not do. But the young men of our country do not stop to reflect on this or step back once they believe in something. All that matters then is the appropriate course of action to achieve their goals and the resources required to make this possible. This is how the revolutionary movement of the youngsters came into being. These young revolutionaries did not wait for any great leader to guide them or advise them on the pros and cons of their plans. It is difficult to find people like these, so steadfast in the face of danger and failure, whose character is so strong that it does not budge from its principles despite all sorts of deterrents. There was no dearth of such people in the revolutionary party and, therefore, they did not lose hope or focus even in the worst of times. And that is why, despite the failure of all efforts in February 1915 to stage an uprising in Punjab, the movement to mount a revolution in India continued.

Two hundred people were arrested and convicted of

treason in Punjab. The revolutionary group in Punjab was thus destroyed. These companions in the game of life and death were all now prisoners of the government. Their existence was that of the living dead. For those who had eluded the first round of arrests, it was like playing with fire. Any day, one's closest companions could be arrested by the police. Today's trusted companion could betray tomorrow, weighed down by the selfish desire to stay alive and forgetting all about duty, courage and ideals. All the centres of revolutionaries in Punjab were, thus, exposed one by one. Homes were searched and arrests were carried out all over Lahore. A bomb was found in one house and wire-cutting tools in another. Very few people knew where Rashbehari was staying, and that is why he remained safe. Circumstances were changing every day. There was no knowing what could happen next and when. And yet, planning for a revolution began anew.

First, it was decided that three Sikhs would leave Lahore to test the waters. These three, while travelling in a *tonga*, were stopped by the police at a turning on the road—the reason being, simply, that they were Sikhs. The police told them that they had to go to the police station and have their particulars noted before they could continue their journey. These men were carrying revolvers. They also knew that they would not be able to give satisfactory answers at the station as they could not tell the police where they were coming from and where they were going. Therefore, going to the police station was as good as throwing yourself into an ocean and drowning. And so, they decided to take one last chance and resist arrest. Many policemen were injured and killed by the bullets these men fired.

Only one of the three Sikhs managed to escape. Of the other two, one was ambushed by a strong-bodied Muslim man and the third was caught by the police. There was nobody in the Sikh community as able-bodied and strong as Jagat Singh, the man who was tackled by the passer-by. His physicality was matched by his valour and determination. He managed to shoot and escape from the police, but he stopped to drink water somewhere. And while he was taking a breath and wiping his face, a Muslim man, even stronger than him, approached and gripped his feet with both hands in such a way that Jagat Singh could not move at all. Losing his balance, he fell. Jagat Singh was sentenced to death after his trial. And this is how many more of Rashbehari's associates were nabbed. There was not a soul now in Lahore who was willing to give Dada shelter. His party was in tatters, and the only companions he had left were a few unknown Sikh youngsters. It was as if he was somehow afloat on a dinghy in the vast ocean. The policemen who died or were injured were Indians; the men who went to jail or were hanged were Indians. And yet there was no personal enmity between them. They had nothing against each other!

Meanwhile the movement towards a revolution had started to take shape amongst the Muslims too, a short while before this. We will discuss and criticize this Muslim awakening further ahead, so it will suffice to say here that there was a new awareness among Indian Muslims after conflict broke out between Turkey and Italy in Europe. I mention this here because our party collaborated with the Muslim group after the failure of the revolt in Punjab. On consultation with them, Rashbehari decided that he would seek shelter in Kabul and control India's revolutionary efforts from there. He got a mullah to teach him to recite the Kalima, which is the Muslim confession of faith, and made plans to go to Kabul in the garb of a Muslim. Some Sikh leaders were to accompany

Rashbehari. Everything had been decided, but one afternoon, a couple of days before they were to set out, Rashbehari said, 'No, I don't think I can go to Kabul. From what I have learnt, there can be trouble awaiting us there. And second, I don't want to delay going to Lahore any more than I can help, for my heart tells me that any delay will only cause misfortune.'

Rashbehari never ignored his instincts and decided right away to just take the night train out of Lahore. Two young men from Kashi were with him. One was Vinayak Rao Kaple, a Maratha who had been living in Kashi for a long time, and let us call the other young man Ganga Ram. He had managed to elude the police for a long time. Rashbehari and Vinayak Rao left by the train at 8.00 p.m. It was decided that Ganga Ram would go to Kashi a couple of days later with a few Sikh leaders. Kartar Singh, Harnam Singh and many other Sikh leaders decided to go to Kabul.

The safest house was that in which Rashbehari had been staying in, as not many people knew about it. Rashbehari had specifically requested that the houses he used to meet people in should be avoided completely. However, on his way back from the station, Ganga Ram decided to look at one of these houses and, if it seemed safe, to pick up some clothes that he had left behind there. The police had already posted their men in these locations. Ganga Ram had barely reached the house when the police nabbed him.

Soon after his arrest, Ganga Ram gave away all our secrets to the police. The police now knew about the house that Rashbehari had last stayed in. On searching the building, they managed to find some papers with his handwriting. From those who had been arrested and interrogated earlier, the police was aware that Rashbehari had come to Punjab once again and had been staying in Lahore. From Ganga Ram, they learnt that he had been in Lahore even while the house searches and arrests were in full swing. They also learnt that Rashbehari came from Kashi and had returned there.

Rashbehari survived many close calls. A long time before this, when he used to have a job in Dehradun, he had gone to Lahore. He had taken leave from work and had travelled to the city via Delhi for some Party work. There were searches and arrests that happened in Delhi at the time, which yielded the address of a young man called Dina Nath from Lahore. The police also recovered Rashbehari's trunk and clothes from another man's house. But they could not decipher where exactly in Lahore Rashuda was. Nonetheless, they arrested Dina Nath. The evening after Dina Nath's arrest, a student from the DAV College came to give Rashbehari the news. He had not heard of it till then. After consultations with some people, it was decided that Dada should leave Lahore that very night. He left for Delhi.

The discussions had gone on late into the night, and the student who had brought the news of the arrest did not go back to his hostel. He stayed in the house that night. In the morning, the police surrounded the house. Three young men were arrested, but Rashbehari was not caught. Dina Nath told the police all the secrets the night after his arrest. Had he turned informer a day earlier, Rashbehari would have been captured.

On reaching Delhi, Rashbehari was about to go to Amir Chand's house, but he spied the latter's servant near the police station. His suspicions were aroused and he beckoned to the servant, asking him where Amir Chand was. The man recognized Rashuda as his master's friend and said, 'Sir, don't go to the house. The police have arrested my master, and I am taking food to him in the police station.' Rashbehari had just enough money on him to buy a train ticket for Calcutta. He immediately went to the railway station and boarded a train for Chandernagore.[20] That was the day Rashbehari's life in hiding had begun. Since then, as if he was 'but a wandering voice', he was nowhere to be found. This was how he would always avoid disaster but land in it yet again, repeatedly.

Chapter 2

THE STORY OF THE KASHI CHAPTER

(1)

In Kashi, we did not learn of the bad situation in Punjab after the revolt failed at first. Nonetheless, we became a bit worried when we did not receive any news from Punjab for a few days. After Rashbehari had reached Punjab, he had said that he would send some Sikh volunteers to Kashi, as it would be better to have Sikhs working with the Sikh platoons in the United Provinces. When Kartar Singh and a few others had come from Punjab, we had also heard them say that Rashuda wanted to send some Sikhs over to Kashi. At that time, we did not have people in Kanpur, Lucknow or Faizabad (Ayodhya). One man had brought information about the date appointed for the revolt, but after that, we had had no news. Some people had come to Faizabad directly from Punjab and some had been sent to Kanpur and Lucknow at different times.

In the meantime, we had started making visits to the cantonment in Kashi. The revolution was to begin on 21 February 1915, a Sunday, and we had visited the Kashi cantonment even on Saturday night. That was when we heard that the date had been changed, and we had no clue why this had happened. On Saturday night, the sergeant and deputy sergeant of the Kashi platoon reassured us that the moment the revolt began, they would join us.

But we were restless with various thoughts. We were embarking on a revolt against the British, and if the revolution were to begin in earnest, what would our families go through? Once the agitation was launched, we would have to take the revolutionary party to Delhi and introduce them to other groups. In that scenario, if the British Army was to attack Kashi, what would happen to our families?

We had also not forgotten how difficult it would be to discipline and control the soldiers who participated in the revolt, not to mention hoodlums from outside. Hence, the responsibility of the well-being of thousands of ordinary people and their families during the revolution was also on us. But we were determined to go forward with our plans and knew that solutions had to be found for the problems, however difficult.

There was another thought troubling us. What if the revolution began elsewhere before it did here? How would we fare, those of us who were already under the police's spotlight? How would we even know when the revolts broke out elsewhere? Would it be appropriate and sensible to involve the Kashi platoon without receiving adequate news about the other centres? We knew that our Party had the strength to attack the English cantonment in Kashi. In such a situation, the Indian platoon here would have to take sides, and we were sure that they would support us. We were sure that we could start the revolution from Kashi, but we did not have the courage to do anything without knowing the situation in other places, especially Punjab. In fact, had we enough arms and ammunitions in Kashi, we may have had the courage to do so.

After considering all these points, we decided that we would go to the railway station and the telegraph office to try and ascertain the reason for the delay in news from Punjab. If the telegram had not come, it would signal that something was up there, for we knew that wires were to be cut shortly before the revolution was to begin. We were guessing that there would be disruptions in the train timetables too, in that case. The moment we learnt that the revolution was afoot at the other centres, we decided to attack the English platoon in Kashi, lock the British men up in jail and free all the prisoners. We thought that if we freed the prisoners, some of them would feel obliged to help us. However, we had not gone to the jails till then and had no idea of the situation there. It is now that I know that this hope was completely misplaced.

Anyway, the plan was that by midnight, we would have got our hands on some ammunition and some money. Right after that, we would send some people to Allahabad and Danapur with news of the revolution. In the morning, we would call a public meeting, collect money from the rich and request the youth of the city to volunteer for us. There were many public meeting committees in Kashi that were run by Bengalis. There must have been at least 250 members in these committees. They were all well-educated, able-bodied young men of good character and gems of the Bengali community. That is why the people of Kashi had a soft corner for the committees. Most of the college professors, school teachers and well-known doctors in the city, even the municipal commissioner, were Bengalis, and somebody or the other related to these eminent citizens was in the committees. The members made such excellent arrangements for travelling, board and lodging at all the festivals and fairs that everyone was filled with admiration. These committees used to help widows in distress, and if there was an illness, they would go to the homes of the sick to care for them. The members also used to set up schools for the education of poor students. The committees had a very strong influence on the Bengali community in Kashi.

Therefore, we had decided that the responsibility of maintaining peace in the city during the revolution would be given to these committees. Although they had not been part of our secret plans, they had ample love for the nation and a lot of organizational power. Regular exercise sessions and discussions on a variety of topics kept them physically fit and intellectually sharp. For these reasons, they were best suited to take charge of the safety and security of the citizens. We were also hoping that we would find volunteers amongst them to be a part of our endeavour, once the revolution began. When we imagined volunteers recruited from the youth of our country walking around every street and lane and riverbank of Kashi, armed with a loaded pistol and a sharp dagger at their waist, we would feel very proud and happy. We had decided that arrangements would be made for the families of the revolutionaries to gather at one place. Our young volunteers would look after the families just as they would keep the peace in Kashi.

We were also anticipating that the moment the revolt began, the soldiers would realize that they were the ones with the weapons and that normal people like us could not do anything without their help. We hoped that they would volunteer to join us. We also thought that they would not be able to rest easy till things were decided one way or the other and would, therefore, feel compelled to ensure the success of the revolution. We were sure that they would prefer to rally behind the educated and able leaders of the revolution rather than serve as slaves in the British Army. Moreover, the plan was to arm as many of our people as possible once we had access to weapons, so that we Indians would no longer be weak and vulnerable.

We were completely ignorant of the strategies of war. One of the reasons was that we had not anticipated that the war with Germany would begin so soon. Hence, we realized that we would have to stage the revolt much earlier than we had planned. Anyway, around the time Rashbehari left for Punjab, I recall that a companion of mine, Vinayak Rao Kaple, and I picked up the *Encyclopaedia Britannica* and started reading up on strategy and warfare, although we used to read all articles related to this topic that were published in newspapers and magazines regularly. In the encyclopaedia, we read that 'generals are made on the fields of battle' and history has proof of this. There is no dearth of such examples in today's times either; take the history of the Russian Revolution, for instance. We knew, of course, that we were not going to become able commanders by reading. Anyway, I am writing about all that we did, and I am not embarrassed about exposing some of our naivete.

I had come to the Kashi cantonment on a bike on the evening of Sunday, 21 February. I also planned to check at the railway station and the telegraph office for any disruptions in the train or wireless services. A sergeant from the platoon was supposed to come to the station that evening. While waiting for him and pacing on the platform, I decided to buy a newspaper. I bought a copy of *The Pioneer* and saw that arrests had begun in Lahore. The police were already setting up pickets in the city like they would in times of battle. I deduced that things had gone downhill and came back to town immediately. There was now no doubt that all our efforts for a revolution had once again come to naught. But that very day, a revolution began in Singapore. We did not have any direct link with Singapore, but I will speak of this another time.

Had Singapore been any place in India, there is no doubt

that the whole country would then have risen up. It was a time when thousands of platoons were being sent abroad, and many Indian soldiers would certainly have joined us rather than fight someone else's war. This was not a naïve or foolish conclusion on our part. It is also not as though we received a positive response from all the platoons. On the one hand, when our young volunteers had informed the soldiers of a Sikh platoon that the revolution would begin soon, they had called a secret meeting and decided that they would definitely join us as soon as things got rolling. On the other hand, a Muslim platoon said, 'Do you think we are children? Is it child's play to fight the English Army? Are there any kings or nawabs in your group? Then what will you do for money? Moreover, the moment the revolt begins, news will spread by wireless telegraph and very soon you will be attacked from all sides by the army. How will you sustain your fight then? What is your martial training? Have you thought of all this? We are not children, nor are we foolish; do not ever come to us with such propositions again. Once the revolution begins, we will not go against our countrymen, but we would rather wait and watch than leap into the fray. But in any case, nothing like that is going to happen!'

The enthusiasm and excitement we saw in the Sikhs was mirrored only to a certain extent in the Punjabi Muslims and Pathans. Having met people from various castes and communities across the country, I believe that there is none as strong, confident and passionate as the Sikh community. The ease with which Sikhs are enthused is incomparable. When Rashbehari was returning to Kashi from Punjab after the failure of the revolution, he got talking to a Sikh soldier. The conversation veered to the present situation in the country. In a very short time, the Sikh got so worked up that Rashbehari and his companions got worried. The Sikh soldier, forgetting that there were various kinds of people in the compartment, loudly proclaimed that he was ready to sacrifice his life for the country. It was with great difficulty that they managed to calm him down.

Everybody blames Bengalis for being excessively emotional. Undoubtedly, the Bengalis are an emotional lot, but the Sikhs have a short fuse and can blow up like nobody else! There is very little difference between what they say and what they do. Therefore, I believe that there is no great task that the Sikh community cannot undertake and accomplish under able leadership. I see only one defect in the community and that is the lack of education. However, to fill that lacuna, every Sikh, rich and poor, is making financial contributions and working towards educating the community. No other community has such a vision. But they are a parochial people and they don't do even a hundredth for other communities of what they do for theirs. Many people in the Sikh community are convinced that if they manage to overthrow the British, they can rule over India. Whether they can defeat an empire or build one remains to be seen, but one thing is certain: if they are not educated, India's future will be dark indeed.

Let us leave this topic and go back to what we were talking about. We were speaking of how we got the news in Kashi of the fiasco in Punjab. We were devastated to see this unfortunate news in *The Pioneer*. We felt as if we Indians are never able to achieve our aims. What we plan never comes to pass. The British always get down to accomplishing what they want and work towards. I wonder what God thinks!

The lives of Indians seem to be a game for the others. It is as if they have no desires or passion, nor the ability to achieve goals. It is as if all the efforts of Indians are wasted and Indian history is replete with the sadness of wasted efforts. Like Indian history, the history of the revolutionary movement is also a history of futility.

(2)

I came back home from the railway station, dejected. My companions were waiting for me and the youngsters in the area were waiting for our orders. The latter did not know about the revolution, but they knew that something big was afoot and they had to be ready to even sacrifice their lives. Everybody listened to my report on the latest developments. We knew that the revolution had ended before it even began. But the next couple of days were spent in anxiety. It wasn't as if we had not anticipated this happening; truth be told, we had been rather apprehensive about our plans being sabotaged all along. So when we saw the news in *The Pioneer*, in our hearts, we all felt, 'This is what we were afraid of; can India's destiny change so quickly?' In another couple of days, we read the report on the tonga incident in Lahore in the newspapers and wondered if the one who got away was Rashbehari. But some people said that it could not be, as Rashbehari's destiny protected him and he was too lucky to fall into disaster. Moreover, it was clearly mentioned in the report that the three men were Sikhs. We spent the next few days worrying about Rashuda and hoping that he would suddenly land up in Kashi. We feared that the repercussions from Punjab would spill over and harm our party in Kashi. Therefore, many of us did not stay in the house but would visit from time to time and gather news about the activities of the police. By then, there was constant police vigil outside the house. One had to dodge them constantly, and that is how we were passing time in Kashi.

Meanwhile, Kartar Singh and Harnam Singh had left for Kabul from Punjab. God knows what made them enter the cantonment there to talk to the soldiers about the revolution. Soldiers were being arrested in various places and, therefore, they seemed plagued by fear. It was not appropriate in such a situation for Harnam Singh to go to the barracks in Kabul. In the end, the soldiers had Harnam Singh arrested. He was brought to Lahore. Despite being manacled, his face had an expression of such valour that both friends and enemies would be entranced. In his book *Aapbeeti* (Autobiography), Bhai Parmanand has described this scene very poignantly. Even high-ranking British officials couldn't be faulted for paying tributes to this brave man. In the days of these early attempts at a revolution, one can say that even the British officials were fans of the courage and goodness of the revolutionaries.

Then one day, we heard that Rashuda had reached Kashi. We got to know about the situation in Punjab when we met him. It was important to deliver the news from Punjab to Bengal, and furthermore, it was not deemed safe for me to stay on in Kashi. So Dada ordered me to leave the city immediately. As a rule, the moment the police started nabbing and arresting our people, we would change all earlier plans. This was because we were aware and acknowledged that no man could tell how he would react once he was arrested.

The police surveillance in Kashi was so strict in those days that no new Bengali could enter the city without their knowledge. The police were going from house to house in the Bengali areas and checking if any newcomers had arrived. Policemen from Chandernagore in Bengal who recognized Rashbehari were now posted at different stations in Kashi. The vigil was constant. Those who were on the police suspect list were watched perpetually. The police would note down the name and address of every Bengali that came into Kashi and then go to the house to verify the information. This was their way of trying to find Rashbehari, and yet he managed to enter Kashi without arousing any suspicion.

Our party in Kashi was alert and well-organized, and, therefore, it was safe for Rashuda to stay for more than a month there. We did not spend too much time at the house. Nobody, apart from a few select people in the party, knew where we stayed. And Rashuda would go from house to house and check on us. Nobody in Kashi recognized Dada. The government had decided to arrest Rashbehari come what may. But Rashbehari had also decided to save the Kashi group come what may. So the youngsters in Kashi stayed inside, quietly, and Rashbehari went from house to house making enquiries. His endeavour was to figure out which of us should be sent out of Kashi and how. Rashbehari made all the arrangements for these exits. Accordingly, I was the first to leave the city, followed by a friend. Thus, many of us reached Bengal. Similarly, our comrades from other parts of the United Provinces left their hometowns too. For example, people moved from Lucknow to Kashi and vice versa.

Our house in Kashi was searched a few days after I had reached Bengal. Another young party worker's house was searched a few days later. This person was still in Kashi but was not staying at his house. The police surrounded the house at three in the morning but came away empty-handed. The youngster heard from Rashbehari that his house had been searched. On the same day, Vinayak was coming back from a dip in the Ganga. Although he used to stay in a rented house, he would often have his meals at his own house. He was almost home when he got the news that several officers were waiting there to meet him. The minute he heard this, he disappeared. Thus, the attempts of the police to nab these youngsters were repeatedly foiled. Rashbehari continued to be in Kashi through all this.

When the government witness started to recount all these details in the Vibhuti Special Tribunal Court, even the judge forgot to take notes and kept staring at Vibhuti. The government counsel and our lawyer-barrister were also listening with rapt attention. From time to time, some people would turn to us and softly say, 'Oh, how brave of Rashbehari!' We, too, would bask in reflected glory. During the trial, I would often look at Vibhuti and try to gauge what he was thinking. I remember regretting the fact that Vibhuti was not a participant in the joy and pride that we felt. I cannot recall now if Vibhuti was proud of his treason or not.

Many youngsters from Kashi ended up in Bengal. Those who had no direct connection with the events in Punjab stayed on in Kashi. They were not a small number, and that is why even in such dire circumstances Rashbehari was able to stay on in Kashi. In such organizations, the greater the number of people who are yet to be identified as revolutionaries and suspected of anything, the stronger and better equipped the party is.

In Kashi, vigilance and caution saved many of us, but in Punjab, almost all members of the Party were arrested one after the other. Only Dr Mathura Singh and a few others managed to escape to Kabul. Pingle was able to elude capture too. He had come towards Kashi after the fiasco in Punjab. But, like Kartar Singh in Kabul, he stopped en route in Meerut to stoke a revolution in the cantonment there. It was in Meerut that he spoke to a Muslim dafadar who showed immense enthusiasm for the revolution and accompanied Pingle to Kashi.

However, Rashbehari advised Pingle not to proceed

with these plans. He told the young man that there was no longer any point in trying to recruit soldiers to the cause, but Pingle was not persuaded. In the end, Dada had to give him permission. Pingle went to Meerut with 10 of the largest bombs. They were so huge that if they were thrown into a barrack, it was certain that nothing would remain of it. The Rowlatt Committee described these bombs as being 'sufficient to annihilate half a regiment'. In the end, Rashbehari was proved right. The dafadar took Pingle to his cantonment and had him caught red-handed with the bombs. Ten or 11 soldiers from the cantonment, too, were accused of conspiring with him and later hanged to death.

Around the time Pingle went to Meerut, Dada sent word to me to go to Delhi for reconnaissance of the bungalows of some high-ranking British officials there. Plans were afoot to carry out a big and daring operation in Delhi. I did not feel right about going there without first consulting Dada in person, but the police were desperate to capture me at the time and a stopover at Kashi spelled danger. Yet I went to Kashi. I had always been imprudent. I never imagined that disaster could befall me, and it was this cockiness that got me captured. Rashbehari was fearless but never cocky.

I ran into an undercover agent at the Mughal Sarai station. My maternal aunt was with me, so there was no question of running. A young man from Bengal was also with me, and he was carrying a few bombs. I had already warned the youngster that he should not board the train with me and should maintain a distance from me at the station as well. Nothing untoward happened at the station, however. I had already told my aunt that if I were to be arrested, she should give a false address to the police and go home. When the train to Kashi pulled into the platform, the undercover agent got into my compartment. For some unknown reason, my young companion also boarded the same bogie. The agent, who knew me, asked who the lady with me was. When he came to know that my aunt was with me, I guess he was reassured that I would be going home and there was no need to pursue me. Moreover, I had heard that he was related to Inspector Jatindra Mukhopadhyay in the secret services department and he was probably only passing the information on to him. That is what the internal arrangement must have been, and it explains how I managed to escape on that journey.

I reached home early in the morning and left very soon after. But my family was sad to see the danger I was in. I categorically told everyone that I could be arrested at any moment. My paternal aunt held my hands and lovingly said, 'Why are you scared, Shachi? I am telling you that nothing will happen to you. Stay at home.' I did not pay any heed to their requests. I left home at daybreak and reached Rashbehari's house. The next morning, I left Kashi. The very same day our house was raided and a search carried out. A secret agent lived opposite our house, and the police had received reports about my having come home. Hence, when they raided my house and did not find me, they were very surprised. Some of them actually assumed that I must have escaped just then and ran around in the streets trying to find me! Later, when I reached Calcutta, I heard that there was a tale circulating in Kashi that I had escaped the police by jumping from one rooftop to the other.

I reached Delhi, accompanied by a youngster from Rajputana. We stayed with a companion from our party. We did what had to be done. There was talk of meeting up with Pingle in Delhi. However, the then home member Sir Reginald Craddock was not in Delhi and, for a couple of other reasons, nothing was done in Delhi.

One day, we were roaming around on the bike till evening. There were notices everywhere that said that headlights should be switched on at 6.30 p.m. So, I turned on the bike's headlight though it was a bit faulty. The moment I took a turn I saw a mounted policeman coming towards me with an air of authority. He signalled me to stop. I stopped the bike and got off immediately. The policeman asked me, 'Why haven't you switched on the headlight?' I realized then that the light was not on. I told the Englishman that it had just gone off, and that he could touch and see that it was still warm. 'Switch on the light!' The policeman finally let me go. As I stared at his retreating figure, I was wondering to myself, 'Dear God, when will we ride horses and ride around with pride?'

Whether Pingle would be able to accomplish anything in Meerut or not, we knew we had a task to carry out in Delhi. Soon we read in the newspapers that Pingle had been captured in Meerut. Around this time, I also fell seriously ill. I had to leave Delhi perforce. I was bedridden for 15 days straight. In the second week of my illness, symptoms of pneumonia were observed. I cannot, for the rest of my life, forget the care that my young companions gave me. I did not have the strength to lift my head. They even cleaned my urine and stool.

Hearings had begun for the Lahore case. There are many interesting things about the case, but I don't have much to say regarding the matter. The first thing that comes to mind, however, is that, in this case, 10 out of 100 revolutionaries forewent their commitment to the revolution and did not hesitate to throw their companions under the bus. There has been a lot of criticism of these traitors. It was because of their faithlessness that the revolutionaries earned a bad name and reputation. But let us not forget that even Jesus Christ's disciples were not above treason, so why should it be surprising when it happens elsewhere? We believe that no revolution takes shape without instances of treason. But where there is treason on one side, on the other there are tales of extreme valour too.

I would like to share with my readers a few instances from the Lahore conspiracy. In court, a Sikh named Jwala Singh raised an objection with regard to the identification of the accused. For this 'offense', the jail superintendent sentenced him to 30 lashes. The surprising thing is that there was no protest in Punjab about this. The second instance concerns the trial of Kartar Singh. He accepted all the charges against him in court, but the British judge did not note anything down on the first day. He told Kartar Singh that his case would be ruined by his admission. Kartar Singh did not change his mind. The judge remarked helplessly, 'Kartar Singh, I haven't heard anything you said today. I give you another day to think carefully and tomorrow you can say what you want to.' The next day Kartar Singh shouldered the entire blame and responsibility for the case. Everyone admired his silent courage. Kartar Singh immortalized the revolution and will remain forever etched in Indian history.

Bhai Parmanand, erstwhile teacher at DAV College in Lahore, was also arrested in this case. He was sentenced to life imprisonment in the Andamans. His cell was near Kartar Singh's in the Lahore jail. All political prisoners were normally kept in the same barracks. They would chat with each other from their cells in the night. It is said that once Bhai Parmanand told Kartar Singh, 'Had I known that this would be my destiny in the end, I would have participated more actively in your endeavour!' Bhai Parmanand's cell was flanked by Kartar Singh's on one side and another Sikh's on the other. He is still alive, and he is the one who later told me about this incident when we were fellow prisoners in the Andamans.

Chapter 3

IN DELHI

A Tale of Courage

The youngster who accompanied me to Delhi was called Pratap Singh. He belonged to the Charan caste of Rajputana. The Charan community respects the Rajputs. Pratap Singh's father was Sardar Kesari Singh. He was close to the monarch of Udaipur. I don't recall the details clearly, but either Pratap's father or his maternal grandfather was a minister in the King's council. His landholding was in the Shahpuri area of Mewar.

There was a time when these Rajput bravehearts were applauded for their valour and when there were great men in this community. As far as Bengal is concerned, Rajputana continues to be associated with bravery, compassion and valour. But of course, the Rajputs of today cannot be compared to their fabled heroes. Yet, even though the community is at its nadir, the values it has inherited are still etched in every Rajput heart. This echoes in my mind whenever I think of the story of Pratap's family.

This family was amongst the few well-to-do zamindar families of Rajputana, but they lost everything owing to their love for the motherland. To begin with, Pratap and his sister's husband were arrested in the Delhi Conspiracy.[21] But they were released as no concrete evidence was found against them. A few days later, Pratap's father, Sardar Kesari Singh, was sentenced to the Cellular Jail in the Andamans for life in connection with another political case. A warrant was also issued for his younger paternal uncle but he had not been captured. Eventually, owing to his poor health, Kesari Singh did not have to go to the Andamans but served his sentence in jails on the mainland.[22]

After being implicated in this case, the entire property of Kesari Singh and his brother was confiscated. Unfortunately, the brother who had nothing at all to do with politics also lost his property. They were reduced to nothing from being owners of large holdings. Pratap's mother was in dire straits and had to stay with one relative one day and with another the next. In the end, she went to her father's place. Even there she had to count her days, especially since her brother was no longer well-to-do.

There is nothing more callous than fate. But those who do not give up their valour in the face of this callousness defeat even fate. Despite all the misfortunes his family had suffered, Pratap continued to work for the movement. His attitude to the work was exemplary too. There is a distinct difference between doing something for doing's sake and working with your heart and soul. I believe that a man should take up work that gives him satisfaction and never out of guilt. He should not do anything that causes him unhappiness and discontent. Any form of work that makes one unhappy is a wasted effort. It is one thing to work because you are shamed into it and another thing because you wish to and are happy doing it. Pratap contributed to the work of the revolution wholeheartedly despite the grave misfortunes that had befallen his family; he was not ashamed or embarrassed at all, and his father was extremely proud of the way his son devoted himself to the cause.

There were many people who contributed to the revolution only for the sake of friendship or out of a sense of duty. One could see that there was no enthusiasm in their work, and they seemed lifeless most of the time. When we saw such attitudes in people, we would not let them suffer too long and provide them with an opportunity to leave. In most cases, they were happy to do so. I have seen very few youngsters like Pratap. It is not merely that he enjoyed his work and life by himself, but he had the capacity to transmit this joy and vitality to his companions as well. It isn't as if he was not anxious about his parents and their situation; indeed, I think anybody who does not feel for their family in such situations is not trustworthy. However, it is one thing to be unattached and it is another thing to not let attachments wear you down. I think I rate those human beings highest who are affectionate and have strong bonds with others but do not let that pull them down or deter them from performing their duties. And that is why, when I would see Pratap unhappy, it would tear my heart. But when I saw Pratap working with his heart and soul, it would give me immense joy too.

There came a time when Pratap had to wage a great battle within himself. After his arrest, he was tortured by the police; they even tried to entice him to reveal our secrets. The police would tell him that if he gave them the information they needed, not only he but his father, too, would be released. Moreover, they promised that the case against his uncle would be withdrawn as well, and the family's property returned. They even offered Pratap a reward. They used emotional blackmail, constantly telling him how much worse his mother's life would get if he was sentenced. In fact, this was not entirely baseless.

In the beginning, Pratap did not talk to the police very much. Slowly, it began to seem as if he liked talking to them. One day, Pratap spoke to the police for three to four hours. All of us in the cell next to his feared the worst and suspected that he would give in this time.

Later when the trial began and we met again, we came to know that Pratap had been very disturbed during these interrogations. So much so that, one day, he told the police that he needed another day to think things over and decide if he would tell all. The next day when they came to question him, Pratap said, 'I have thought a lot. And in the end, I have decided to not say anything. So far only my mother is suffering. But were I to reveal all the secrets, so many mothers will suffer similarly and so many will weep instead of just one.' Only a thinking person can understand how difficult it is to let yourself go morally, and then not fall and climb back up to your earlier position.

I don't know how many fathers in India today would sacrifice their sons willingly and knowingly for the country. It is India's great misfortune that a youngster like Pratap is no more. His body could not take the torture meted out to him in Bareilly jail by the British. It was this Pratap that I had gone to Delhi with and had the honour to work with. He must have been about 22 years old then. I will talk about the work we did in Delhi in another chapter.

The Story of the Muslim Revolutionary Group

I have mentioned earlier that we were first introduced to the Muslim revolutionary group[23] after the failure of the Punjab revolution. We had the opportunity to get to know them better while working in Delhi.

Our countrymen do not know anything about this group. Their work was not visible to anybody. It began in India at the time of the Italo-Turkish War. During that war, probably in 1911, the Indian Muslims had sent a medical mission to Turkey to care for the wounded there. Most of the people who went were Muslims. The editor of *Zamindar* in Punjab, Zafar Ali Khan, was also part of the mission.

This group earned the love and respect of the sultan of Turkey and other Ottoman commanders and courtiers. A Muslim friend of mine used to tell me that this respect had made them arrogant. It is but natural that men who were insulted and disrespected at every step they took in India became arrogant when the king of Turkey accorded them respect. Until then, the Muslim community in India had never showed any kind of social or political consciousness. But as the mission travelled around Turkey and was exposed to the freedom there, and they saw how people of their own religion had preserved their sovereignty in a European country—and above all when everybody, from the young to the old, had received them with love and respect—it was if they woke up from a deep sleep. After the Italo-Turkish War, there were signs of a widespread awakening and self-recognition in the Indian Muslim community. In Kashi, I saw that the tea seller, weaver and cart driver were busy discussing the latest on the Royal Turkish Debate. Muslims shouldn't have to earn empathy from the other religions; this is their birthright. The Rowlatt Report says that the discontent amongst the Indian Muslims was caused by the fact that the British did not help the Turks in their war with Italy. But I disagree. Even if the British had helped the Turks, this awakening of the Muslims was inevitable. The medical mission to Turkey certainly sowed the seeds of revolution in their midst but an entire community does not gain this awareness because of an attack from outside or by dint of some empathy from foreigners. The relations this community had with the British are another matter.

Anyway, many youngsters from the medical mission had already been initiated into the faith of the revolution before they went to Turkey, and once they came back, they began to actively spread the fire of rebellion in the Muslim community in India. The Turkish government appointed some people of their choosing from the mission to the Turkish consul in India. The people of India did not have a clue about these developments at the time, but the government of India knew this and much more.

However, the Muslim revolutionary group had always looked to Muslim powers abroad for support. Their hopes were concentrated outside India. One of the gentlemen I spoke to in Delhi from this group said that they had requested Kabul to attack India many times. I had, on that day, voiced my opposition to such plans very strongly. They had tried hard to convince me that India could not succeed in its revolution without outside help, and I had tried to explain to them that external aid should not involve some foreign country mounting an attack on India. They had tried to tell me that the Afghans would not take over or stay permanently; they will liberate us and leave, they had said. Many Muslims in India believe this.

Nonetheless, on occasion, these Muslims also helped us financially. From my conversations with them, I have understood that their revolutionary group was operating as a united entity throughout the country. The group was active from the borders of Punjab to distant Brahm Desh in the east (Myanmar). On the other hand, our revolutionary party in Bengal was riddled with factionalism. But fortunately in the north of India, outside of Bengal, ours was the only group that existed. Maybe that is why there was no factionalism.

The main difference between us and the Muslim group was that our concept of a free nation, though it meant self-dependence of Hindus, did not involve the domination of Hindus. The thought of excluding Muslims from our endeavour was never on our minds. In fact, we were constantly making efforts to draw them into our group. And if they did not come even when invited, it was because the Muslims did not love India in the same way as the Hindus did. Our interactions with the Muslims of our country made us realize that they were more attracted to Turkey, Egypt, Arabia, Persia and Afghanistan. This was their thought process, and that is why they established a separate revolutionary group. Many Indian Muslims had accepted pan-Islamic principles, inspired by Turkey, and that is why the Muslim Revolutionary Party preferred not to be called a part of the Indian Revolutionary Party. Apart from these two groups, there was one another group in Delhi. It is probably still there. This group was no secret commission and it is discussed later in this book.

Story of Delhi's Nishkalanki Group

How Indraprastha, Hastinapur or Delhi casts a spell on Hindus! So many different dynasties, so many communities, came and gave it new forms. The history of Delhi is the rise and fall of so many peoples, and the history of India, too, has flowed with that of Delhi. The jewel of Hindu pride, Delhi, was marauded by foreign invaders, and in this great city, over different epochs, different dynasties were tested, through endless struggles and innumerable revolts. It was through many such revolutions that modern Delhi took shape. Besides warriors and martial groups, the city has also witnessed the appearance of many saint communities. For example, during the Muslim rule, the Satnami sect came into being near Delhi. Similarly, the Nishkalanki group was formed during British rule.

Like the Satnami group, this too was a small community. It came into being 30 years ago and still survives in the city. Over the past three decades, the group has been continuously praying for India's freedom and for the return of Satya Yuga.[24] These days, they preach that Lord Kalki (the final incarnation of Lord Vishnu) has taken birth and will soon make an appearance. But they cannot say exactly how soon this will happen, that is, in how many days he will make an appearance. They say that when Vishnu had taken birth in the form of Ramchandra, only 12 sages knew that he was the incarnation of the Lord. Had other people known about it, they would not have believed it.

Similarly, in our times, there are a few people who believe that God has taken birth in the present epoch. They say that many great men have been born in India in recent times, although most of them are not aware of their own real form. The day the emperor of these great men presents himself will be the day they realize their power and the truth of their past lives. Some of these great men are very powerful and think that they are incarnations of God themselves. The believers say that God has taken birth in the house of a brahmin this time and, because of this, they too shall be revered. In previous epochs, these incarnations had appeared in the homes of kshatriyas, and that is why, despite being God incarnate, they had to bow to brahmins. This time, by being born brahmin, he will receive the respect of all. Moreover, due to his bringing up in a brahmin home, his conduct will be such that no one in the country or abroad would be able to point a finger at him. The character and behaviour of the earlier incarnations was hardly without blemish, but this time, the demeanour of the person would be akin to that of God. They believe that despite being a swordsman, Kalki Dev will not take up arms against anyone.

These people claim that this time, for India's freedom, the Hindus will not have to take up arms because India's enemies, the sinners whose nature is that of wild beasts, will fight amongst themselves and die. Those who survive will die of illness and starvation due to epidemics and famine. This way, earth will be rid of vice and only good men will endure. And there shall be Satya Yuga on earth. According to them, the move towards this golden epoch has already begun, and within a few years, the world will be cleansed of its taints.

While they go about their worldly tasks, they continuously chant Kalki Dev's name, along with a public and private prayer for the well-being and freedom of India and the world as a whole. They say that our only task is to approach God, the Supreme Being, and seek his blessings and protection. And they are not saints or monks either. I cannot say for sure whether they suffered from weakness of character or possessed unusual mental strength because I have not had the occasion to interact much with them. Before my visit to Delhi, I had heard of this group but had never met anyone from the Nishkalanki Dal. I had heard that they would occasionally proclaim on the streets of Delhi that Lord Kalki Dev had been born; hence, sinners should beware and everyone should immerse themselves in God, chant Kalki Dev's name and take refuge in him, and so on. This time when I was in Delhi with Pratap, I managed to meet the leader of the group on a couple of occasions; everyone referred to him as Balmukund or Hanuman ji.

He was a simple, poor brahmin and did not know how to read and write. He used to cook his own food and wash the dirty utensils too. Everybody in the sect respected him. There were not many educated people of the middle class among his followers. None of them knew Hindi, and they were dead against cow slaughter. Their hero, Balmukund ji, left his human body five or six years ago. But now, even English-speaking middle-class people are becoming members of the sect and participating in its activities.

I have heard about the appearance of God's incarnation from people other than the Nishkalankis. A sadhu visited my maternal uncle in Gorakhpur after I came back from jail, and like the sect in Delhi, he said many things about the incarnation. During the last war, when America did not join the British against Germany, the sadhu had met my uncle and prophesized that the United States would eventually enter the fray and the allies would win. My uncle had written to me when I was in the Andamans, recounting all this. I still have that letter. Erstwhile lawyer and author of the book *Brahmavid Rishi O Brahmavidya*, the respected Tara Kishore Sharma, has also been predicting the same for a long time. Upen Babu, the editor of *Jugantar*, has also heard similar things from various sadhus. All of them said things in different ways but they all meant the same thing.

The Reorganization of the Delhi Group

Two prominent workers from the Delhi group, Avadh Bihari and Amir Chand, were far superior to other revolutionaries in many aspects. Both men had a strong sense of duty that was rooted in religion. Very rarely has such an amalgamation of deed and duty been seen in Indian revolutionaries. Avadh Bihari had been involved in revolutionary activities from the age of 23 or 24, or maybe earlier than that. Even at that age, his sense of duty was extraordinary; it seems to have been an inherent quality. He was very fond of an Urdu poem that I will quote here.

Ehsaan naa-khuda ka uthaaye meri bala
Kashti khuda pe chhod doon langar ko tod doon

(My affliction can bear the kindness of the captain. Left to myself, I would leave the boat to God and break the anchor.)

And he lived by it, setting his life adrift in the middle of the ocean with faith and courage.

Amir Chand was 20 years older than Avadh Bihari. He was a teacher, and Avadh Bihari had grown up in his care—first as a student, then a disciple and then a friend. Amir Chand himself was a disciple and follower of Swami Ram Tirath. The Swami knew him well, and he was the first to talk about the Swami's teachings. It was under his influence that the workers of the Delhi group became religious. Important to mention among these followers of Amir Chand are Mr Lachhmi Narayan and Mr Ganeshilal Khasta.

I was not close to Amir Chand and Avadh Bihari because they had already been arrested when I arrived in Delhi with Pratap. But around this time, I had occasion to meet with and get to know Lachhmi Narayan and Mr Khasta. Avadh Bihari and the others in his group knew everything about the Nishkalanki sect, but amongst all of them, it was Lachhmi who had a soft spot for them. He was a student of Indian medicine and, like the Nishkalankis, had little to do with the English language.

After the arrest of Amir Chand and Avadh Bihari, the responsibility of the Delhi revolutionary group fell on Lachhmi Narayan and Ganeshilal. The latter was well-versed in Persian and wrote excellent poetry. Lala Har Dayal published several of Ganeshilal's poems in the *Ghadar* newsletter. He was later sentenced to seven years of rigorous imprisonment for writing a passionately patriotic poem. Mr Khasta was not literate in English either; all his knowledge was imbibed through the Persian language. He was especially fond of philosophy and his unquenchable desire for learning was a remarkable trait.

During this visit, I had noticed that after the arrest of Avadh Bihari and others, our work in Delhi was not moving forward. Even Lachhmi's and Khasta's enthusiasm was waning. After the hearings in the Delhi Conspiracy Case had ended, Lachhmi was most enthusiastic and would meet us when we visited the city despite many dangers. In the beginning, he would not let any difficulty deter him from carrying out the tasks for the group, but slowly his enthusiasm petered out. It soon came to pass that he would try to avoid public meetings, and soon, those that he met lacked enthusiasm too. The truth is, around this time, there was another sentiment taking root in Lachhmi Narayan. This change had come about due to his increasing proximity to the Nishkalanki group. He was less and less involved in the tasks assigned to him, and slowly started spending more and more time in prayers. He started ignoring the work of the Party. His energy was now spent on converting the people he had recruited into the revolutionary group to the beliefs and practices of the Nishkalanki sect. As a result, our work was no longer his priority. Finally, we heard that Lachhmi Narayan would use his voice or his pen only to take God's name and nothing else, and his followers too were the same.

After the failure of the revolution, this was one of the reasons Pratap and I came to Delhi. We had to ultimately put off one of our main tasks as Mr Craddock was not in

Delhi, but we threw ourselves into the reorganization of the Delhi revolutionary committee with full vigour. Apart from arranging a rented house for our stay and introducing us to the old workers of the unit, Lachhmi Narayan did nothing else, which is to say that he decided to hand everything over to us and wash his hands off the revolution.

We stayed for 15 days in the rented house in Delhi. Rajputana is not very far from Delhi; while I stayed in Delhi, I sent Pratap there twice. We wanted to bring some youngsters from the region to the city and train them. Hence, while Pratap was recruiting for the Party in Rajputana, I was meeting workers in Delhi and picking those who seemed appropriate to me. Our work in Delhi reignited the fire in Ganeshilal Khasta's heart, and he recovered his former enthusiasm. We realized that he would be the best candidate to take over the leadership of the Delhi unit from Lachhmi Narayan. Thanks to his efforts, we also got to know the Delhi Muslim revolutionary group more closely.

Our agreement with the Muslims was that they would provide us with pistols, revolvers and bullets, and we would give them bombs. Plans were made for both the groups to work in tandem. After a long time, work seemed to be happening in Delhi. Whether it was by purchasing bombs from us or by other means, the Muslim group also helped us financially.

Just when the work in Delhi picked up in earnest, I fell very ill. I took the helpless Pratap and came back to Bengal; there was a warrant out for me and I thought it was better to go to Bengal rather return to the United Provinces.

It was disappointing to see that Lachhmi Narayan had given up working for the revolution in order to chant the names of Kalki and Kali. There was no doubt that he was a believer, but we did not like his growing disinterest in the cause. This came from the Nishkalanki group, and apart from Lachhmi Narayan and some of his friends, we distrusted the beliefs of the sect immensely. All of us have faith in God, and although we have learnt from the teachings of the Nishkalankis, we do not believe in their ways.

We have all too often heard that religiosity has brought ruin to this country. Sadly, we have to accept that, in our experience of revolutionary work over the past 10–12 years, 99 per cent of those who claim to be very religious are disinterested in working for social welfare. However, the true test of religious belief is in what you are willing to sacrifice. And when it comes to sacrifice, these so-called religious beings often turn vengeful and selfish. I believe that in the Vedic philosophy, there are two main principles: *Adhikari-bheda*, which refers to the distinction between qualified persons or to the difference of various aspirants capable of apprehending the same truth; and *Guruvaad* or authoritarianism, which ignores these distinctions. When we approach religion from the latter perspective and spend all our energy on religious deeds, we are destined to misfortune. And then under the guise of morality, we often give way to vengefulness. In the name of religion, we promote irreligiosity.

Lachhmi Narayan was a capable man, and he prayed with a true heart, but he could not maintain the balance between worldly affairs and religious faith. And I have no doubt that under his influence his friends also took up Nishkalanki beliefs wholeheartedly. But when disaster struck and all of us were arrested, these very same companions of Lachhmi Narayan who chanted God's name endlessly gave testimony against us to escape the clutches of the police. In fact, the cherry on the cake was that they did not spare Lachhmi Narayan either.

Before misfortune struck, Lachhmi used to say of the Nishkalankis that they are rapt in God's embrace and to think of God is their only task; hence, they must not be forced into working for the revolution. 'We don't have to do anything,' he would say, 'but when God appears before us, it is our main task to seek his refuge.' Lachhmi Narayan had been involved in the revolutionary effort for a long time and in the most difficult situations. That is why he had the mental fortitude that was lacking in most of his companions, and for the same reason, when disaster struck, he did not forget his true essence. But the people he had tried to guide took the wrong path and could not abide by the most basic humanitarian values.

Avadh Bihari was also a follower and a regular in the Nishkalanki sect, but he did not give up his duty and managed to maintain a balance between the worldly and otherworldly aspects of life. There is a notable lack of equilibrium between worldliness and spirituality in Indian society.

Chapter 4

IN BENGAL

Rashbehari Gives Up India[25]

I arrived in Bengal with symptoms of malarial fever. The revolutionary committee in Bengal had a centre in a village near Calcutta. For various reasons, I still cannot mention the village by name. I was confined to the bed for 15 days in this place. It was the youngsters in this place who looked after me with love. Pratap left me in Bengal and went off to Rajputana. The plan was that I would join him there once I had recovered, and this time, we would work hard to set up a centre in Rajputana. But when I met him again both of us were in jail.

When I was ill and confined to bed, Mr Nagendra Nath Dutt who was also known as Girija Babu, a leader from East Bengal, used to visit me often. After conferring with him, it was decided that Rashuda would not be allowed to live in India any longer. Things were difficult, and by God's grace, he had been safe till now, but it was no longer safe for him to remain in the country. Our group was constantly besieged by loss, and we were not able to expand. The moment we made some decent progress, there would be a catastrophe, and it would take us days to recover and regroup. First, it took us a year to recover from the Delhi Conspiracy Case, and just when we had repaired the damage and were planning a big strike against the government, the Lahore Conspiracy collapsed. This crippled us completely. Our groups in Punjab and the United Provinces were shattered. Various centres in Bengal had to suffer blow after blow. In such a situation, it did not seem sensible for Rashbehari to stay in India. The Party was weak in this moment; it was not possible to stand up to the might of the organized government machinery. We had been able to keep him safe for so long only because of our organizational strength.

A reward of 7,500 rupees was announced for the capture of Rashuda after the Delhi Conspiracy Case. A year later, Rashbehari's roll of honour was published in the Lahore Conspiracy Case. As a result, the Punjab government offered another 2,500 rupees. Now the total amount of reward money added up to 10,000 rupees. The government of the United Provinces increased the award by another 2,500 after the Banaras Conspiracy Case. The consolidated sum was now 12,500 rupees. Keeping all this in mind, we decided that Rashuda had to be sent abroad.

We tried to look on the bright side. So far, the fact that we were not adequately armed for a revolution had often sabotaged our plans. We had thought that the revolution was still a long way off, and we did not, therefore, arrange to bring in arms and ammunition from abroad to that end. But when we saw the situation in the country, we soon realized that if we had better access to weapons, it would not take much to start the revolution. And that is why it was decided that we would send Rashbehari abroad and begin anew the preparations for the revolution. Before leaving, Rashuda had also said, 'This time, each young man and woman of the country should be armed, and then we will see how the British continue to rule India.'

Rashuda did not initially agree to the plan of going abroad and wanted to wait a few more days. But in the end, he gave in to our entreaties. The logistics of where, when and how were then discussed with Rashuda. It was decided that he would send the required quantity of Mauser pistols and bullets for us, and later, after arranging for the arms required for the revolution, he would come back to the country. The plan was to consult people abroad with the relevant experience about the transportation of the weapons and then work out the logistics.

Rashuda first came to Nadia with Vinayak Kaple. Till he left for foreign shores, he stayed somewhere near Calcutta. A few days before leaving, he shifted to Calcutta, and one afternoon, Girija Babu and I accompanied him to the port where his ship was ready to set sail. We are talking of April 1915. Rashuda and I were in one car and Girija Babu in another. Rashuda was extremely fond of me. On the way, he pulled me close, put his hand on my shoulder and said, 'I can't even begin to tell you how much it hurts me to leave the country. Listen to me carefully ... When you are done organizing the matters of the country, you also come and join me.' This was the last conversation I had with him.

So it was planned that once the organization was in place and functioning well, I would to go abroad and join him, for there was a warrant out for me as well, and if I stayed in the country, I was very likely to be arrested. A warrant was a very serious thing under the circumstances; even if the police was merely suspicious about you, it was impossible to get any work done. Had there been someone else who could introduce the revolutionaries in different parts of the country to each other,

I could have gone abroad with Rashuda. Unfortunately, there was no other person who could fill this role, and, therefore, I had to stay on in the country despite all the dangers that I faced. Before he left Kashi, Rashuda had made my mother promise that she would pay 1,000 rupees for my travel abroad. My mother had known for a long time that I was involved in revolutionary activities, and she was sympathetic to my cause. I must have done good deeds in my past birth to be born to such a mother in a Bengali home.

It is not yet time to write about the details of Rashuda's journey abroad; all I can say is that it may appear to be a mysterious escape, but in fact, the plan was simple. The only things required to travel, thus, were courage and faith in God. When Rashbehari went abroad, the War was raging in Europe, and it was no mean feat to travel abroad or back home from there. Moreover, it was very dangerous for a person like Rashbehari to roam from one place to another. In India, he had always carried a loaded pistol, and at least one of us was always with him. That is why it was difficult to capture him alive. But above all, he survived with God's blessings. The last time he came to Calcutta, he had not even wanted to carry a revolver. He was stout, and so I believed that he could not really run. One day, I asked him, 'If the police came to catch you, would you try and run or not?' He laughed and said that he wouldn't be able to run at all; he would, therefore, just surrender peacefully. Similarly, in answer to another question, he said that he was not destined to be captured alive. However, no one had any control over destiny.

Rashbehari is now in Japan. He teaches English, edits the monthly magazine *Asian Review*, lectures about India all over Japan and writes for various news magazines. He would have long ago been captured by the British in Japan, but the help of a high-ranking officer in Japan staved off that threat. He has married a Japanese woman from a refined family. They have a son and a daughter. The son is called Bharat Chandra. Obviously, his wife, our sister-in-law, has learnt Bengali. Rashbehari is now a citizen of Japan.

Many people must know by now of the article that Rashbehari sent to *Young India* and other magazines. His current views can be gauged by those. Apart from this, the letters he has written to his companions, excerpts of which I am presenting here, also show his opinions, thoughts and state of mind.

(1)

Tokyo, Japan
12 April 1922

My dearest …

… The idea that I could not protect … all from the inhuman … they were subjected to makes me restless. Of course, I consoled myself with the fact that by passing through the agony of fire … have come out a better and purer soul. But I did not like the tone of permission that pervaded some parts of … letter. There is eternal life, so work is eternal. You need not be anxious about impurity even if there is any … of course there is no necessity of secret work, and I quite agree with you. Hitherto, our knowledge of the international situation has been very meagre. We mostly confined our attention to India. But now I have come to understand a bit of international politics. This has greatly altered my former ideas. Please remember that we shall have to—rather we are destined to—tackle the problem of the world. It is India's mission to usher in a new era of real peace and happiness in the world. India's freedom is but a means to this end, it is not an end in itself …

(2)

Tokyo
9 July 1922

My dearest …

Your letter … reached me yesterday. What did you wish me to write? And what was your heart's desire? I think I was sufficiently clear in my letter. Of course, there are many things that I cannot write in letters for obvious reasons, and your curiosity about them must remain unsatisfied till we meet again. The most noteworthy thing, however, is that my whole outlook has been broadened, and I have given you a hint in this connection in my last letter. Independence, India must have, for her independence is essential for the regeneration of the whole world. It is not the end in itself but it is the means to an end, and that end is the destruction of imperialism and militarism and the creation of a better world for all to live in. It is India's mission, and therefore yours and mine. … I like Japan, and I have come to adore her because I am convinced that she will stand for Asian independence when the time comes. When I first came here, the Japanese had little knowledge of the state of affairs in India. It is chiefly through our efforts and sacrifices that today the Japanese are closely following the trend of events in India. I have got many Japanese friends, from cabinet ministers and members

> of Parliament down to lawyers, journalists and students. Many books in Japanese about Gandhi and the Indian movement have been published, and the papers and magazines regularly carry articles on India. This month, a professor in the Tokyo Imperial University published a voluminous book in Japanese on India. Next month, I am engaged to deliver lectures on India. Situation for three days … today most of the young men here are staunch advocates of Asian Independence. Even older men and responsible officials are in sympathy with the new awakening everywhere from Persia to China. The most remarkable national trait (here) is patriotism. This is the reason that we are given protection. But for Japanese sympathy and love, I would have been dead long ago … about going back to India, well brother, I do not want to return till India is free … Your *boudi* is learning Bengali.

The Centre's Story

Rashuda had left India and gone away. Girija Babu and I put him on his ship and came back to the centre. We did not have a close relationship with this centre, and there are many reasons for that.

First and foremost, we did not agree politically with the leaders of the centre. From the time of the inception of the revolutionary committee, they were in favour of terrorism. They had not made any efforts to start an armed revolution so far. They believed that if high-ranking officers of the British government were killed with revolvers and blown up with bombs, the government would be forced into making concessions and giving us more political freedom. And, therefore, it was possible to obtain self-rule by force and violence, one concession after another. But they were deluded in thinking this. Self-rule for India would mean the first step to independence because it would not be difficult to work towards obtaining freedom once Swaraj had been achieved. They also said that without self-rule, brought on this way or any other way, it was not possible for India to gain complete independence. They believed that with anarchist terrorism, they could quickly and easily establish self-rule. They had learnt these views from a well-known and popular leader in Bengal. But even to succeed in this strategy of anarchist violence, they were not able to organize the group in the manner that was required. For example, if they wanted to assassinate a magistrate, they would send a youngster armed with a revolver to the concerned place, even though the organization did not exist there.

No mission can succeed without the support of a disciplined, efficient and powerful organization. The leaders of our centre in Bengal did not comprehend the need for a strong and vast organization to achieve the difficult and mammoth goal of self-rule as a means for attaining complete independence. Therefore, under their leadership, no cohesive group or revolutionary network could be formed in Bengal. These were puny groups whose range of operation would be limited to the villages they were based in. Working in this manner dimmed the chances of success considerably; based on their failed efforts, one can say that terrorism was not the way forward. I had constant and strong arguments with them about these ideas and strategies of theirs.

∽

Many young men like me did not participate wholeheartedly in their activities because the group focussed on terrorism as its main goal. Such goals cannot, in the long run, motivate youngsters. Without high, strong and generous ideals and beliefs, no person will put his life on the line and work for the nation. And it was not possible to have unanimity on the principles of terrorism. Everyone was kept in the dark about the working of the revolutionary committee. Only some people were roped in, and they were made to undertake tasks that involved terrorism. This was against our wishes. On the first day that I was introduced to these leaders, after my association with Rashbehari and his effervescent young followers, I was absolutely taken aback and wondered what kind of a group I had got entangled with! I objected to their views the very next time I spoke to Rashbehari. That day, Rashuda instructed me to not speak to them about anything other than work and faith.

Rashbehari had been in their company from his childhood, but his nature was unlike theirs. When he was a bit older and went to Dehradun to work, he created his own method of work and carved his own path. Just as Mother Nature creates her work unnoticed, Rashuda put together a huge organization, while his leaders in Bengal were oblivious of the fact. It was only when his work had progressed somewhat that they were informed of it. Being opposed to infighting and factionalism, he tried to work with them as far as possible, but he was not in agreement with their views about terrorism, and, therefore, his mode of operation was completely different.

∽

There was another reason for our differences with the centre. These leaders believed that only they had unravelled the secret of spirituality. So, if we had any difference of opinion with them, they would push our views aside by declaring that we were completely besotted with Western thoughts and principles. As if to say that a clean revolution could only be inspired by Western ideals while anarchism was rooted in Indian beliefs! This attitude of rejecting the opposing view without consideration seems to be the norm today.

They would preach in various ways that the best route to spirituality, to God, was not through asceticism or meditation. They preached that the best way to live was not to renounce the world, but to carry out one's tasks, duties and responsibilities, albeit in a detached manner. But in reality, this was not their attitude. They indulged in political intrigues within their small, closed group and did not want to include people. This caused a constant strife between them and us. The day that the Punjab revolution plan failed, when we had sought refuge at the centre to breathe a bit, they had sarcastically remarked, 'Enough playing around, why not sit quietly and meditate a bit?'

I think their nature was opposed to the true ideals of a revolution, and that is why they got involved in various other things and distanced themselves from the movement. Although they preached about maintaining a balance between duties and detachment, they tried to avoid any political commitment that would mean a sustained confrontation with the British government. Undoubtedly, while these people had been in contact with other revolutionaries and helped them, while they did not mind putting themselves in grave danger sometimes, their nature was essentially different, and, in the end, they left the movement. Just as great men who are inclined towards asceticism in the beginning often involve themselves in worldly matters but slowly, with their inclination taking over, renounce all worldly attachments one by one, our leaders at the centre were, at first, intimately involved with the revolutionary committee but, owing to the pull in another direction, slowly became distant from our ideas and activities. Finally, yes, they gave up working for the cause of the revolution, but it must be said that they did not renounce the world; they gave up politics but not social work.

I did not get along with them for all these reasons. As long as Rashbehari was in India, he managed to keep a distance from them, yet accord them a certain respect. He had, after all, risen to his present stature under their guardianship. But his nature had changed so much that when he visited one of the leaders for the last time before leaving India, on perceiving his personal magnetism and charisma, the latter had remarked, 'How do we keep him hidden? Whosoever lays eyes on him will not be able to look away; to behold him is to think that one is seeing a real man. A real human.' When this incident took place, some repairs were being done on the leader's house, and the labourers were walking in and out. He had addressed the comment to these men. There was a time when this man was Rashuda's guru, but today, the teacher was impressed by the student. After Rashbehari left India, we became more and more distant from these leaders. At that time, everyone in the Bengal revolutionary group was working in close contact with the revolutionary group from Dhaka.

The Story of the Dhaka Anushilan Samiti[26]

The perception among the revolutionary groups in Bengal was that the Dhaka Anushilan Samiti was not interested in collaborating with the other groups and, therefore, no revolutionary committee of theirs could work with the Dhaka unit. But these people were unaware that the Dhaka Samiti had already merged with the Chandernagore Samiti and with

Rashbehari's group, and that this merger had happened before the World War. As far as I know, I can say that despite all its drawbacks, this unit from Dhaka was better than all the revolutionary groups of Bengal. There was no other Anushilan Samiti in Bengal with as big a working committee. They also had branches in every district of East Bengal and North Bengal. Everyone agrees that in terms of number and diffusion theirs was the largest organization in all of Bengal.

However, the leaders of the West Bengal revolutionary group thought the East Bengal leaders lacked intelligence and, therefore, did not trust them. The youngsters from the West Bengal revolutionary group considered themselves to be more cultured than their counterparts from East Bengal. Moreover, because they were bigger than any other revolutionary group in the region, the East Bengal group was regarded with envy and jealousy. It is for this reason that, other than Chandernagore and Rashbehari's group, no other committee from Bengal was willing to work with the Dhaka Anushilan Samiti. Pride is a dangerous quality. Just as it helps to elevate man, it can bring him down too. It is very difficult to control the ego. Many a great civilization has been destroyed because of arrogance. In this case, the main reason that the many small revolutionary groups of Bengal could not unite to form one big and effective organization or work together efficiently is the petty egotistical attitude of the leaders of these different units. In fact, the leaders seemed to outnumber the workers. Anybody who could cobble together 10-odd persons would turn into a leader. And none of these leaders wanted to merge with any other group because they felt that would mean the loss of their independence and individuality. And I think they were all opposed to working with the Dhaka unit because they feared they would be lost in that big group. I personally tried many times to unite the Dhaka Anushilan Samiti and many revolutionary groups in Bengal but was not successful. There was another big reason for this not coming to pass. There was no leader who was impressive, powerful and charismatic enough to bring them all together.

ഗ

In short, all the groups in Bengal were unhappy with the Dhaka revolutionary committee. It must be pointed out that the members of the Dhaka Anushilan Samiti too were proud to the point of arrogance that theirs was the biggest group. I came to know that revolutionary groups from West Bengal did not have the same antagonism for smaller groups from East Bengal. There was a reason for this. The Dhaka unit was set up by Pulin (Behari Das) Babu. And our dear Pulin Babu was quite autocratic. He could not bear to be in a situation where his authority was not unquestioned or even a degree less than he wanted it to be. The willingness to compromise, which is required to be able to work with others, was missing in him. What was more, in this respect Pulin Babu and his fellow leader in the unit Barin (Barindra Ghosh) Babu, were similar in nature. Hence the Dhaka group, under the able leadership of Pulin Babu and Barin Babu, kept their distance from the other committees; meanwhile, the dissatisfaction of the groups in West Bengal with Pulin Babu and his Samiti grew until it became ugly.

But when Pulin Babu was jailed, there was no strong leader to take control of the Samiti. And since then, this committee became a kind of a republic. Most of the groups in Bengal were known by the name of their leaders—for example, Jatin Babu's group, Bipin Babu's group and so on. However, this group had always been known as Dhaka Anushilan Samiti. But it is also not true that the lack of a single leader weakened the group because it has gone through fire and storm like no other group and emerged strong. It has managed to resurrect itself time and again after undergoing various difficulties and tragedies. This is a characteristic of youngsters from East Bengal. Once they commit to a cause, it is for life and with all their heart and soul. However many faults the people from West Bengal find in their eastern compatriots, I feel that the young men of East Bengal are more simple-hearted and determined than anyone else. The people of West Bengal are less passionate, and if we look critically at the history of the Swadeshi movement, we can see that East Bengal was far ahead of West Bengal in its participation in the national movement. The young men from East Bengal are capable and committed, but they can prove to be difficult at times. Often, they seem to fall prey to a kind of narrow-minded regionalism.

In spite of these drawbacks in their mentality, the leader who took the reins of the Dhaka Anushilan Samiti after Pulin Babu realized that if the different revolutionary groups did not come together and work as one, the country would not benefit at all. That is why they were desirous of meeting other groups at this juncture, and it probably explains why the Samiti merged with the Chandernagore group from the time of the Barisal Conspiracy. The Kashi group also met Rashbehari's group from North India through the Dhaka Samiti. Hence, our group had a network that was active from East Bengal to Punjab. Most of the news and information about the planning for the Punjab revolution was sent to various groups in Bengal through the Dhaka unit. The revolutionary groups in Lahore, Delhi, Kashi, Chandernagore and Dhaka came together in this manner. Unfortunately, other groups in Bengal did not understand the importance of this.

When thousands of youngsters were arrested unceremoniously under the Defense of India Act, all the groups felt powerless and decided to work as one. For some time they did. Had this unity been achieved earlier, the result would have been very different. When Rashbehari was in the vicinity of Calcutta before he left India, he had sent a proposal to all the groups to merge and work together. But no group in Calcutta paid any heed to this suggestion. Finally, and with great sadness, Rashuda had to give up his plan. Anyway, after Rashbehari's departure, we continued to work with this group from East Bengal as before. In fact, it was the Dhaka Anushilan Samiti that had organized 1,000 rupees for Rashuda's travel expenses.

At the time that Dada was sent abroad, there was much competition amongst the groups as to who would be more daring or effective, thereby outshining the others. When Rashuda went to Japan, we thought that we were the first unit to work on getting arms from abroad, but we did not know that Jatin Babu had also sent his men abroad at the same time for the same purpose. However, although all the groups in India were working separately and in a spirit of rivalry, it seems that they had met and united abroad.

I am not very conversant with all that went on abroad because, a couple of months after Rashuda left, I was captured by the police. From Girija Babu of East Bengal who had come to Kashi after his capture in November 1915, I heard that Rashuda had sent word that he would soon be back in the country. The understanding was that he would return to India only after all the arrangements had been made for getting arms and ammunition into the country. Therefore, when we heard that he had said he was coming back, we assumed that he had managed to arrange for arms to be delivered to the country.

Just then, we learnt from another source that the government had got wind of the plan, and a couple of ships carrying arms had also been seized near the Indian coast. Many other things came to light when I read the Rowlatt Committee Report. This part of the history of the revolution has been discussed in detail and critically in Mr Nalini Kishore's *Banglay Viplavvaad*. I will present my readers with some excerpts from Nalini Babu's books.

Revolutionaries Abroad

All the revolutionaries accepted the fact that it was important to accept help from foreign powers to bring about a successful revolution in India. They knew that the various enemies of the British would not hesitate to help India, given the opportunity. And if capable leaders were to emerge in India, they could create an international problem, provoke jealousy and competition amongst powerful empires, and, taking advantage of the situation, lead India to independence.

There is no dearth of examples where subject nations have managed to loosen the grip of strong and powerful governments due to quarrels and issues amongst bigger powers. Compared to the past, it can certainly be said for our times that there is no country on earth at present that, despite its ups and downs, the good and the bad, does not have a relationship with other countries. Awareness of this fact prompted the revolutionaries to look outside. But these foreign powers who were approached for aid also knew that if Indian revolutionary forces were not requisitely strong, the help extended by them would be wasted. If a person seeking help cannot use it, then nothing and nobody can help. The Indian revolutionaries knew well the difference between help offered by the powerful and the intent of the powerful to gobble up the weak. And that is why till they were a force to reckon with, they did not look to these powers for help.

But had there been efforts to secure foreign help right from the time the planning for the revolution began, our efforts would not have been wasted during the German War. Unfortunately, there was no leader among us who had the long-term vision to get the country ready and to decide the right time to establish contact with foreign powers.

Shyamji Krishna Verma was the first amongst the Indian revolutionaries to travel abroad. His efforts inspired many young Indian men living abroad to embrace the idea of a revolution. In December 1905, Shyamji decided that he would give six deserving Indians an amount of 6,000 rupees so that they could travel to America, Europe and other places around the world, and learn how to disseminate the idea of independence and freedom among Indians who lived there. Around the same time, a gentleman from Maharashtra by the name of S.R. Rana wrote to Shyamji from Paris, offering a sum of 6,000 rupees for three Indians to travel abroad. These allowances would be issued in the names of Rana Pratap Singh, Shivaji and some well-known Muslim ruler. The aim was to pick and choose educated Indians, take them abroad and train them as workers for the revolution. But I can't really say if this effort bore any fruit.

In 1906, a talented brahmin from Maharashtra, Vinayak Damodar Savarkar, went to London to study law. After his arrival, Shyamji Krishna Verma's work moved ahead with much speed. But even he was unable to establish any contact with a foreign power or authority which could help India in her cause. Vinayak Damodar was living in London when the famous Hem Chandra Das from Bengal went abroad.

But Hem Das had gone there to learn about making bombs and other incendiary devices and did not try to petition any foreign authority for aid in the revolutionary struggle. The well-known Lala Har Dayal from Punjab also went abroad at the same time, and he was deeply inspired by the fervour of the revolutionaries he met there to contribute to the cause back home in India, but even he did not think to look for support from governments or other political organizations in these foreign countries.

∽

Meanwhile, the powerful tides of the Swadeshi Movement had deluged Bengal and the restless youth of the region, unmindful of any adversity, plunged into the herculean struggle for self-rule with all their heart and soul. So far only the children of the rich would go abroad to study law, train for the Indian Civil Services or to just travel under the influence of the Bengal Renaissance, but increasingly, many young men inspired by the idea of serving the motherland—even those who were not known as good boys—met up in America to plan and organize support for the revolution. Amongst them was Mr Tarak Nath Das, a name we are all familiar with. Around this time or a bit earlier, a young man from a revolutionary group in Bengal was sent to Berlin but he could not exert any influence on the German government. This young man obviously lacked the charisma and personality required to make an impression on a powerful foreign authority.

Shyamji Krishna Verma was forced to flee to Paris after working for some time in London. At the time, there lived in the city a young, female revolutionary who was known as Madam Cama. In the meantime, Lala Har Dayal made a visit to India and then returned to America. For some time, he taught Hindu philosophy at a few American universities. At the same time, Tarak Nath also began teaching at a university in America. There was another Bengali gentleman teaching in an American university at this time. I cannot say for sure whether it was Surendra Kar who is mentioned in *Banglay Viplavvaad*. After the Ghadar Party was established in America, Lala Har Dayal and the Bengali teacher met with the president of America and requested help for Indians to be trained in warfare and other subjects. The latter did not accept any of their requests. After this setback, they petitioned another government and their request was accepted this time. This incident is mentioned in the first part of Nalini Kishore's book. But this revolutionary group in America had no contact with the revolutionary group in India.

However, a few days after the Indian revolutionary group in America managed to establish a connection with a foreign power, the World War broke out. Lala Har Dayal, Tarak Nath and others fled America and went to Europe. That is how their efforts to stage a revolution failed. Lala ji first came to Constantinople and then he travelled via Geneva to meet with other revolutionary groups in Berlin. A well-to-do landlord from Aligarh, Mr Mahendra Pratap Singh, went to Switzerland a few days after the beginning of the World War. Lala Har Dayal met him there when he reached. He came to Berlin with Lala Har Dayal, and that is how Mahendra Pratap became a part of the revolutionary group.

After Lala Har Dayal and others left America, the responsibility of maintaining the revolutionary group fell to Dr Chakraborty and Viren (Virendranath) Chattopadhyay, among others. Viren is the son of our very own Dr Aghorenath Chattopadhyaya (Chatterjee). Srimati Sarojini Naidu and the present editor of the *Shama* magazine, Srimati Mrinalini

Chattopadhyay, are his sisters. Virendra has married a Roman Catholic,[27] and although they are much in love, their religious beliefs were so strong that it caused a lot of animosity between them. As a result, they started living separately. Even now, neither of them has married again and their love for each other has not diminished despite the distance between them. The lady still takes care of Mr Chattopadhyay's expenses even today.

After the beginning of the World War, leaders of various revolutionary groups based in America and Europe gathered in Germany and started setting up the Indian revolutionary organization in consultation with representatives of the German government. The names of all those who met in Germany—Har Dayal, Tarak Nath, Barkatullah, Chandra Kumar Chakravarty, Herambalal Gupta, Virendra Sarkar, Mahendra Pratap and Champakaraman Pillai—can be found in the Rowlatt Committee Report. Pillai was the president of the revolutionary party in Switzerland. We have often seen the name of Viren Chattopadhyay in many papers.

Har Dayal and other gentlemen published a magazine in Europe, most probably from Stockholm. The purpose of this publication was to evoke empathy in Europeans towards the cause of the Indians and to tell them how the British were still ruling the country in the twentieth century. Our leaders have yet to understand the advantages and benefits of promoting India's interests in Europe and America. If they realized this, they would be doing so today.

Our country has still not learnt from the British how to spend huge amounts of money on self-promotion and appoint appropriate people to do so. And even today, while some Indians abroad talk about our country wanting independence, leaders here in India are busy praising the British Empire! Anyway, forget it.

Around the time the propaganda work began, Indians also started procuring arms and ammunition for the revolution. But nothing happened on time. The German consul general in Shanghai, China, was tasked with sending the arms and ammunition. He was working under the directions of his counterpart in Washington. Meanwhile, the Indian revolutionary leaders were working with German government representatives and war secretaries to kindle the fire of a revolt in India. The German government arrested Indian students studying in various institutions in Germany just as the war with Britain broke out and convinced most of them to work for the revolutionary cause, sending them back to India with a lot of money. However, it is probable that the bonafide Indian revolutionaries in Europe had not yet spoken to the German government. Therefore, those who came back with money from Germany gobbled it all up. Only a couple of them came and met the revolutionary groups. Had the Indian revolutionary group in Europe been more careful and alert, such unfortunate incidents would not have taken place. On reading the report of the Rowlatt Committee, it does not seem as if there was a powerful presence of Indian revolutionaries in Europe. The Ghadar group from America did whatever they possibly could.

Anyway, after consultations with German experts, it was decided that young Indian revolutionaries would be given some martial training near the Burmese border and that they would launch an attack on Burma. And by whatever means possible, arms and ammunition required for the revolt would be made available to the Indian rebels. There were many Sikhs living in America, China and the Malay Peninsula at the time. The attack on Burma was carried out through them. Indian revolutionaries were constantly visiting Batavia (the capital of Java), Manila (the capital of the Philippines), Bangkok (the capital of Siam), Shanghai, and other cities, setting up a network over time.

As the Ghadar Party started getting organized, the revolutionary groups in India began making stronger efforts to contact and merge with groups abroad that were dedicated to the cause. In February 1915, Bhola Nath Chattopadhyay of Jatin Babu's group went to Bangkok, but I have no idea how much progress he made. It is only when a young man by the name of Jatindra Nath Lahiri came from Europe that Narendra Nath of the Jatin group went to Batavia in April and work began in earnest. Rashbehari was also in Shanghai in April. All the arrangements in Batavia and Bangkok were made in consultation with the German counsel general in Shanghai and with the help of the Ghadar Party. Contact was also established between the Ghadar Party in Batavia and the Bengal group.

On 29 April 1915, a ship called the *Maverick* left the San Pedro port of California for the Indian subcontinent. This ship, earlier used to transport oil for the Standard Oil Company, had recently been bought by a German company based in San Francisco. When it left the port, there were 25 so-called employees and five workers on the ship. They had declared themselves to be Iraqis but were actually Indians. This ship had been sent with the efforts of the German counsel and Ram Chandra of the revolutionary group. It had been decided that a smaller ship by the name of *Annie Larsen* would meet the *Maverick* on its route with arms and ammunition, and these supplies would be transferred to the *Maverick*. But they did not manage to reach the right place at the appointed time. Consequently, the *Maverick* reached Batavia with just some Indians and German experts. The high-ranking port officials of Batavia had the *Maverick* searched but found nothing objectionable on it. On the other hand, the *Annie Larsen* reached Washington at the end of June and the American government confiscated all the arms and ammunition on board. The German counsel in Washington made a claim to the cargo, but the American government rejected it. The *Maverick* later returned to America from Batavia and Narendra Nath (whose present name is Manvendra Nath Roy, or M.N. Roy) managed to flee to America on it.

Another ship by the name of *Henry S.* managed to reach Manila, but the Philippine authorities unloaded the arms. There was a German general by the name of Boehm on the ship, and it is said that he had been given the responsibility of training the Indian youth at the Burma border. He was arrested in Singapore. Narendra Nath, in consultation with the German counsel, had made arrangements for the arms and ammunition from the *Maverick* to be unloaded near Raimangal in Bengal. All arrangements were in place in Raimangal, but the *Maverick* never arrived. In July 1915, the British government got wind of everything, and the arrests and captures began in India.

But Rashbehari was undeterred, and he tried to once again send arms to India. Plans had been made for a revolt to begin in December 1915 in India. The arrangement was that one ship, laden with weapons and ammunition, would free all political prisoners in the Andamans and directly mount an attack on Burma. Two other ships would reach Indian shores with more supplies. A Chinese gentleman was coming to India with 66,000 guilders (silver coins from Holland) as financial aid for the revolution. He, too, was caught in Singapore. In addition to the money, he was found to have the address of a Bengali in Penang and two others in Calcutta. Another revolutionary, Avani Mukherjee, was arrested in Singapore. His notebook had Rashbehari's Shanghai address; addresses of two Chinese collaborators; the address of Matilal Rai from Chandernagore; some addresses from Calcutta, Dhaka and Kumilla; and the address of a Sikh engineer, Amar Singh, from Siam. Raids were carried out in Shanghai; a number of revolvers and thousands of bullets were recovered from the addresses of the two Chinese gentlemen. In an earlier arrangement, the *Henry S.* was supposed to have been met by Amar Singh, and some of the arms and ammunition on board was to be given to him. The Rowlatt Committee Report says that Amar Singh was hanged to death, but I met the man—this very Amar Singh—in the Andamans. It is true that he was sentenced to be hanged, but like many other revolutionaries, his sentence was also changed to life imprisonment in the Cellular Jail.

Among the ships that managed to make their way towards India, it is said that one was captured by the Dutch government under International War rules, and one hears that another was drowned by the British warship *HMS Cornwall* near the Andamans. I don't know what happened to the third ship. In the meantime, another young man from Jatin Babu's group managed to reach Shanghai but was arrested on arrival.

∽

This is how the third attempt at a revolution failed. A year after the beginning of the World War, it was not difficult to travel to and from India. But when the British government got wind of the preparations for the revolution, it became increasingly difficult to travel abroad. Therefore, the ships carrying arms also could no longer escape government scrutiny. Moreover, the Germans were now busy with their war and could not pay much attention to the Indian cause. Moreover, the Indian revolutionary group had not been able to establish its identity as a major player to attract the attention of the foreign powers. Had the group worked on strengthening these relations well before the war, I am sure things would have been different.

People who think that the Indian revolutionaries' desire to look for help from the imperialist enemies of the British was nothing but folly and a dream should know that it is because of these European enmities that China has not been colonized despite being in such a bad condition. Countries like Afghanistan, Iran and Turkey have also become powerful owing to the help and sympathy they have received from various foreign governments. The Germans had helped the Boers with arms and ammunition during the Boer War. And in the last war, when Turkey was practically annihilated, Kemal Pasha had declared a revolt against the government and nullified its treaties with friendly powers, but this was possible with help from the French. Today, in order to not be completely dependent on the French, Angora is trying to make overtures to America.

The truth is that if someone stands with their head held high, there is no dearth of help. It is when one is weak from inside that problems arise. As it is rightly said, 'Anybody can give, but to accept is a challenge.'

Chapter 5

THE BURMA STORY

This plan for a revolt in Burma with the help of Indians wasn't the first; the freedom-loving Burmese had tried to organize one many a times before. There were many Burmese in the Andamans, sentenced to the Cellular Jail for such political crimes. They were all released after the end of the War. The British government did not think of them as a threat. One learns that this was probably because the unrest in Burma did not really represent the awakening of a community. There was no unity around the revolutionary cause in this region, and that is why it was not all that powerful. But with the help of the Indians, a great deal of planning went into the revolution in Burma. The Rowlatt Report says, 'Burma however has not been altogether free from criminal conspiracy connected with the Indian revolutionary movement. It has been the scene of determined efforts to stir up mutiny among the military forces and to overthrow the British government.' I will give you a few brief examples of what these 'determined efforts' were.

As I have already mentioned, during the Italo-Turkish war, a medical mission comprising Indian Muslims had gone to Turkey to help with the wounded. A young man by the name of Ali Ahmed Siddiqi had joined the mission without informing his guardians of his plans. Just before leaving Indian shores, he sent a letter announcing to his family that he was going to Turkey as part of the Indian Medical Mission.

He spent four months with Anwar Pasha in Turkey on the battlefield. He heard many mysterious stories about Anwar Pasha's life. During the Italo-Turkish War and the Greco-Turkish War, the people of Turkey experienced firsthand certain British strategies of war that reshaped the history of their country. It was British intervention in these wars and in the political life of the Turks that created the Young Turk party, which would eventually mould the destiny of Turkey. How the Young Turks first appeared in Turkey and how the party rejuvenated a moribund Turkish society, led a revolution, and defeated the cruel and powerful sultan of the Ottoman Empire, Abdul Hamid, establishing a new political order in the country—Ali Ahmed would listen to all these stories, entranced, sitting alone with Anwar Pasha. His heart would overflow with joy and he would be restless with dreams of a proud and bright future for the Muslim community in India after listening to these innumerable and inspiring stories of the Islamic world, stories of extraordinary courage and humaneness. When this man, one of Turkey's most high-ranking generals who was well-known throughout Europe and one of those instrumental in moulding Turkey's political destiny, would speak so frankly with a young man from India, on the one hand Ali's heartbeat would quicken with joy and on the other he would recall the insults and degradation that Indians suffered every day. His heart would then fill with disgust and hatred towards the British, and he was drawn more and more to the revolutionary groups and their ideals.

When Ali Ahmed and other Indians expressed their wish to see more of Turkey, government officials in various places organized big events and showed them their country, escorting them with state honours. When the streets would be lined with Turkish people cheering them on and pretty girls would shower petals from windows, it was not surprising that the Indians would embrace Turkey more as their own than India. They could not help comparing the attitude of the Turks with the treatment meted out to them by the British government in their own country. That is how Ali Ahmed was inducted into the revolutionary fold and, like many other Indian Muslims, joined the Young Turks.

During this Italo-Turkish War, another young man by the name of Abu Sayyed went to Egypt from Rangoon and, from there, to Turkey. It was on Abu Sayyed's request and proposal that a member of the Young Turks, Taufiq Be, was sent to Rangoon in 1916. Taufiq Be nominated a Muslim businessman, Ahmad Mulla Da'ud, as Turkey's consul general in Rangoon.

As for Ali Ahmed, he returned to India after the Balkan War had ended and the World War had begun. After spending some time at home, he sold off his wife's jewellery and moved to Rangoon to do business there. In December 1914, the Turkish sent another Indian Muslim by the name of Fayam Ali from Constantinople as a representative of the Young Turks. Fayam Ali and Ahmed Ali met in Rangoon and started planning a revolution in Burma under Turkey's leadership. In a few days, they had collected 15,000 rupees in donations from the local Muslim community. I would like to mention here that in Bengal, the rich would not contribute at all to the revolutionary cause, and that is why it had become imperative to carry out political dacoities in Bengal.

While this pan-Islamic group was planning and organizing a revolt, the Ghadar Party in America was not lagging behind either. Khemchand Daamji, a Gujarati gentleman, had, at some point, gone to America from Rangoon and joined the Ghadar group the moment he reached there. In the beginning, the *Ghadar* newsletter was sent only to Burma with the aid of this gentleman. During the war, this magazine was published in Gujarati, Hindi and Urdu. There was unrest among Muslims in Burma during the World War, and the *Ghadar* newsletter worked as oil in fire. It was during this time that a soldier from the Baloch Regiment killed his British officer, and, as a result, this regiment was held back in Rangoon and not sent to Europe. The Muslims in Rangoon kept talking of an uprising among these soldiers through writings in the *Ghadar* newsletter, and, consequently, in January 1915, this regiment was all set to declare an open revolt. But the moment the British Army officers got a whiff of the news, they meted out harsh punishment to the regiment. Two hundred Balochis were sent to various prisons in India.

There were two Indian regiments in Singapore. The Muslim revolutionary group of Burma managed to come to an arrangement with one of them. Qasim Mansoor, a Gujarati Muslim settled in Singapore, wrote to his son in Rangoon, enclosing a letter addressed to the Turkish consul general there. The letter stated that a regiment in Singapore was ready to revolt and side with Turkey, and that it was imperative that a Turkish warship be sent to the city. This letter ended up in British hands, and the Singapore regiment in question was posted elsewhere.

Meanwhile, people from the Ghadar Party in America had also landed up in Singapore. They started their propaganda in the other regiment and also sent their representatives to Burma. In early 1915, Sohanlal Pathak and Hassan Khan of the Ghadar Party came to Rangoon from Bangkok and established a centre in the city. It must be noted that the Ghadar Party included Muslims, but there was no place for Hindus in the Muslim revolutionary party.

The result of all this propaganda work in the Singapore Army was that the revolution soon began in earnest. Although there was no connection between the Punjab plans and the Singapore plans, it is surprising to note that the revolt in Singapore began on 21 February 1915 and the scheduled date for the revolt in Punjab was the same day. On this day, the soldiers in Singapore openly rose up against the British, in defiance of years of training and obedience to the rules. For a week, Singapore was held by the Indian Army, but the city was not in India, and, therefore, the fire of revolt could not spread. In a week, English, Russian and Japanese warships surrounded Singapore. For a week, the revolutionaries had fought the British Army and the latter had conceded defeat in that battle. But when the warships came, the revolutionaries had to give up in two days and flee. They took shelter in the forests for a while, but there was no way to escape from Singapore, and all of them were caught by the British in the end. The English newspapers printed that there were riots in Singapore, but the British government and the Indian revolutionary party both realized that it had not been difficult for the revolutionaries to influence the Indian soldiers and win them over.

After the mishap in Singapore, Pathak and Khan of the Ghadar Party in Singapore moved to Rangoon, and, once again, they started campaigning among the Indian troops stationed there. On the one hand, efforts were being made to spread the word about the revolution in the Rangoon regiments and on the other, on Burma's border with Siam, a revolt was being planned with German help. A railway track was being laid in North Siam under the aegis of German engineers. Most of the labourers were Punjabi. A plan was hatched to attack Burma using this railway line. Sikhs and Punjabis returning from America and China began gathering at the Siam border.

A Punjabi Sikh, Shiv Dayal Kapoor, came to Shanghai from America. Through him, a German in Shanghai sent a large sum of money to the German consul in Bangkok. Some of this money was spent on the Sikhs going to Burma and the rest was sent to revolutionaries in Bengal through a Bengali lawyer.[28] It is said that this Bengali lawyer turned informer and revealed the plans to the British government. All these plans and arrangements should have been made well before the start of the War. It is because they were carried out in haste during the War that such unreliable people had to be inducted. God knows who had recommended this Bengali lawyer as a go-between. Anyway, whosoever that might have been, the result was that the plans for a revolt from abroad failed. Yet, in Burma, one more effort was made.

Sohanlal Pathak and Narayan Singh once again started talking to soldiers in various cantonments in Burma about a revolt. Sohanlal began working up hostilities towards the British in a group of gunners by telling them that there was no point in sacrificing one's life for the British, and instead those lives would be worth more if laid down for the motherland and for one's own religion. That would be a matter of pride. The soldiers did not respond to him, but one day, he was caught by an Indian captain. No one was there other than Sohanlal and the officer. Sohanlal had on his person at that moment a couple of revolvers and several bullets. God knows what state of mind he was in, but he did not think of using his weapon to get rid of the captain.

All he could say at that moment was. 'You are going to get me arrested? Are you forgetting that I am your brother? Will a brother tell on a brother? What kind of a brother are you, getting one of your own arrested?' But the captain did not let go of Sohanlal and kept dragging him along. It is true that Sohanlal was not a physically powerful man. But it is also true that no man can completely overpower another without help, however strong he may be. Had Sohanlal wanted, he could easily have used the revolver and fled. Yet he did not resist the captain, despite knowing well enough the consequences of being handed over to the British. Only God knows what his thoughts were; it seems as if he was in an otherworldly frame of mind that day.

Sohanlal was sent to jail, but he did not follow any rule there. When all the prisoners would stand at attention for the inspection by the jail authorities, Sohanlal would refuse to comply. He would say, 'When I think that the British rule is unjust and a tyranny, how can I follow their rules in jail?' When the Laat Saheb[29] heard of the capture of Sohanlal and came for an inspection, the jailor had, with much hesitation and trepidation, requested Sohanlal to show deference to the Saheb, but he did not agree. Sohanlal was an exceptionally courageous man, well-known and respected, but he was also unfailingly humane and kind to others. He was never rude or nasty. He spoke politely to any man who approached him. If someone stood up and spoke with him, he, too, would stand up.

That is why the jailer stood in front of him and started speaking to him just before the Laat Saheb arrived, thereby managing to maintain the Saheb's image and dignity. The Laat Saheb spoke to Sohanlal for two hours. He asked Sohanlal to apologize; he told him that a single mercy petition would spare him the death sentence. Sohanlal spoke to him about all the injustice and oppression that was being carried out by the British as they were ruling by force. If anyone should apologize, he pointed out, it was the Laat Saheb.

Just before Sohanlal was hanged, as he stood on the platform before the noose, the magistrate had once again told him that if he were to once offer a verbal apology, his death sentence would be cancelled. The official said that he had been instructed to request the prisoner one last time to apologize. The jail staff were all staring stupefied at Sohanlal, who stood only a few steps away from death. Sohanlal started to slowly smile and then said, 'If someone has to apologize, then it should be the British who should apologize to us. Why should I apologize?' The English official once again requested Sohanlal to apologize and told him that there was no point in sacrificing his life like this. Sohanlal thought for a bit and said, 'If you are willing to let me go free, without any restrictions and conditions, I am willing to think about an apology.' The English official said, 'We don't have any such authority.' Sohanlal replied, 'Then why waste time? You do your duty and let me fulfil mine.'

Sohanlal was hanged to death.

The Muslim revolutionaries in Burma planned another revolt for Bakr Eid. But since the arrangements could not be put in place, the plan was deferred to 25 December. Some revolvers and dynamite were recovered from a barrack of the Burma Military Police, and all those who were suspected of involvement were jailed under the Defense of India Act. That was the end of the unrest in Burma.

Chapter 6

RESULT

All the efforts of the revolutionaries were wasted one after the other. The result was that they were targeted by governments in the country and abroad, and there was no limit to the harassment they faced. In India, under the India Security Regulation, groups of young men were either jailed or put under house arrest in villages at the slightest suspicion. Even a smidgeon of proof resulted in heavy punishment. Many sacrificed their lives to the hangman's noose, and many were sent to the Cellular Jail. Many young men resorted to suicide after capture, unable to bear the atrocities of the police or the tough life in jail, and many a mother's heart was torn to bits. The revolutionary groups were scattered and broken. The leaders of the revolutionaries were either imprisoned or hanged to death. The encounters with the police that the different revolutionary groups had in various places after they broke up will be remembered always in the history of the revolution.

When the seriousness and the extent of the revolutionary activities in Punjab came to the government's notice, they realized that they could no longer underestimate it. The eminent and politically enlightened leaders of the country had all along been saying that the efforts of the revolutionary movement in India were juvenile. But the British government had realized that if these revolutionaries were given any leeway and allowed to carry on as before, there would be an unprecedented situation in the country. Unlike the Indian political leaders, the British had understood what the revolutionaries were capable of doing. I spoke many times to English officials about this before I was sent to the Andamans. I learnt that, amongst the various movements in the country, the government was only worried about the revolutionary movement. And, therefore, all their force and poison was being used to annihilate it. For instance, the moment they got a whiff of the revolutionary movement in Punjab, they introduced the India Security Regulation to enforce a strict administrative rule there.

History was repeating itself in India. What had always happened throughout the ages was happening here too. When a suppressed community starts to wake and rise up, strict measures are enforced to quell all rebellion. However, nothing can hold back the true awakening of a people and any form of repression that it may be subjected to is only a test of its strength. If the community is strong-willed, repression is a stimulus and not a deterrent in its awakening. The anger caused by such political repression is God's blessing. The Indian revolutionaries, in all honesty, never held the British responsible for their oppressive policies. Rather, they were convinced that God was testing them, and this was His way of testing their mettle and reawakening them. They understood that a subjugated community could only be free after going through these rigours, as if they were milestones a subjugated race must cross on the path to freedom. The strictness of administrative policies was but an indicator of their community's progress on the journey towards self-determination. That is why they bore all the misery and hardships that the struggle brought and did not flinch while giving up their lives.

Summary trials began after the Defense of India Act was issued. Three conspiracy cases were prosecuted in Punjab one after the other. Sixty to seventy people were accused in each case, and, in the end, twenty-eight people were sentenced to death. Eleven soldiers from the Meerut Platoon were hanged, as well as many men from the 7th Rajput regiment in Delhi. Those who escaped the noose were sentenced to life imprisonment in the Andamans. Even amidst such a crackdown, the surviving revolutionaries in Punjab started to plan another revolt. Some Akali Dal members were plotting to free the revolutionaries from jail.

Another Sikh group turned their attention to procuring more arms and ammunition. Armed policemen used to patrol under the bridges near the big railway stations in those days. Apparently, a group of seven or eight revolutionaries armed with pistols mounted a sudden attack on the policemen under the bridge near the Amritsar station. There were 15 policemen, 15 magazine rifles and 750 bullets. The revolutionaries carried off all the rifles and bullets. But because there was no organizational network in place, five of the revolutionaries were caught with the guns and all of them were hanged. Even after this incident, yet another group of Sikh school teachers tried to keep the fire of revolt alive. I guess these efforts are carried on even today.

Dr Mathura Singh and other revolutionaries like him left India and went to Persia and Mesopotamia via Afghanistan. They campaigned for the revolution among the Indian troops stationed there. Dr Mathura Singh was eventually caught at the India–Afghanistan border. He too was hanged. Those who escaped both the noose and life imprisonment in the Cellular Jail had to face internment. During that period, no other state witnessed the kind of internment that Punjab and Bengal experienced, and the maximum number of hangings and life sentences were seen in Punjab.

After the Banaras Conspiracy in the United Provinces, the revolutionary group managed to resurrect itself in about a year with Mainpuri as its centre. It was exposed within a year or two. In Russia, no revolutionary group could work undetected for more than two months. They would then be either punished by the State or forced to flee the country and seek shelter abroad. I would like to point out that in India, the working period of revolutionary groups before they are identified and pursued or captured by the government is about two years. In Bengal, during this period, internment was more common than hangings and life imprisonments. As a result, the Bengal revolutionary group more or less broke up and dispersed to different parts of the country. Had these revolutionaries possessed adequate reserves of arms and ammunitions at the time, they could have made it impossible for the British government to survive.

Rashbehari was in Kashi at the time. One day, there was a message from the centre that the well-known revolutionary leader Mr Jatindra Nath Mukhopadhyay, who was in hiding, had expressed a wish to live in Kashi. We conferred about this and concluded that it was not difficult to keep him in Kashi without arousing any suspicion. But we were also apprehensive about the fact that any slip-up from his group in Bengal could cause grave misfortune for Kashi. If one is in charge of all the arrangements, it is easier to spot loopholes and fault lines and to rectify them. One can, therefore, also take responsibility for any mishap that occurs. But how is one to control such mishaps if the organization is not in one's hands?

It is true that many small groups had come together under Jatin Babu's leadership, but they had not merged with the East

Bengal Anushilan Samiti or the Chandernagore revolutionaries who were part of the Rashbehari group, nor did they make any efforts to do so. Rashbehari made many attempts to meet them before he left for Japan, but for some reason or the other, the meeting did not take place. Whatever the case, we accepted the responsibility of hosting Jatin Babu. But we have no idea why he decided eventually not to come to Kashi.

He stayed put in Calcutta. One day, he was visiting a house in Pathuriya Ghat where many revolutionaries in hiding stayed. A man they had known for a few days also happened to come there at that time. They suspected him of being a spy, and without any confirmation, one of the revolutionaries shot him the moment he saw him. This young man most probably shot the outsider in order to save Jatin Babu. The latter did not fire the shot, but the man in his dying declaration accused Jatin Babu of shooting him. Therefore, a death sentence was handed out to Jatin Babu. I don't understand why, if the man had to be shot in the first place, he was left alive to make a dying declaration to the police.

The helpless Jatin Babu now had to go elsewhere. A secure place was found for him. When it was time for him to go there, he told his companions, 'Till I am convinced that arrangements have been made for such secure spots for you all, I cannot accept this arrangement. We are all discharged soldiers who are waiting to hear our death sentences every moment. Therefore, we should all stay together so that we can carry out an effective struggle which will create a moral impression on the people.' In the end, the arrangements were made according to his wishes. Five of them moved to Baleshwar, where they set up a new centre. The revolutionary movement in the state had not shut down. Jatin Babu continued to steer the work of the movement from faraway Baleshwar.

Had the revolutionaries not tried to get back to their work and stayed hidden and quiet instead, I believe no one would have been arrested. But revolutionaries always choose to carry on their tasks while in hiding, and that is why they are forever exposed to danger and misfortune. However, it was never their primary concern to salvage their lives. What good was life, according to them, if it did not serve the motherland? When the Bangkok lawyer, whom I mentioned earlier, snitched to the police, there were several raids and arrests in Calcutta. The police managed to acquire Jatindra Nath's address through this source. Jatin Babu also came to know that the police had his address. If he wanted to, he could have run away. But merely saving his own life was not a priority for him. He could have gone to another safe spot, but he was not willing to leave his companions behind. He did not differentiate between his own life and safety and that of his companions.

When they decided to leave, two of their companions were 12 miles away in a dark forest. It was decided that they could not be left behind at any cost. In the middle of the night, Jatindra Nath left with the others and took a path through the hills to find his companions in the jungle. It would have been impossible to traverse 12 miles on an unknown path and return, and then go to another place the same night. But to undertake the impossible was his mission in life, and that day too, he decided to do the impossible. By the time they were on their way back, it was morning. Police posts had been set up along the river in the villages bordering the jungle, and yet, they managed to enter one of the villages on the route to Baleswar. Chitpriya, Manoranjan, Neerendra and Jyotish were with Jatin Babu.

Meanwhile, the police had told the villagers that a group of dangerous dacoits was hiding in their area, and they would be richly rewarded if they captured them or assisted in their capture. Jatindra Nath had neither eaten nor slept for two days, but he kept walking in the hot afternoon sun, crossing villages, rivers and canals. While crossing a river, he asked the boatman to cook them some rice as they were starving. But the poor man, chained to centuries of tradition, feared that he would go to hell if he, being of a lower caste, offered food or even a utensil to cook the food to a high-caste brahmin. Soon, the police got the information that Jatindra Nath was in the vicinity of a particular village. An armed police group set out in pursuit of the fugitives on this route. If the revolutionaries had had a network in place in this region, they could have defended Jatin Babu and his companions in this hour of trouble. But its absence meant that they had to run from one village to another.

They reached a jungle near Baleshwar by evening. There, the magistrate and the district superintendent awaited them with searchlights, all set for the skirmish that would take place. Meanwhile, the police had divided themselves in two groups, and they were closing in on Jatin Babu and his companions from opposite directions. Jatindra Nath realized that it was not possible to flee the jungle. Another night passed and morning dawned. The police were closing in further. Jatindra Nath's companions implored him to run away even if it meant that they died in the process. But Jatin Babu did not accept this option. He said, 'My dear brothers, think about this. We have left the comfort of our parents' love, our wives and children, and the security of our homes to work together. Isn't that so? So why should I abandon that thought in this hour of misfortune? No man is immortal. Everyone must die someday. Then why die like a coward?'

They decided to fight to the end. On one side were more

than a thousand villagers who were siding with the armed police because they thought dacoits were being captured, and on the other, just these five revolutionaries! They left the jungle and entered the village. They were exhausted by hunger, lack of sleep and being on the run for so long. They did not have the means to buy two morsels of food. Just then, the two factions saw each other. Shots were fired from both sides. One of the policemen got a tad too close to the revolutionaries, and Chitpriya shot at his cap, which flew into the air. The policeman did not advance any further. The revolutionaries were lying on uneven ground and shooting from there. There was constant firing from the police as well. How long could five tired, hungry and sleep-deprived people fight against such a powerful enemy? The revolutionaries were fast running out of ammunition. They were all injured. But they did not give in.

Then a bullet took Chitpriya to the world of everlasting sleep. At that moment, Jatindra Nath said to his companions, 'There is no point in wasting more energy. Chitpriya is gone and I, too, shall go. Don't waste your lives; maybe they will serve a good cause in the future.' But his companions too were determined to lay down their lives fighting. Jatindra Nath wanted to save their lives. In the end, they accepted his request and surrendered. Jatindra Nath collapsed because he had lost a great deal of blood and his throat was parched. In a fading voice, he asked for water. Manoranjan was bleeding profusely, but he wanted to fulfil his leader's last wish, so he left to wet a sheet and bring water from the nearest source.

A police officer was also moved by this scene. He told Manoranjan to sit, and since there was no other receptacle, he brought water in his cap and gave it to the dying man. The moment the water went into his throat he smiled and told the police officer, 'I am the one responsible for this whole incident. My companions were only following my orders.' Jatindra Nath passed away in a hospital in Cuttack. Manoranjan and Neerendra were hanged. Jyotish was sentenced to life imprisonment in the Andamans. It is from this Jyotish Chandra that we learnt of the whole episode and could tell our countrymen of the same. Unable to bear the torture in the Cellular Jail, Jyotish Chandra lost his mind. Apparently, he is now in a mental asylum in Berhampur.[30]

To read the letter that Neerendra and Manoranjan wrote home to Calcutta, sitting at death's doorstep in a dark corner of the jail, charges one up emotionally. They wrote:

> Chitpriya and Dada have gone. We are also on our way to join them. We hope you will carry on the work as before. May God grant you success. It is the end of the road for us. Farewell! Goodbye! There is no way to bring back those who have gone forever, but what can be done for Jyotish, his companions must think about.

This letter reminds me of another one. Despite being a follower of Jainism, he chose the path of armed revolution for the sake of his country. When he was sequestered in a jail cell for the murder of the Mahant of the Nimej Bazar temple,[31] they wrote a letter to his revolutionary companions the gist of which was: 'Brother, I am not scared of death and there is no greed for life. I shall be happy in whatever God decides for me.' These two young men were Moti Chand and Manik Chand or Jai Chand.

These revolutionaries were like ascetics, not bothered about life or death. Even their opponents, the British, could not help but praise them. In reference to Jatindra Nath, the then head of the secret service and present police commissioner Mr Tegart had apparently told the prestigious lawyer the late Mr J.N. Roy,

'Though I had to do my duty, I have great admiration for him. He was the only Bengali who died in an open fight from a trench.' But after Mr Tegart made this statement, there were many Bengalis who fought valiantly in similar circumstances, and I would like to present them to my readers.

Jatin Babu and his companions lost their lives in a direct confrontation with the police on 9 September 1915. But many revolutionaries showed the same mettle in the years leading up to 1918. In 1916, there was a third and successful attempt on the life of the deputy superintendent of the secret service, Basant Kumar Chattopadhyay. He had managed to miraculously escape the previous two attempts. In 1917, the revolutionaries were involved in a skirmish with the police in Guwahati, and in 1918, there was yet another armed confrontation in Dhaka, in which two revolutionaries were killed. There was a small skirmish in Pabna, and apart from this, dacoities and murders were committed regularly.

I will speak briefly about these armed clashes. In 1916, Nalin Vukich was sent by the revolutionary group to a college in Bhagalpur to study and promote the cause. He was a good student who was granted a scholarship. Very soon, the police took notice of this Bengali. Nalin abandoned his studies and ran away. He was a good student, receiving a scholarship. He left because the scholarship trapped him, not allowing him to participate in the movement. But who wanted to deal with the trappings of availing a scholarship? He travelled from one city to another in the guise of a Bihari. In a few days, the police identified him again. When Nalin returned to Bengal in 1917, it was a very dangerous time—there were raids and arrests all around, internments, deportations and a veritable rain of bullets! It had become unsafe for the revolutionaries to live in Bengal. The group decided that all the good workers would be kept as a reserve force in some safe place in Assam. Consequently, Nalin Vukich, Nalin Ghosh, Naren Banerjee and others took refuge in Guwahati, Assam.

They slept with a loaded revolver under their pillows and took turns to keep guard at the window through the night for two hours each. The Calcutta police managed to get their Guwahati address from a revolutionary they had arrested there and surrounded the house on 9 January 1917. The one who was watching at the window woke the others but silently. All of them picked up their revolvers and pistols, came out of the house and fired at the police. The sudden attack caused the police to disperse and the revolutionaries were able to make their way to the hills. But in the afternoon, innumerable armed policemen came and surrounded the entire hilly area. There was firing from both the sides. Many were injured and caught, and only two managed to escape. One of them was Nalin.

He walked for six days, crossed a mountain and eventually reached Lumding. It was a backbreaking journey without food or sleep—always evading the police, sometimes by climbing up a tree or a steep hill, and catching two winks on some rock. He had one revolver on him. His hands and feet were cut and bruised from walking great distances at such a pace and from climbing mountains and trees. And walking was not the only travail. A species of tick that was peculiar to those mountains stuck to Nalin's forehead and back, and could not be pulled off, try as he might. Its poison is painful, and Nalin was in excruciating pain. Somehow, he escaped the Assam police and reached Bihar, but it was not safe for him to stay there either. Once he saw that, he went to Bengal. At Howrah station, he did not see any one of those he was expecting to be met by.

Where should he go? It had been more than a fortnight since he had had a normal meal or slept. His body was collapsing, and the poisonous ticks were still stuck to his forehead and body. In Howrah, his fever went up. Helpless, and with no solution in sight, he fell asleep under a tree in the fort grounds. He lay there like a corpse for three days and nights. By chance, another revolutionary who knew him happened to see him there. His face and body seemed to be riddled with the marks of smallpox. The condition of the revolutionaries in Calcutta at that time was piteous. Almost all of them had been caught; nobody had any money and the few that were free were roaming around the city in a pathetic condition. Nalin was taken to and kept in a small house in Calcutta. The pox covered his mouth, his eyes and his tongue. He could not speak for three days. There was no money for treatment, so all they could do was wait and watch. There was only one other revolutionary hiding in that house. Everyone wondered how they would have enough people for the cremation, if required.

Yet Nalin did not die of smallpox. Death was in fact waiting for him in Dhaka, where he decided to go in order to rekindle the fire of the revolution once he got well. Nalin and Tarini Majumdar were staying at the same address. At dawn on 15 June 1918, the police surrounded the house. Once again, there was firing from both sides. Tarini was shot many times and fell dead there. Nalin tried to run despite having been shot and fell when yet another bullet hit him.

Nalin lay in the hospital, fatally injured. And the police were frantically trying to get his name and address as well as a dying declaration. Lying on his deathbed, the brave revolutionary was in excruciating pain and all he wished for was his death. In such a situation, it would be impossible for a normal human being to keep hiding. He would want the whole world to know his work. He would want those for whom he is giving up his life to know that he did so. But a revolutionary is extraordinary and tries to hide his true self till the very end. This is not possible without education and training. There was no desire even on the deathbed, no wish that everyone should know him or realize his value. Unwept, unhonoured and unsung—that is how they wanted to go. A true revolutionary does not want anyone to shed tears for him, remember his name or sing his praises. And that is why this young man, the revolutionary lying on his deathbed, had just one answer for the police despite all their questions and attempts to extract information from him, 'Don't disturb me, please, let me die peacefully.'

Have our countrymen ever thought about these people who learnt to live in the shadows and embraced death willingly? They live detached from the world and die quietly, without any personal desires and ambitions; they crave no fame or laurels. The satisfaction they derive from their work is for their own soul and they have no expectations of or from anybody. They are selfless and generous to a fault. What can we call these revolutionaries? Maybe they were mad, or merely confused and unwise children, because that is how the great, politically savvy leaders of this country see them.

Apparently, the biggest fault with these revolutionaries was that they did not succeed in achieving their goal. Month after month and year after year of untiring work, and all they produced was failure? Is that not a confused path which leads only to futility? Is this failure worth anything? The Indian leaders and critics of the revolution keep posing such questions.

But we only think of one aspect of failure. We do not perceive how the riches of the world are hidden in failure, how failure harnesses strength and how success comes through failure. Revolutionaries are always ridiculed and laughed at in all societies and through the ages. This is because in almost all the countries of the world, the first efforts of revolutionaries have nearly always failed, and the intellectuals invariably measure their worth against this failure. Hence, the revolutionaries in India were also considered a lost, confused lot. And these 'intelligent', 'far-seeing' critics do not hesitate to refer to them as idiots. The sagacious editor of India's illustrious *Modern Review* magazine said, referring to the revolutionaries, 'If there are even a few armed revolutionaries in India, then we should definitely doubt our sense.'

The revolutionaries and their critics differ in only this respect—the revolutionaries have immense, unshakeable faith in their goal and they have spent their lives trying to achieve it whereas the critics have made it their life and business to sit in the comfort of an armchair and find fault. Criticism is their business. True, many things must be calculated to earn a living, but too much calculation may result in the death of truth. Another huge difference between the revolutionaries and the critics is—what the revolutionaries think of as 'faith', the critics think of as 'opinion'. And opinion can never get over its obsession with success. But those who are setting out to make history do not care about these 'opinions'; they are faithful and devoted to the cause. Failure does not deter them. That is why history remembers them—for it is only the devoted and the faithful who manage to achieve anything. With reference to the Indian revolutionaries, the illustrious lawyer Mr Norton had once said, 'These revolutionaries have not been successful in achieving their goals, and that is why, today, they are criminals for the government; had they succeeded, they would be praised, lauded and worshipped in the world as the most patriotic beings.'

It is impossible to say whether India will win her freedom through the path chosen by the revolutionaries or not. Maybe their way is all wrong, but it is hardly fair to call them idiots for choosing such a path. Who knows whether, in the end, the world has sided with the revolutionaries in India or with their critics! But we do know that when a handful of Italians had reared their heads in opposition to the great and powerful Austrian empire, they too had had to face derision and criticism. And we know that after 60 years of untiring efforts, crossing innumerable hurdles and facing catastrophic failures, today the Russian revolutionaries are about to realize their dreams. Italy has also achieved independence after 40 years of striving for it, through many sacrifices and misfortunes.

How many insults the first travellers along the path of revolution have had to bear! In this context, I remember what Terence MacSwiney said, 'Any man who tells you that an act of armed resistance—even if offered by 10 men only, even if offered by men armed with stones—any men who tell you that such an act of resistance is premature, imprudent or dangerous, any and every such man should be at once spurned and spat at, for remark you this and recollect that somewhere and somehow and by somebody, a beginning must be made and that the first act of resistance is always and must ever be premature, imprudent and dangerous.'

I have tried to write a chronological account of the history of the Indian revolutionaries to the best of my ability. But history is based on judgement. Without the judgement, history is but a chronicle of events. And that is why I have, at times, deviated from incidents and spoken of other things. And just because I have praised the revolutionaries, it should not be taken to mean that I am promoting armed revolution. I want to say that even if we differ with them, we should not curse them or hate them. Even the British government, their opponent, has praised them, and this did not make the British armed revolutionaries!

I am sitting down to write history. I have already spoken about how Indians generally view the revolutionaries, as well as about how we should perceive them and why. I don't know if the revolutionaries were indeed mad, but speaking of the madness, I am reminded of Rabi Babu's (Rabindranath Tagore) poem:

Kon aalote praaner prodip jwaaliye tumi dharayaaso
Saadhokogo, premikogo,
Paagologo, dhorayaaso.

(While you come down to earth, from which source do you light up your lamp, O hermit, O lover, O crazy dear? Pain and misery in this vast world rings the lute within your soul.)[32]

Chapter 7

WHY DID THE REVOLT FAIL?

Why did the Ghadar revolutionaries' efforts fail? To answer this, it is essential to understand what it was that they wanted. Without a clear understanding of their goals, it is difficult to understand both the extent and the causes of the failure. Therefore, it is important to critically look at their aims and objectives before analysing their lack of success.

It is not possible to carry out a complete analysis and criticism of the Indian revolutionary movement because that will require a historical overview of its emergence throughout India. That would be so huge a task that we will have to digress considerably from our main topic. We will, therefore, leave that for some other time. In this narrative, I will deal with only what is essential.

Whatever the differences among the various revolutionary groups in the country, they were all unanimous in the opinion that India had to achieve its independence at the earliest. That is to say, no non-Indian or foreign party should interfere in the governance of India, and the welfare of the country should be the responsibility of Indians and Indians only. What is good for Indian society, what relations should India develop with other countries, what is best for India in terms of commerce and business—all these decisions should be taken as Indians see best. No other nation should have a say in these matters.

This is what the Indian revolutionaries wanted and worked towards. India could not be free to take these decisions as part of the British Empire; just as a child instinctively knows its parents, the revolutionaries, too, knew this. In a nutshell, at the root of all the efforts of the revolutionaries was the desire to make India powerful and self-reliant enough to get rid of all kinds of external controls and influences. Among these countries, Britain did not have an exceptional status in the eyes of the revolutionaries, although the struggle began with the British, as they have the closest links with Indian life, society and business.

The revolutionaries feel that to achieve freedom it is important to awaken the masculine power, the inner warrior of India's martial race (kshatriya), and it is with this belief that they planned their strategy. Much before the emergence of Mahatma Gandhi on the national scene, our revolutionaries have had to deal with criticism and flak from the "brahmins" for this ideology that invokes the "kshatriya" ethos of the warlike and the masculine. I would like to take this up in detail at some point, but this is not the place for a philosophical debate of this nature. Nonetheless, it would not be amiss to point out a couple of things. The truth is that there is no difference between the kshatriya and brahmin ideals. The ultimate goal of both is the same. When the brahmin and the kshatriya lead their lives, each adhering to the respective laws of nature meant for each, both achieve the same goal in the end.

That is to say that this world is a reflection of the Almighty, Brahman. And this reflection is sometimes manifested and sometimes formless. This cosmos that changes constantly is a reflection of Brahman, the Universe, as well as that which is indescribable, that which cannot be expressed, that which is incomprehensible to the mind, that which no adjective can qualify—that is to say, the formless essence of Brahman—are one and the same. That is the ultimate truth, and the ultimate duty of both the brahmin and the kshatriya is to achieve this knowledge. If we follow the truth of Vedanta, then the duties of all sections of society are the same, but not everybody accepts this truth.

Not all the sects in India accept that it is possible for the Almighty to have a form. They say that it is not possible for Brahma to have a form, for he is the only reality and everything else is transient. Anything other than Brahma has no existence. Hence, everything in creation is just an illusion. And that is *Maya*. Where did this illusion come from and what is its form? They say that it is that which cannot be expressed. That is why the main goal in life of those who subscribe to this notion of Maya has been to renounce the world, to give up all earthly concerns and go live in ascetic solitude—in the jungle, on the mountain, in a cave—in order to meditate and concentrate on God. Many believe that this is the essence of Brahmanism, the ideology of a Hindu society which is led by brahmins, and that those who hold such beliefs are true brahmins. And this is what I too call the brahmin dharma or duty. But when I speak of the kshatriya dharma or duty, I refer to a system of beliefs that does not regard this ever-changing cosmos as an illusion or Maya, and does not accept that the only reality is the Almighty. And where you do not renounce the world but accept the good and the evil, the violence and the nonviolence, and the other contradictions that it presents, and live on the battlefield in a struggle to attain the ultimate truth. To be one with God while living in this world and accepting that everything, good or bad, is a manifestation of the Almighty and following the path of your righteous duty is what I call the kshatriya dharma.

There has always been an opposition between these two systems of belief. They are different ways of life which lead to the same goal. The ideal for one is Gautam Buddha, and it is Sri Krishna in Kurukshetra for the other. Sri Chaitanya is the ideal guru for one, Guru Gobind for the other. The principles of one ask you to give up the world for the realization of the ultimate truth, and to follow the principles of the other, you have to be a part of the world—if need be, break it, crush it and reconstruct it from scratch. Sometimes by lighting up the world with knowledge, sometimes by spilling blood with the sword, and sometimes by bathing it in love, the beautiful creation that is earth must be coloured and brightened. This conflict of beliefs was not just a conflict of words or language. People chose what they believed in and lived their whole lives by it. That is why so many left their homes and became ascetics, and so many others spent their entire lives bearing with fortitude the criticism and torture meted out to them by family, society and the government machinery.

It was the kshatriya dharma that the revolutionaries upheld and that is what they preached to the people of India. But they were not able to take into account how they would express their desires to the poorest people of the land and how the desires and dreams of the latter would be safeguarded. They did not consider how they would deal with the conflict in society rising out of the chasm between the rich and the poor, between the landlords and the peasants, between the industrialists and the labourers, between Indian and foreign businessmen. They did not think of how the crises arising out of all these conflicts could be resolved. They did not stop to reflect on how they would reconstruct the country from scratch after the revolution had been realized so as to construct an equal and just society. They believed that all this could be sorted out after freedom had been achieved.

Nonetheless, most of the revolutionaries believed that the structure of governance in a free India should be based on the principles of a republic. Most of them did not see any place for a king in this future nation. I say 'most' because there were some who believed that if there was any king who was willing to sacrifice his life and fought with all his heart and soul for India's freedom, then it was worth nominating him as the monarch. In such a scenario, the structure of the government could be like that of the British—a constitutional monarchy, with both king and Parliament. The Abhinav Bharat, a secret society in Maharashtra (founded by Vinayak Damodar Savarkar and his brother Ganesh Damodar Savarkar in 1904), clandestinely published and circulated a booklet titled *Choose, Oh Indian Princes!*. This booklet specifically mentioned the Maharaja of Gaekwad in the context of nominating a future king. Meanwhile, many Sikhs in Punjab wanted to establish a Khalsa state in India. Most of the revolutionaries were Hindus and some of the groups secretly harboured the wish to establish a Hindu state. But later, this sentiment completely eroded away, and although they moved forward with the support and self-assurance of the Hindus, they did not favour any religion or community above the other. That is to say, even though the revolutionary effort for India's freedom was made largely by Hindus, their political belief was that all religions and communities would be equal in independent India, and the interests of each would be safeguarded.

Many in our country are of the opinion that the revolutionary movement was a wasted effort and that its failure was inevitable. According to them, with the advancement of technology, it is impossible for a subjugated people to wage a successful revolt against an imperial government by using martial means. They believe that to even think about defeating a powerful enemy like the British through an armed revolution is madness and setting oneself up for failure. Therefore, they considered the Indian revolutionaries to be mad and imprudent, and continue to do so. If their belief is true, then India will be in shackles forever—partly because these critics are also not able to produce an alternative recourse for attaining independence. It cannot be denied that, in recent times, revolutionaries in Russia and Germany have defeated mighty states. Therefore, it would not be right to say that nobody can defeat a powerful government by means of an armed struggle. And when comparing our situation with the German and Russian uprisings, we must not forget that they were fighting against their own people, while we are fighting against a foreign power that has occupied our land. Hence, the likelihood of receiving empathy and support for our cause from our countrymen is much greater.

It is easier by far to wage a war against a foreign oppressor than to wage a civil war. It is also true that India's efforts at a revolution failed while those of Russia and Germany succeeded. But I have a disagreement with many people over the reasons for this failure, and I am going to talk about it. I am not going to debate whether Indians should choose the path of a (armed) revolution or not; I will simply try to critique the logic given by the other side. I would like my readers to remember that I am analysing events from the past. It is important to do so while writing history. However, I do not in any way wish to comment on how this would affect the future or what should happen in the future.

To return to our topic, why did the revolution fail? Many people say that it was not the right time yet. In other words, the situation in India was not yet conducive to a revolution;

the people were not prepared. But I don't agree with those who say that the people at large did not support the revolutionaries because nobody, either openly or secretly, called upon the farmers and labourers and workers to participate in the revolution. Whenever the educated class of the country has called upon the masses to rally for such a cause, they have responded with innumerable sacrifices. What educated people don't do despite understanding their duties, the uneducated do instinctively or by relying on their common sense. Obviously, the latter cannot sustain sacrifice and hardship over a long period of time, but it is not possible to achieve anything by relying purely on the thoughts of an educated elite. There are people who say that the revolution failed because the majority of the people in this country are uneducated, and that till education reaches all, all efforts at a revolution will be wasted. I show them the example of Russia and say that the success or failure of a revolution does not depend on literacy or illiteracy.

Then why did the revolution fail in India? Is it true that all those sacrifices, all that tremendous courage were an utter waste? The revolutionaries bore so much misery, suffered so many betrayals, stood firm in the face of torture and unspeakable travails despite repeated failures—was all this futile?! Did the country not gain any prestige from these warrior (kshatriya) instincts? Has not the fear of death left the Indians? Could the revolutionary movement not influence any of the other movements in the country? Did it make no impression on world politics, on other civilized nations of the world? Did India's honour in the world increase? I would like my readers to pay attention to books like the Harvard University professor Roland G. Usher's *Pan-Germanism* and Ben Hardy's *Germany and the Newest War.* Then perhaps they will understand what I am trying to say.

Many people say that the revolutionaries spawned more disaster than success and that the British government found excuses to torment the people because of them. They argue that the government could, because of the actions of these revolutionaries, enact strict laws that caused problems for more legitimate movements and agitations. But truth be told, the revolutionary movement and its endeavours have started to come to light only after the legitimate movements and protests have been quelled. The British have revealed all this unknowingly in the Rowlatt Committee's sedition report, proving that they have allowed for certain political rights in India only after the actions carried out by the revolutionaries. Many people recognize this fact.

In the end, what the revolutionaries wanted did not come to pass. They wanted to free the country but could not. Their goal was not achieved.

I believe that the absence of an impressive leader is the biggest reason for their failure. In the Russian and German revolutions, there were and are many people who were worthy to be counted amongst the most eminent intellectuals in the world. But there was no discerning person in the Indian revolutionary movement who could be called a thinker. Hence, the revolutionary movement could not spread its message with sufficient eloquence and therefore did not have the kind of influence it should have had. It is true that some of Vivekananda's ideas animated the movement and many of the revolutionaries were inspired by this great man. But unfortunately, there was nobody of the stature of Vivekananda to lead the movement. Had Mr Aurobindo Ghose or Lala Har Dayal stayed on with the group till the end, maybe the movement would have been more effective, but they too left the Party. An acquaintance of mine used to recite a poem in reference to this very Aurobindo, and I can't stop myself from quoting it here:

> He is gone to the mountain
> And he is lost to the forest;
> The spring is dried in the fountain.
> When the need was the sorest.

The movement lacked the support of versatile, thoughtful people like writers, journalists and poets. The few magazines that were published clandestinely by the movement were full of calls for a revolution. There was no fresh thinking in these articles and no new ideology or principles for life were presented. These writings will find no lasting place in Indian literature. This is another reason why the revolutionary movement was destined to fail. The only exception was the *Jugantar* ('Jugantar' in Bengali) magazine, founded by Barindra Kumar Ghosh and Bhupendranath Dutt during the first epoch of the movement. The influence of this magazine can be seen even today. And that is why Barindra would proudly proclaim in the Andamans, 'The path that I etched out, Bengal is following even today. It is sad that no one else has managed to carve a new path.'

Apart from this, the revolutionary group could not make any mark in the space other than the underground world. There was no leader in the group who could participate in the open movement and earn the same respect as Gandhi and Tilak. Thus, the movement got alienated from the masses and was confined to a few. They had no means of communicating with the [uneducated] public, attracting them towards their ideology and convincing them of their objectives and methods. Either the leaders of the revolutionary movement did not realize this or maybe they ignored it. Moreover, leaders of other political parties have often been able to exploit the revolutionaries because they did not have a strong and discerning leader. This may not have harmed the country, but it has caused tremendous misery for the revolutionary party.

But after the failure of the Ghadar revolt, many Indian revolutionaries showed exemplary communication skills. The countless nameless young men whom no one bothered with, who found no role in the leadership of the revolutionary groups, whom the people of the country called uneducated or simple—many stories of their valour and sacrifice can be heard abroad. In the civilized world, they may not occupy a place above the well-known leaders of our country, but their place is not any less. It is said that these revolutionaries are regarded with more respect than other big leaders. The reason for this is that when these young men came in contact with senior leaders abroad and experienced the freedom there, they realized that their secretive, narrow route was not the only way forward. And when they stepped onto a new path, their hidden strength blossomed with the stimulus and space that was now available to them.

From the stories of these revolutionaries living abroad, we learn that there were so many unknown young men in the revolutionary party that our countrymen are not aware of and who could have, given the opportunity, been some of the best thinkers in the world. Intellect does not come from reading books and passing exams. It is one thing to read a book and another to be a thinker. Herbert Spencer, one of world's greatest thinkers, knew only his mother tongue and French and no other language. But there are many learned men who know many languages and yet are no match to Spencer. In our country, there were far more learned men than Vivekananda, but how many thinkers of his calibre have there been? If we look at the lives of various thinker-poets and those of the philosophers, we understand that scholarship and intellect and the power of thinking are two different things. Just as the tree does not know when it will flower and the bird does not know when it will want to sing, those who are cogitative in nature, the truly brilliant and emotional thinkers, show their sagacity even if they have not had a formal education.

Many people refer to the revolution as madness or the product of an impaired intelligence. They say that no one who does not suffer from mental illness can be part of a revolutionary group. But Rabi Babu says, 'Intelligence is something that is found on earth but a madness that transcends the normal, and is one of a kind, is from the heavens. That is why things built from intelligence break and wither away. And the things that madness brings in plants the seeds for jungles in a jungle.'

Part 3

The Revolutionary Movement in India after 1920

Chapter 1

THE NEWS OF RELEASE

I still remember that day vividly. It was the month of February in the winter of 1920. I was unwell and in the Cellular Jail hospital. A prison officer came and informed me that the jailer had summoned me to his office. I was livid when I heard the familiar words. I could foresee the same scenario repeating itself—more threats of violence. It was common in the Cellular Jail for the jail authorities—from the jailer to the superintendent—to look for an opportunity to torment the political prisoners somehow or the other. Such situations often escalated into physical fights. There had been instances of political prisoners dying in these fights. All this was part of jail life in the Andamans. It is enough to mention here that both during and before my time there, the jail authorities in Andaman treated the political prisoners cruelly because they had sanction from the higher-ups in the political administration to do so.

Therefore, when a prisoner-officer came and told me that the jailer had asked to see me, my first instinct was rebellious anger. Here I was, lying ill on a charpoy, and the man was ordering me to his office. My only thought at the time was that the jailer intended to humiliate and trouble me. If I didn't go, there would be a showdown with the jailer, and if I did go, I would face insults of all kinds. If I were to swallow the treatment meted out to me to avoid a nasty fight, I would lose the respect of my friends. All these conflicting thoughts were running through my mind in a matter of moments; I was faced with a conundrum. But almost immediately, I found a solution as well.

I told the messenger that I was too weak to get up and go to the jailer's office. The officer left, but soon came back to say that it was urgent and that the jailor was insisting that I go to his office. I became extremely worried on hearing this. Various thoughts ran through my mind: had he managed to get his hands on one of the many secret letters I had written or was this provoked by some new confrontation that had taken place in the world outside? Why was he insisting on calling me to his office when I was lying in the hospital, clearly unwell? In any case, I did not have much time to think. I did not have fever that day, nor was I so weak as not to be able to get up and walk around. At home, one did not debate about getting up if one really needed to meet someone. Here, it was a matter of self-respect. In any case, a showdown seemed imminent, although I decided that I would not let matters escalate. Only a few days ago, there had been a major fight. Therefore, pretending to be weaker than I was, I slowly walked to the jailer's office. The latter welcomed me in a much too friendly fashion and asked me to sit on the bench next to his chair. I was surprised at his attitude as I had been expecting a storm. I had barely sat down when the jailer suddenly said, 'Cheer up, man, you have been released.'

I had not expected to hear these words right then, though I had been convinced that I would be released within a few days. I had reached the Cellular Jail on 18 August 1916, and since that day, I had maintained that I would definitely be released by the time I turned 28. I was convinced no power could keep me in jail after that. There was no political prisoner in the jail who did not know I believed this or had not made fun of me for saying it. My belief was based on a prediction made by the Bhrigu Saṃhitā,[33] about which I will write elsewhere. After the end of the World War, when many prisoners who were incarcerated on petty charges were let off and the political prisoners were told that their sentences had been reduced by only a month, I was disappointed. It was in such a scenario that the jailer gave me news of my freedom.

I was not jumping with joy because I had always felt that I would most certainly be released. Hence, when it happened, it did not seem like anything out of the ordinary. Therefore, I received the news with equanimity. Looking at my unnaturally calm demeanour, the jailer said, 'What is the matter with you, young man? It seems you do not want to go home. Cheer up, you are a free man.' I smiled and went back to the hospital. Slowly the joy of being released spread through me. In the hospital, right under the spot where I lay on my charpoy, was the verandah of Barrack 1. Well-known revolutionaries like Barindra Ghosh, Upendra Nath Bandyopadhyay and Hem Chandra Kanungo used to cook their meals on this verandah. These men were convicted in the famous Alipore bomb conspiracy, the first-ever case against the revolutionaries in India, and deported for life to the Cellular Jail in Andaman.

After some years in the jail, the difficulties they faced debilitated and changed them. There were many showdowns between the political prisoners and jail authorities during my time there, but these people did not participate in any hunger or work strike. In fact, as far as I could see, they had turned into confidants of the jail administration. They seemed to believe that if they behaved in such a manner, it would result in an early release from jail. Hence, they always sided with the authorities in any protest that the rest of the political prisoners mounted. The latter did not, therefore, think much of them. These men believed that the others would realize their foolishness when it would be time for the authorities to consider their pleas for release.

However, since the day I had stepped into the Cellular Jail, I had always been with the political prisoners in any showdown with the jail authorities. When I received the joyous news of my own release, my first thought was to go and tell these cautious and scheming people about it. I wanted to tell them that it does not always pay to be wary and calculating. With these thoughts in mind, I went and stood on the balcony, called out to Upendra Nath and gave him the news of my release. He came out, heard my news, and before a smile could touch his face, he went back inside with his head hanging low. I came back to my charpoy and lay down. Today, 18-and-a-half-years-later, I don't remember what I thought of while I was lying there. All I can recall is that I was not exuberant on hearing the news of my release. Throughout the time I was in jail, I had felt that I was only there momentarily, a guest who would leave soon. But one thought kept tormenting me: how would I face my companions? I thought of all my friends, and it became unbearable when I realized that they were facing a lifetime in prison. It was this thought, perhaps, that did not allow me to be jubilant at the news of my release. I cannot now recall if there was any other political prisoner with me in the hospital at that time.

The jailer had informed me that I would have to stay on in the jail for another 20-odd days. The ship that was to transport the released prisoners to the mainland was on another voyage. I would be put on board the ship when it came back, but till then, I would have to live in the jail, eat the food there and sleep in a cell like all the other inmates. I had tried to request that I be allowed to at least have a look around the Andaman Islands. I had come here with a life sentence and stayed inside the prison for four years. Now, before leaving for the land of my birth, I wished for the opportunity to see the islands like a free man. My request was denied. It was a strange situation; I had been released but could not step out of the jail, and I continued to eat, drink and live like a prisoner for the next 20 days.

The day that I had been counting the minutes down to had finally arrived. So, why was I not overjoyed? Even today, I find it difficult to answer this question. I had seen other prisoners being released; their joy had known no bounds. They would run around uncontrollably. I don't know if I was overwhelmed or not. It is possible that I checked my emotions thinking of what my companions must be going through. It was in such a frame of mind that I left the hospital and came back to the barracks where my friends were.

By the time I got back to the barracks, news had spread through the jail that the prisoners from the first conspiracy case—Barindra, Upendra and Hem Chandra—had also been released, and they would be returning to the mainland with me on the same ship. Like me, they too would have to stay in jail for another 20 days.

When I reached the barracks, all my companions came and stood all around me, asking me the details. It was exactly as I had imagined it. The people who had been so close till then suddenly seemed distant. I felt that they inhabited another planet. This was not something to be said aloud, but all of us were feeling this. On the one hand, there was a subdued joy in me, and on the other hand, there was agony. It would have been criminal to express joy in such a situation, and I kept trying to not let my feelings show. As for my companions, they may have been feeling hopeful of their own release or maybe they were agonized with doubts of ever being released.

The youngest fellow there asked me for a book as a keepsake. At that moment, I would have willingly given anything away. I happily gave him one of my books and, after that, I gave away all my books as keepsakes to the political prisoners of the Cellular Jail. Nothing was dearer to me than my books. I was not rich. My father died when I was 14 or 15 years of age. We had got some insurance money on his death and that is how the five of us, our mother, my brothers and I, managed to make ends meet. Some of those books are out of print today and cannot be replaced, but that day, I could have given anything away in the joy of being released from that tomb. I kept just one book with me. This was a copy of the Bible which was signed by my father. Some of the books that I gave to my companions, the titles of which I do remember are:

1. *The Liberation of Italy* by Countess Evelyn Martinengo Cesaresco
2. *Voltaire* by John Morley
3. *Rousseau* by Morley
4. *The Life of William Ewart Gladstone* by Morley
5. *Budhha Jeevani* by Dr Ramdas Sen
6. Files containing Indian and foreign monthly magazines and newsletters, collected over two to three years.

There were eight or 10 other books, but I don't remember their titles. Amongst the ones that I have mentioned, save for the first one, the others are not available even in libraries. *Budhha Jeevani* is, in fact, out of print. While I was in prison, I used to try and read as much as possible. I had been working in Barindra's press for about a year before the release. I would work till ten o'clock in the morning, then have a bath, eat and spend the rest of the day reading. It always upset me if some official work came in after the morning meal.

Barindra and Hem Chandra had more than 200 books each, and all of them were wonderful. They took all the books with them. A few days before the ship was due to arrive, news came in that 18 prisoners sentenced under the Martial Law of 1919 in Punjab had been released. They, too, were to go back to the mainland with me.

It was only when I got back to the barracks that I learnt the jailer had spoken to Barindra, Hem Chandra and Upendra around 10 or 11 a.m. on the same morning, and given them news of their release. Barindra and Hem Chandra used to visit the office many times a day. There was a small printing press in the office, and Barindra was entrusted with all its work. Binding was also done in the jail. This work was entrusted to Hem Chandra. Both later said that when they were informed of their release, their legs started trembling and they forgot where they were. They could hardly feel the solid ground beneath their feet. They didn't hear a word that the superintendent said regarding the work he had assigned to them for the day. They were stupefied. They came back to the barracks, gave everybody the good news and went back to the office to understand their instructions once again.

Barindra and the others had been very hopeful the day the World War had ended. The jail superintendent, Major Murray, had kindled this hope by saying, 'It is possible that you people may be released. I have made a strong appeal to the Bengal government to release all of you.' Barindra and the others were optimistic after that and would often talk amongst themselves about how being on the right side of the authorities had paid dividends. I would, of course, feel sad when I heard all this. But I also had the conviction that sooner rather than later, the political weather in India would change, and then it wouldn't be possible for only a couple of people like Barindra and his companions to get out while all the others languished in jail.

Moreover, I don't know if this was superstition or a strong belief, but based on my astrological charts, I was convinced I would be free from the clutches of the enemy in my twenty-eighth year. I also believed that I would get married around the same time. I still believe in astrology. And even if it is a superstitious belief, what is the harm? In those days of strife and distress, it gave me strength.

Before I was arrested, my mother told me that she had shown my birth chart to the Bhrigu Saṃhitā people in Banaras. All that they had said about my past, present and future had turned out to be true—the time of my arrest, the period when I would live surrounded by enemies, the time of my release and my marriage, even the time when I would get arrested again. The thought of marriage calmed me at the time. For how was I going to get married in a situation where I was running from the enemy or under their control? Obviously, it shall have passed for me to be able to get married. Before this, no temptation on earth could lure me into marriage. But because it was predicted on my astrological chart, the idea of marriage seemed to point to an end of troubled days and strife. I now felt there was no harm in getting married. Why not, if marriage helped to lighten the mental and emotional baggage of the tough times in the Cellular Jail?

A life sentence in the Cellular Jail is no laughing matter. Many political prisoners were crushed in body and spirit by the gruelling experience, and resorted to different means to try and survive it. Poor Barindra and his companions had chosen to trust the oppressor, while other prisoners clung to the adage, good things happen to those who wait. Unfortunately, the superintendent who had given them hope about release was also the one who summoned Barindra and the others to his office when the ceasefire was declared and told them that the government had reduced only a month of their sentence. And those of us who were constantly fighting with the jail authorities were told that if we behaved for the whole year, a similar reduction would be made in our case too. This news devastated Barindra and his companions, but we were all happy to hear it. At least, while I cannot state that with certainty for the others, I can speak for myself with conviction.

The English, by way of celebrating the end of the World War, released all political prisoners in Burma. Even the older prisoners who were not serving political sentences were let off. The Indian political prisoners were undoubtedly disappointed, but I had not lost hope. Hope is what keeps a man afloat. Mine was based on truth and conviction, but there were times when I too felt my hope faltering. But these moments were like birds that flew overhead—they came, and they went.

I kept myself busy with reading. I was then reading Mill's *Principles of Political Economy*. I had just finished the book one day at around three in the afternoon when a telegram from Reuters came in for printing. The incomplete language of the telegram suggested that the King had made some announcement about the release of political prisoners. And that was the end of reading and learning for some days. There was only one topic of conversation; all our talk and thought revolved anxiously and constantly around who would be freed and when, and what would happen or not happen. Barindra made tremendous efforts and procured from the office a copy of a newspaper called *Bengali*, which had printed the King's decree. There was hope in our hearts now, and yet there was also fear, because although the King had decreed that the maximum number of political prisoners be freed, there was nonetheless one sentence in the decree that was cause for worry. It said that if the viceroy of India felt that releasing a prisoner could cause upheaval and disturbance, then he could be further detained. Our hearts were in our mouths. What would the viceroy decide? This ambiguous order hovered over us like a nightmare that wouldn't go away.

Despite the general restlessness, my hopes had soared even higher now. When I had come to the Cellular Jail and told my companions about the astrological forecast of my release, they had all laughed at me. In fact, Upendra and friends had categorically said, 'You will never be released while the English are ruling us.' I had then replied, 'If the condition for my release is that the English rule has to end, it will end because what is certain is that I will be freed.' Obviously, all this was said in a tone of light-hearted banter. It was a good way to distract ourselves. Barindra and Upendra had said to me, quoting Ullaskar,[34] 'This time we are facing tough men. They will skin us, eat us and make drums with what is left.'

After the King's decree I asked these men, 'What do you have to say now?' But then days passed, and nobody was freed or released. There was no respite; reading didn't distract, and work brought no relief. Then one day, Barindra came and said that the chief commissioner had received a telegram from my brother, asking if the political prisoner Sachindra Nath had been released. Once again, we were swinging between hope and despair. And yet again, nothing. I think a Sikh political prisoner was released during this time. Then I fell sick and was sent to the hospital, where I finally received the good news.

Chapter 2

LEAVING THE CELLULAR JAIL

The 20 days of waiting for the ship also passed. As the date of my leaving the prison drew near, I felt happy and miserable in equal measure. I was constantly besieged with guilt about leaving my companions helpless and unwell in this difficult place. I promised all of them that the moment I got back home, I would leave no stone unturned in my efforts to free them. This seemed to be the only consolation I could offer my friends.

Bhai Parmanand was suddenly confined to a cell in the dungeons. This is the same man who is today a fiery leader of the Hindu Mahasabha. Apparently, his wife had got something published about him in the newspapers in Punjab, and that is why he had been locked up in solitary confinement. I promised my companions that I would also campaign for Bhai Parmanand's release.

Finally, preparations were on for our departure. I remember clearly how the 18 prisoners sentenced under the Martial Law in Punjab as well as Barindra and Upendra were jubilant. And I was trying not to cry. We were given the clothes that one is given on being released from jail. Barindra had already arranged for some clothes in anticipation of his release. He gave me a dhoti and a coat from those. If I remember correctly, I think he also gave me three rupees. The rest of the expenses were to be borne by the government. At the time of release, we were all made to stand in a queue in pairs. And even when we stepped out of the prison, we walked to the gate in discipline.

The day I came to the Cellular Jail, I was smiling outwardly but my heart was heavy. On this day, when I was leaving, it was the same; the smile on my face hid a heavy heart. I remember vividly what I was feeling the day I had arrived in the Andamans. I was convinced without an iota of doubt that I would soon be free. I was also sure that Barindra, Upendra and other political prisoners who had been there for a long time would make it easier for the new prisoners. Therefore, I was not miserable or agitated even though I knew a difficult time awaited me. But I was disillusioned in no time. My despondence increased with each passing day. On the day of my departure, I was happy, and with each passing hour, the joy kept increasing. Yet, thinking of the companions I was leaving behind, it was difficult not to cry.

As soon as we stepped out of the gate, one of the Sikh political prisoners let loose the loud war cry of '*Jo Bole So Nihal*'. And the others, in one voice, replied '*Sat Sri Akal*' (He who recites the name of the Lord shall forever be victorious). Inside the gates, there was strict discipline. Outside, too, it was a kind of prison, but when the war cry was raised, the jail authorities could only look on askance. The hair on my arms stood up with each slogan. It was morning, and there was silence everywhere. The sea spread out in front of us in its vastness and we could see small mountains adorned with trees and plants. The Sikh war cry echoed all around. But as the volume of the slogans increased, my heart ached thinking of what the prisoners inside the jail and those languishing in the cells must be feeling.

The queue was maintained, and we still stood in pairs. When enough sloganeering had been done, we moved forward. The war cries were now replaced by songs in Punjabi. I still remember a bit of a song: *Chidyanaal main baazladava, giddran ton maisherbnawa, swa lakh se ekldawa, tab gobindsingh naam dharawa* (the sparrow shall fight the eagle, the jackals shall turn into lions, one man shall fight a hundred thousand, and then I too will be called Gobind Singh). A couple of men would start singing and then the others would join in to complete the chorus. My eyes filled up. A desire buried deep in my heart came to the fore. Every day that I spent in the Cellular Jail, I would tell myself that once I got out of there, I would train myself for a career in politics. The day I was told about my release, my first thought was that the moment for which I was training myself had arrived. But was I ready? The songs being sung by the Sikhs brought alive in the imagination scenes from the Mughal era when Guru Gobind Singh's sparrows had defeated the eagles. Today, we were in great need of a Guru Gobind Singh.

I was wondering if I was prepared for the new responsibility that was coming my way. I had thought my life was over. Did I have any right to this rebirth, this new lease of life? Should I not be dedicating my life to the betterment of society now? I was agitated by these thoughts. We had, by then, reached the edge of the sea. I touched the water and thought that this very water was also touching my beloved motherland. The water, too, seemed like a mother's protective bosom, touching the motherland at one end and me at the other. We took a small boat and travelled to the ship. Some old acquaintances of Barindra had brought flowers for all the prisoners who had been released.

The column for character or conduct on our release

certificate said 'Fair', meaning neither good nor bad. Under the column where the reason for release was stated, it said, 'Released in view of the Emperor's announcement'. In connection to the release, it also said, 'Correspondence ending in a telegram'. The remarkable thing about my life is that nothing has ever happened simply or without glitches. I have always had to face and overcome several barriers. In this case, my release came about only after the telegram had arrived. Afterwards, when I restarted life's journey after this rebirth, I had to face problems at every step of the way. In fact, even for my marriage, I had to walk for miles before I could finally see the girl.

On our way to the Cellular Jail, we had been stuffed like sacks of commodities in the luggage compartment. On top of that, our legs were chained, and armed guards kept an eye on us. On the day of liberation, it was different. We went and sat on the deck; there were no chains on our feet, and there were no guards. The realization that we had been released had finally begun to sink in. I wondered if we could walk around, look anywhere we wanted? And I realized that there was nobody to forbid it. This was the first taste of freedom. I roamed about the ship, looked around and observed everything—what kind of people were travelling on the ship, where was the engine, where was the kitchen and where were the toilets and the bathrooms?

Then the worry about food began. There were no arrangements for Hindu meals on the ship. The choice was either to eat some dry snacks or eat the food prepared by the Muslim cooks on board. Barindra managed eventually to make some arrangements for the four of us—Barindra, Upendra, Hem Chandra and I—with the ship's steward. It is important to mention here that we did not believe in any discriminatory food habits, although we never ate cow's meat. When we actually think about it, it is difficult to comprehend the difference between eating pigeon's meat and the meat of a cow! Ideologically, it may not be right for some to consume any kind of meat; in fact, it is categorically wrong, and in many cases, it may be harmful too. I eat meat as I love to eat it, and often because of peer pressure. As I have mentioned before, I gave up eating meat several times but because of the company I kept, I always started to eat it again.

We had reached the Andamans during the monsoons after spending four days and three nights in the ship. On the way back, we spent the same duration of time on the ship. The sky was clear throughout the voyage and there were no movements on the horizon. As far as I remember, the prisoners who had been convicted under the Punjab Martial Law had been segregated from us. They were most likely chained by their legs, having been told that they would be officially released only once they reached Punjab. Unfortunately, my recollection of these details is not very clear now. It is possible that I am mistaken. What I remember clearly is that the four of us were together on the journey and the other prisoners were elsewhere on the ship.

On the ship, I watched the British children running around fearlessly. There were a set of stairs near the edge of the ship to go from one deck to another. A child could easily fall into the sea running up and down, but these children were unmindful of any danger. There was nobody keeping an eye on them. This made a huge impression on me. I was amazed at how laidback the parents were and how they spent time apart from their children. Could Indian parents ever be so unconcerned? I think of myself as being rather brave, but even today, I don't have so much courage. I remember another scene vividly. I was a student at Queen's College in Banaras, crossing the college campus on my way somewhere one day at around three or four o'clock in the afternoon. Walking just ahead of me was the principal, Mr Mincent, with another professor. One of Mr Mincent's children, a toddler, was playing on the ground. An ayah was sitting close by. The child tried to climb a tree and the ayah tried to stop him, but the principal told her that the natural curiosity of children shouldn't be stifled. 'If he wants to climb the tree, let him,' said Mr Mincent, 'just ensure that he doesn't fall off.'

I was not mentally aligned with the men that I had to spend four days and three nights with. Everyone's inner world is different in such moments. I was in my own world during that journey and I'm sure they were in theirs. We did talk and laugh, but we were unable to touch each other's hearts. Although this was unsaid, all of us knew it. It was as if a curtain had been drawn in front of each of our hearts and we spoke to each other from the confines and safety of this curtain. I would, at times, tire of this situation and make my way to the Sikh contingent. But there was no peace there either. Everyone seemed to be in a different frame of mind and busy with their own thoughts. I felt very solitary even in the company of so many men. I am trying to convey to my readers how unhappy and lonely I was in those happy days.

A British deputy commissioner of the Andaman Islands and some Bengali medical officers were also on the ship. Barindra and his friends knew these people. After a long conversation with these officials, Barindra came to us and said that the situation in India was precarious. One could no longer tell the difference between friend and foe. School principals, teachers, doctors and students—all sections of Indian society had been infiltrated by the secret police. It was impossible to say which neighbour or acquaintance was a spy for the government and which was not. Regarding the deputy commissioner, Barindra said, 'Mr Louis is a good man. He spoke to me at length. He was very sincere when he said that Ullaskar was a man of high ideals and large heart. We spoke of the Sikh political prisoners too. He was all praise for their bravery and their strength to stand up to the opposing power.' In saying all this, Barindra seemed to accept that the political prisoners who had resisted the jail authorities, fighting for their self-respect, were indeed brave and worthy of admiration. He acknowledged that he was weak in comparison to them.

It is important to talk about Ullaskar here. His father was a professor in an engineering college in Shivpur. He had set up a laboratory in his house before he joined Barindra's group of revolutionaries. He used to experiment with explosives in that lab. It was after they had begun to associate with Ullaskar and his friends that Barindra's group had become robust. During his trial, Ullaskar had taken pride in saying that such and such bombs that had wreaked havoc at such and such places were made by his own hands. Ullaskar had everybody spellbound by singing a patriotic song in a courtroom. He was betrothed to one of the daughters of a well-known national leader, the late Bipin Chandra Pal. But before the wedding, he was arrested in the Alipore Conspiracy Case and sentenced to the Andamans. Once Bipin Pal's daughter got to know that Ullaskar had lost his mental balance in jail, she decided to not marry at all. As far as I know, that girl never did marry.

One day in the Cellular Jail, Ullaskar suddenly wondered aloud why he should be subservient. The honourable and true way for a rebel was to rebel in prison as well. And, therefore, he broke the rules many times, and suffered the consequences and was punished severely. Once, he refused to work in the brick kilns outside the jail in the scorching heat. Ullaskar and his companions were brought back to the jail, where they were cuffed and chained in solitary cells and left standing. Law states that this punishment can be imposed only for eight hours in a day and not for more than seven days running. But when the jail authorities wish to torture a prisoner, they do not care two hoots about the law. The paperwork in the office records that everything has been done according to rules and regulations, but the reality is totally different. It is impossible for a prisoner to prove any of this in a court of law as there are no witnesses to these tortures.

Ullaskar, while cuffed and standing in his solitary cell, had a fever of 103–104 degrees. His handcuffs were not removed; nonetheless, and he remained standing. He was sent to the hospital only when he passed out. And when he regained consciousness, it was found that he had lost his mental balance. This is the same Ullaskar who used to say that we are now confronted with men who will chew us up, hide and bone. I got to know all these things about Ullaskar when Barindra came and told us about his conversation with Mr Louis, the deputy commissioner of the Andamans. The latter had a very high opinion of Ullaskar.

I was stupefied to hear all this. I have so many stories of atrocities and torture at the Cellular Jail, but I do not have the courage to write about them as I have no evidence to prove them in a court of law.

Nature was at its worst when I had come to the Andaman Islands. That was in the month of August. Sitting on the lowest deck of the ship amid rainstorms and thundering cloud, it had seemed as if the world was headed towards annihilation by drowning. On our way back from the Andamans, all was quiet and peaceful as if even nature rejoiced in our release.

One night, we decided that we would watch the sunrise in the middle of the sea! When I woke up, the sky had a red hue. I got out of bed immediately, thinking that it must be time for the sunrise. I saw that Hem Chandra had also woken up. I wanted to wake the others as well, but Hem Chandra said to not do so and to wait until the sunrise began. The two of us went and stood on the deck. We kept staring at the horizon, holding the railing tight. The sea was churning. Neither of us had a watch and had no idea what time it was. We stood there until we were very tired, but there was no change in the sky. None of our other companions had woken up yet.

Hem Chandra and I then walked around the ship, trying to find out what time it was. I think it was the steward who told us that it was only 3 a.m. I thought of going back and lying down for a little while, but Hem Chandra dissuaded me. So, we sat on the deck chairs or maybe somewhere else from three o' clock till about half past five in the morning. What was surprising was that the sky was ringed with the glow of sunrise for nearly three hours. At around 5 a.m., the rest of our companions also made their way to the deck. The sky grew lighter but the source of the light was still not visible. We were getting impatient. The wait became annoying but how could we leave without seeing what we had been waiting for hours—a sunrise in the middle of the sea?

Suddenly, everybody was invigorated and pointed to the horizon. All of us saw a flame rise out of the sea. There was water all around as far as eye could see. A feeling of limitlessness suddenly engulfed us. The sun was rising, and mankind could only look on quietly. It was a meeting of peace and infinity. A limitless sky above us, an endless sea below us and our ship trying to move forward in a fixed course towards infinity. And the flame-like sun, rising in its calm ascent to infinity! We were just lost wanderers in all this immensity.

The ball that was the sun was now clearly visible above the sea. But sunrise in the middle of the sea was not as beautiful as a sunset seen from land, I realized. There was not a cloud in the sky, and maybe that is why this sunrise was not colourful. What surprised us was that the flame, which seemed to be floating on water, had suddenly detached itself and established itself firmly in the sky as the sun. There was no objective beauty in this sudden detachment. Some people said this *was* the charm of a sunrise over the ocean. But we felt we had wasted three hours. Returning to our quarters, we spent time together, chatting and laughing.

Looking at the horizon, one could not tell which way our ship was headed or if in fact it was moving at all. But looking at the water below, you could tell that it was moving in some unknown direction. Being on our ship in that vast ocean gave me a sense of being one with infinity, but it also gave me a sense of disquiet and helplessness. I went towards the stern of the ship, and standing there all by myself in that deserted space, I saw how our ship created a minor turbulence in the vast body of water and was moving ahead on its path. If we sank here, there would be no help, I thought. Again, I thought of how my life had ended once before. What right did I have over this new life? I started daydreaming. Would I be able to dedicate myself to the cause of the nation once again? I remembered that my mother was a widow and the fact that, till date, I had not been able to help her or provide for her in any material sense. Would I be able to do anything for my mother once I went back? She was going to insist that I get married. I was willing to get married, but would I be able to walk the path of sacrifice after that? I was lost in all these thoughts, and when I looked up, I found Hem Chandra standing next to me. When he asked me what I was thinking, I shared my thoughts with him.

Hem Chandra Kanungo was a gentleman, a good soul. He must have been young when he went to prison. I can't forget my first glimpse of him sitting on a stool on the day that I had stepped into the Cellular Jail. His beard, reaching his chest, was now more grey than black; he wore glasses and his complexion had faded. I had thought of how this gentleman had lost his youth in the struggle for India's independence, having been in jail for years. He was engrossed in reading a book and his face looked serious and lost in thought. Hem Chandra was unaware of this young man, newly arrived in the Cellular Jail, who was staring at him unblinkingly. For me, this is a vivid memory: a young man meeting an elderly one in a prison on a small island, miles away from the motherland. This was the Hem Chandra who had sold off his property and gone to France to learn how to make bombs. At that time, no national leader had been able to fathom that such revolutionary ideas were spreading like wildfire in the hearts and minds of the young men.

Hem Chandra Kanungo was now going back home after spending 12 years in the Cellular Jail. He had a wife and son at home. He was taking back with him, for his son, all the books that he had collected over the years in prison. Today, a few days after his release, he was talking about the ship and about his aspirations with the young man who had been stricken to see him as he had stepped into the Cellular Jail.

The days went by. It was our last night on the ship. We were close to the motherland now, although we had not yet caught a much-awaited glimpse of her shores; hopefully, we would see them the next day. There were a lot of electric lights on the ship, enhancing the darkness all around. The horizon wasn't clearly visible, and the ocean seemed to spread out to infinity. It seemed that the endless sea had merged with the limitless sky. Our ship moved on the waves and under the stars like a bubble over this infinity. The darkness in the middle of the sea was frightening. I was standing at the railing of the deck. Below me, I could see the waves dancing; lit by the electric light of the ship, they seemed terrifying. Without the lights they wouldn't even have been visible.

This was a sight I can never forget. One had only so far heard the shloka '*Bhayanam bhayam bheeshanam bheeshanaam*' ('terrible, more terrible and even more terrible'), but it seemed to manifest itself in the sight of those waves. It was as if darkness had acquired form with the help of some light. For the first time, I experienced that darkness, too, had a form. The waves were dancing but they didn't seem to be water. No one can know where he will end up if he was to fall into the deep. A monstrous shadow of time seemed to hover over the waves. It is possible to see in darkness. Those who have the sight will vouch for it.

We seemed to have acquired a navigator in the night. The next morning, I remember seeing, far away, a thin line that was the motherland. I could not recall when we had crossed the meeting point of the river and the ocean. I still couldn't say whether we had made the crossing at all. On the fourth day, I saw seabirds fishing. A couple of times I also saw the fish fly a short distance. These seabirds were seen for about 200 miles from the Andaman Islands and about 100 miles off the Indian coast. I am not sure, but I don't think I remember seeing them anywhere in between. The European men and women on the ship would throw food to the birds, and that is why they would fly close to the ship. Thanks to the magnanimity of these good folks, we got to enjoy the antics of these birds.

Hem Chandra told us that we had crossed the Ganga Sagar confluence in the night. It was not definite that the thin line which seemed to be visible at a distance was land. We got to talking about how long it would take for us to produce our own pilots, captains, and so on. The strip of land on the horizon seemed to be getting closer as the day progressed. It was a mesmerizing sight. The coastline was now clearly visible, but the expanse behind us seemed to be oceanic. The vast ocean spread out on one side, and on the other, there was a tantalizing glimpse of the coast. The coming together of this finiteness and infiniteness is very poignant. We can't make do with only infinity and neither can we be fulfilled with the finite. The sky and the ship were my companions in that endless ocean. The passengers on the ship were also my companions, and maybe that is where the finite and the infinite met. It makes one nervous to face infinity. It is possible that there are still worldly desires latent in me and that is why I fear the infinite. Once, when Swami Vivekananda had a spiritual experience in the presence of Sri Ramakrishna Paramahamsa, he became scared and said, 'I still have parents and siblings!'

The day moved on and we approached the dusky coastline. Seeing the figures of men at work, silhouetted against that strip of land, made us happy. To see these men was to see their families. I saw them rooted to their work through the ups and downs of their life. Soon, we could see that there were women among the men, walking with them. Many tributaries empty themselves into this estuary. There is farming on its banks in various places and villages nestled between these farms. The river was full, and the coastline was decorated with lush green trees. The greenery on the shores and the water flowing in between made for a beautiful view. I felt a certain joy in the sight of the river, the trees and the villages that, I think, came from a nostalgia or longing for family life, which I had been denied for some time. Maybe for this reason, or maybe because of a cultural ethos ingrained in us, my heart sang when I saw man in a domestic setting with his wife and child. It is possible that, unknown to myself, I had moved into the stage of life when I was ready to get married and start a family; hence, I was enchanted at the sight of these domestic scenes.

As the sun was setting and the day turning into night, our ship was sailing through a narrow stretch of river where the banks were crowded with people. Hem Chandra and I were standing close together on the deck. Big boats, laden with merchandise, were plying on the water. These were rowed by half-naked boatmen, clad only in some cloth wrapped around their waists and ending above the knees. They worked hard from morning till night, exposed to the sun and the water equally. Looking at these boatmen, Hem Chandra remarked that the prisoners in jail at least got clothes to wear, and they were not made to work in the sun and the water. At least there was a limit to the work they had to do. But our countrymen who are not in any prison are working under such tough conditions.

He had spoken the truth, but I did not like it. I felt as if Hem Chandra was putting forth an argument in favour of the Cellular Jail and its officials. I was not willing to forgive or in any way think well of the heartless and cruel jail authorities of the Andamans. My thoughts must have been visible on my face. I told Hem Chandra that it was acceptable to bear any hardship of one's own free will, but if one is forced to do so, even a molehill seems like a mountain. I don't remember what Hem Chandra said in reply to this. Night was falling and the river was getting narrower. Calcutta seemed to be close now.

Throughout the years I spent in the Cellular Jail, surrounded by the enemy, the memory of this bustling capital city kept enticing me. As it drew near, I felt the joy and excitement of freedom.

We knew that nobody on the mainland was yet aware that the political prisoners from the Cellular Jail were coming back. We were coming back to a life of affection after a lot of hardship. In such a situation, all one wanted was to meet a loved one at the moment of setting foot on the homeland, but this would have to remain a mere wish. I remember when we used to entertain ourselves in the prison by talking about this moment. Upendra Nath had once drawn for us a scene of our release—a white elephant with its trunk holding up a garland of flowers and young apsaras, dressed in all their finery, were blowing conches to welcome us. When imagination was all we had, why scrimp on that! This is how the deprived make do in life. Today, when I was being reborn, as another life was beginning and the Calcutta metropolis approached, there was also a shadow of melancholy on the joy one felt. There was a very strong desire that there be a loved one present when I stepped off the ship, but I knew that was not to be.

Chapter 3

IN THE LAP OF THE MOTHERLAND

We had hoped to reach Calcutta in the afternoon. But it was past evening when we reached there. Our travails had not yet ended. It took us more than an hour to disembark from the ship, and once we got off, we were made to stand in pairs. This was followed by a walk of a couple of miles to the police station. When we were being taken to the Andamans, it had been a similar routine. That morning, we had had to walk to the ship in a queue of twos from the Presidency Jail with chains on our feet. In Tolstoy's novel *Resurrection*, there is a touching description of prisoners journeying on foot. Yet, this was happening to us even when we had been released. Fortunately, there was a team of CID officers who had come to meet the first-ever political prisoners who had been convicted in a bomb case—Barindra, Upendra and Hem Chandra—and they could go straight home afterwards.

As always, my bad luck did not desert me. The rest of the freed prisoners were brought to the Matiya Burz police station, and we were left wondering if we had really been released or not. But we were not manhandled, nor was anything said to us, so we deduced that this must be a matter of routine. No one stopped us when eventually we stepped out of the police station. We walked a bit further ahead and then decided to eat something. Apparently, the police had not made any arrangements for feeding us. Barindra had given me three rupees, and I managed to buy some food. Whatever it was, it tasted terrible. We felt we were so close to Calcutta and yet so far. All one wanted to do was to run to the city. Yet, we didn't want to jump into the fire from the frying pan either. Somehow, we passed the night and, in the morning, we came to know that we would get money for rail travel from the Laal Dighi police station. And that is when we would finally be free of the clutches of the police.

Morning brought with it a strong desire to set foot in the bustling streets of Calcutta. We were told that we would be taken from Matiya Burz police station to the Laal Dighi police station, but only after a couple of hours. On enquiry, I found out that the police had no objections if I went off to the Laal Dighi police station by myself and joined the group of freed prisoners there. I immediately decided to take the tram. Soon, I reached Kalighat, where a paternal cousin of mine lived. But I decided to first visit the barrister B.C. Chatterjee.

Mr Chatterjee had fought many political conspiracy cases in Bihar and the United Provinces. He was the son-in-law of the eminent leader Surendra Nath Banerjee. He had defended the accused in the Banaras Conspiracy Case, and I had got to know him well at that time. As far as his political ideology was concerned, he was a follower of Aurobindo. In the difficult times that followed the Bengal partition, Aurobindo and Bipin Chandra used to publish a daily newspaper titled *Bande Mataram*. This is an important document of our national movement. B.C. Chatterjee was an associate of Aurobindo's and a contributor to this newspaper. All the lawyers and barristers of the Calcutta High Court, including Chatterjee, had appealed to us to give up dacoity. They promised to collect the money that we required. But after a few days, they said,

'Do what you want, as nobody is willing to contribute any money. We had hoped to collect a large sum for you all, but we have been disappointed. You are free to do what you think is required.' In short, Mr Chatterjee was deeply empathetic to the revolutionary cause, and it was to his house that I decided to go as soon as I stepped into Calcutta after attaining my freedom.

I was not sure of the exact location of his house. I got off the tram at Kalighat and asked a young man for directions to B.C. Chatterjee's house. The young man seemed very pleasant, but, at first, he tried to ignore me and gave me vague directions. When I told him I had just got off the ship from the Andamans and that I would be eternally grateful if he could show me Mr Chatterjee's house, he hesitated a bit but went with me to the address in the end. He accompanied me from Kalighat to Ballygunge and then back to Kalighat; the two places are rather far from each other.

Mr Chatterjee did not recognize me at first, but within a few moments, he jumped out of his chair and came forward to embrace me. He made me sit with him and showed me a letter that was in his possession. It was a letter that I had written to my brother from the Andamans. I saw that it was blacked out in so many places that it was impossible to read. Among other things, I had written that a new administrative law would be implemented in India. The authorities were saying that India would soon be given certain opportunities for political progress. If this is true, I had argued in the letter, we too could have political evolution and upliftment like England and France; why would anyone be mad enough to choose the path of violence and bloodshed, putting one's life at risk by taking up arms? The revolutionaries are not mad, I wrote, and if the authorities truly mean what they are saying, they should release all political prisoners. My brother had sent this letter to Mr Chatterjee, who, in turn, had sent it to his father-in-law Mr Surendra Nath Banerjee. The latter had on the basis of this letter made a strong appeal in the Assembly for the release of all political prisoners. He had also shown the letter to many important people. Mr Chatterjee told me that he had personally met Mr Montagu in this regard.

He then mentioned that he was arguing the Mainpuri case when the Emperor's announcement regarding the release of political prisoners had been made. The deputy inspector-general of the CID, General Sands, was with him at that time. Mr Sands asked Mr Chatterjee to get my mother to write a clemency appeal and said that he would recommend it. Mr Chatterjee then sent a telegram to my maternal uncle informing him of the same. My uncle got my mother to write the letter, and, consequently, I was released from jail and had the good fortune to hear Mr. B.C. Chatterjee recount it all to me.

Mr Chatterjee had last seen me when I was 23 years old, and now I was 28. My hair was long, and my beard was like that of a goat. That is why the barrister had not been able to recognize me when he first saw me. He wanted to send news of my release to my brother by telegram. I told him not to. I wanted to just turn up at home. I took leave of Mr Chatterjee with a light heart and went back to Kalighat with the unknown young man who had accompanied me. On the way, I spoke to him about politics. I wanted to start recruiting young men for our cause immediately. Instead of going straight to my cousin's place, I went to see the young man's house. But sadly, my first effort at recruitment failed miserably. This young man did not join the movement. When I came back to Calcutta later, I tried to follow up with the fellow and to convince him, but I got no response.

I reached my cousin's house and was asking at the door if he still lived there when he looked out of the window and said, 'Sachindra! You are back! Come in! Come in!' He kept staring at me. I laughed and said, 'It's been many days since I have shaved or cut my hair!' The barber was called, and I was groomed. My cousin told me that my younger brother had come from Banaras to take me home from Calcutta, but they had no information as to where the ship had docked and so he had gone back to Banaras. After I had a bath and ate the first home-cooked meal after my release, the feeling of having been freed finally started sinking in. My taste hadn't changed even after five long years of eating jail food, day after day. In all that time, I had not taken to it. This just proves that repeating something day after day does not form a habit and that the desire for appetizing food never goes away. Actually, human life is not affected by physical changes until the mind changes or our desires change. Life is driven by desire and passion.

My cousin, too, suggested that we should send a telegram home and inform my younger brother that I had been released. I don't recall who finally sent the telegram—this cousin of mine or Mr Chatterjee. But I remember being upset about my brother having come all the way to Calcutta and then gone back alone. My cousin also advised me to leave the past behind and think of getting married; I was only getting older, after all, and would later regret having let time slip by. I rested for a while and then went to Laal Dighi. A car drove into the police station carrying Calcutta's well-known barristers, I.V. Sen and V.K. Lahiri. They had come in search of Barindra and his companions. I told them that they had gone onto their destinations the previous night. Now, I am not so sure if it was I.V. Sen or J.M. Sengupta. Mr Lahiri mentioned that he was somehow connected to my family.

When they did not find Barindra and the others, these gentlemen requested me to accompany them to a Khilafât conference being organized in Calcutta that day. I was nervous thinking that this was only the first day of my having stepped onto Calcutta soil! Not yet free of the clutches of the police, and I was already accepting an invitation to a political conference, that too in the vicinity of the police station! It is true that I had been released without conditions. On my release certificate, it just said that I should contact the district collector of the place I was going to and inform him that I had returned from the Andamans. I asked the esteemed lawyers if it was all right for me to go for the meeting since I was still in the police station. Was it important for me to go? Mr Sengupta and Mr Lahiri insisted that I should go, and, eventually, I gave in. They bundled me into the car and soon I was at the venue.

After the conference, I went to meet Maulana Shaukat Ali. My companions had met Maulana Shaukat Ali and Maulana Mohammad Ali for revolutionary work before I had been arrested, and that is how they knew me. Maulana Shaukat Ali now requested me to join the fight openly and said that the time for behind-the-scenes warfare was long past. I heard them out and then went to the Punjab camp. They all insisted I eat something, and I was tempted with all the delicious fare on offer, but I was scared that I might not be able to digest that food. In the prison, our diet had been very different. It was impossible to find even a few drops of cooking oil in it, let alone the smell of clarified butter, which is the staple of good Indian food.

In any case, from this scene of vibrant activity, I returned to the detestable police station. We had to wait a long time for us to have our names noted and be given the fare to travel. This time spent waiting weighed heavy on me. I had started detesting even the shadow of a policeman. The police had been the cause of much misery in my life; maybe that is why I could not stand them. These five hours in Laal Dighi seemed to be more difficult than the five years I had spent in the Cellular Jail, but finally the torture ended. The policemen took us to Howrah railway station afterwards, the consolation being that we didn't have to walk in a queue of twos. The policemen bought tickets for about 40 to 50 released prisoners with the official documents that they had. The Anglo-Indian lady at the counter soon became irritated and started cursing. I had been standing at the front of the queue and was probably smiling, amused at being counted amongst rogues. I was a little worried about the police accompanying me home, but when they handed me my ticket and went away, I was relieved. It was a big worry off my back. In that small railway compartment, I felt truly free for the first time. The train seemed too slow to me; maybe I would only have been satisfied if I could ride a storm to reach home. I don't remember how I passed the night. It was winter; I had neither a blanket nor warm clothes. All I had was a coat, a dhoti, and some money that Barindra had given me. I also had some clothes from the prison.

I remember clearly that I reached Banaras at dawn. The true joy of having been released hit me only in that moment. There is no other place as dear to me as Banaras. It is my birthplace; I don't remember my childhood here, and I wasn't here in my youth, but the best years of my life, of being aware of my life, have been spent in this city. Banaras holds my happiest memories in its air and in its soil. As I left the station and made my way home, my joy kept increasing. When I stepped off the tonga and into the lane where my house was, it felt as if the ground beneath my feet had melted. I did not walk home; instead, I ran home. From the time I left the Andamans to the time I reached home, the attraction to home and motherland kept increasing—so much so that in the end, I just had to run. The window in the downstairs room was open, and I went and stood like a statue at the window. I could see many young men lying there, and my brothers Rabindra and Jitendra were also amongst them. Rabindra saw me and immediately screamed, 'Dada is here!' He jumped up as if someone had pushed him from under the bed. They all came and embraced me. This was my rebirth.

My youngest brother Bhupendra's Upanayan ceremony[35] had been held the previous day. No one at home knew that I would be arriving that day. I asked everyone where mother was. She had gone to the neighbour's house on some errand. When she came back, she saw me and cried for sheer happiness, saying, 'My son! My son has come home!' Moving her hands over my head, my shoulders, and all over me, she said, 'How much you have borne!'

I was taken aback when I saw my youngest brother. I had left home when he was eight years old. Now fourteen, I still remembered him as that eight-year-old. I could not relate that memory with the reality that I now saw. As for the older of my younger brothers, Jitendra and Rabindra, I could not imagine seeing them as anything other than what I remembered them as.

One chapter in life had ended, and a new one was beginning.

Chapter 4

WORRYING ABOUT MY COMPANIONS IN PRISON

A couple of hours after I reached home, a young man came to see me. His name was Jitendra Nath Mukherjee, and he had been my classmate in college. Just as I had embraced my brothers, I embraced him too. None of my other companions of yore from Banaras came to meet me. Jitendra and I began talking about politics. I had not forgotten what I was supposed to do once I got back. I asked him, 'So where is Malviya ji these days? I have to meet him.' I told him of the situation in the Andamans, about how the prisoners were suffering there, and how Bhai Parmanand had been locked up in solitary confinement in a dungeon. Since the islands were not connected to the mainland, such news did not travel at all. What could be done for the political prisoners? How? These were the questions that occupied me now. Jitendra Mukherjee told me that Pandit Madan Mohan Malviya was in Banaras, and we could meet him at the Hindu University. It was decided that I would do two things after lunch. One was to meet Pandit Malviya and the other was to inform the Magistrate of my arrival.

We reached the Hindu University after lunch. A meeting was on. I wrote a note on a slip of paper and sent it to Pandit Malviya:

Bengali Tola Intercollege, Varanasi, established in 1854 by the Sanyal–Lahiri family. Photo taken in November 2022.

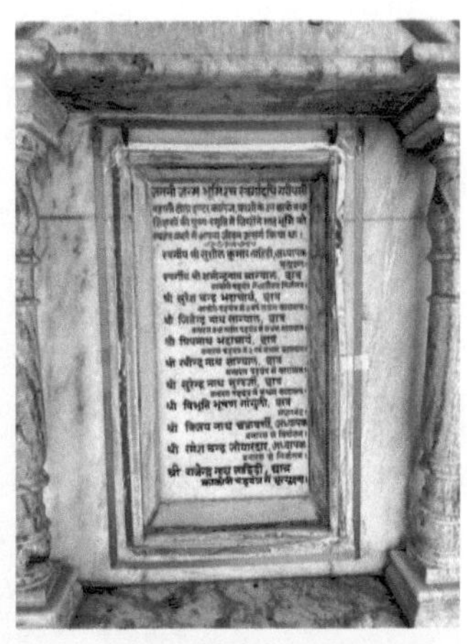

Plaque of freedom fighters associated with Bengali Tola Intercollege, Varanasi. S.N. Sanyal's name is second from the top, following Sushil Kumar Lahiri's. Photo taken in November 2022.

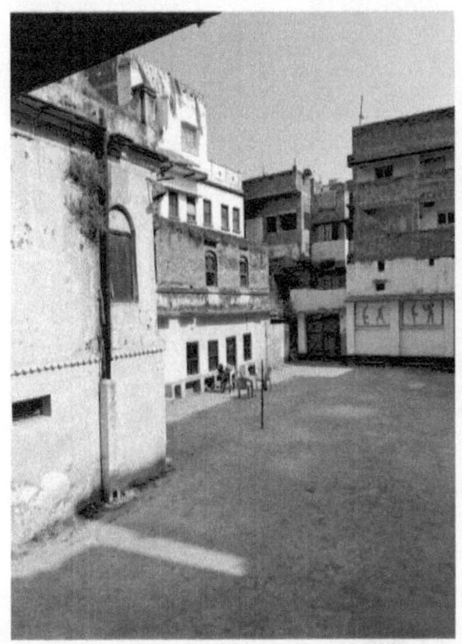

Akhada in Bengali Tola, Varanasi, next to the ancestral homes of the Sanyal clan. Their properties were confiscated or forcibly acquired by the British after the Kakori case. Photo taken in November 2022.

Sachindra Nath Sanyal with wife Pratibha and newborn son, 1922.

Photo taken soon after Sachindra Nath Sanyal's wedding in 1921. Top (left to right): Jitendra Nath Sanyal, Rabindra Nath Sanyal and Bhupendra Nath Sanyal; middle: Sachindra Nath's mother (left) and two aunts; bottom: Sachindra Nath and his wife Pratibha.

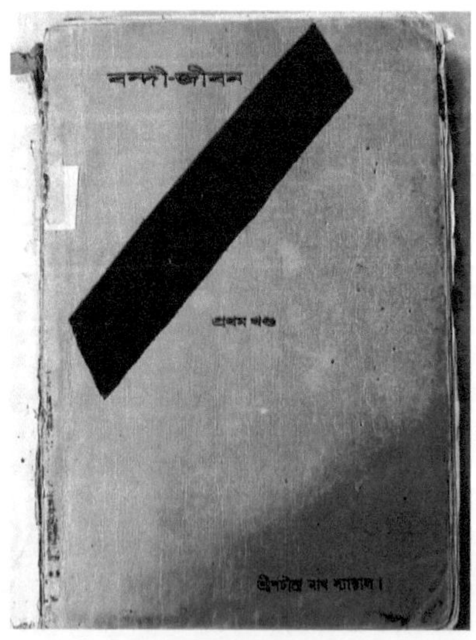

The cover of the first edition of Bandi Jeevan *published in Bengali circa 1923.*

ORDER UNDER SECTION 3 OF THE PUNJAB CRIMINAL LAW (AMENDMENT) ACT, II of 1935.

No. A. 5?? S.D.S.B. WHEREAS in the opinion of the Governor of the Punjab there are reasonable grounds for believing that Sachindra Nath Sanyal, son of Hari Nath, of Allahabad, has acted, or is about to act, in a manner prejudicial to the public safety or peace, or in furtherance of a movement prejudicial to the public safety or peace;

NOW, THEREFORE, in exercise of the powers conferred by sub-section (1) of section 3 of the Punjab Criminal Law (Amendment) Act, II of 1935, the Governor of the Punjab is pleased to direct that the said Sachindra Nath shall remove himself from the Punjab before the expiry of twenty four hours from the time of service of this order, and thereafter shall not enter, reside or remain in the jurisdiction of the province of the Punjab;

AND FURTHER, in exercise of the powers conferred by sub-section (2) of section 3 of the said Act, the Governor of the Punjab is pleased to direct that this order shall remain in force for a period of twelve months with effect from the date of issue.

By order of the Governor of the Punjab,

Sd/- J.D. Penny,

Chief Secretary to Government, Punjab.

Dated: Simla E.,
The 29th , September, 1937.

Attested:-

Superintendent of Police, Special Branch II,
C.I.D., Punjab.

Official order expelling Sachindra Nath Sanyal from Punjab after he began to revive the revolutionary movement post his return from Cellular Jail (his second stint) in 1937.

Office of the Chief Commissioner, Delhi.

ORDER

Whereas I am satisfied that there are reasonable grounds for believing that Sachindra Nath Sanyal son of Hari Nath of Madanpura, Benares, Allahabad and Gorakhpur, is about to act in a manner prejudicial to the public peace;

Now therefore in exercise of the powers conferred by section 3 of the Punjab Criminal Law (Amendment) Act 1935 (Punjab Act II of 1935) as extended to the Province of Delhi I hereby direct that the said Sachindra Nath Sanyal

(a) shall remove himself within six hours from the Delhi Province and shall not return to the Delhi Province;

(b) while in the Delhi Province shall abstain from all forms of political agitation and from participation in any procession or meeting.

I further direct that this order shall remain in force for a period of six months from the date thereof.

Chief Commissioner, Delhi.

Delhi,
Dated the 2nd December, 1937.

The British government banned Sanyal from staying in or entering Delhi Province as well as from all political activities.

GOVERNMENT OF BENGAL.

Whereas in the opinion of the Government of Bengal there are reasonable grounds for believing that...Babu Sachindra Nath Sanyal.........

son of....Babu Hari Nath Sanyal...

by caste.......–...............................of village...Santipur, Nadia and of 276,

police-station...Madaripara, Benares, Colonelganj in the district of Allahabad and 126 Notified Area, Gorrakhpur is a person in respect of whom an order may lawfully be made under sub-section (1) of section 2 of the Bengal Criminal Law Amendment Act, 1930

The Government of Bengal in exercise of the powers conferred by the said section 2, are pleased to make the following order :—

Order.

The said....Babu Sachindra Nath Sanyal son of Babu Hari Nath Sany shall not reside in, or enter, or remain in, any area within the Presidency of Bengal.

By order of the Governor ~~in Council~~,

Asstt. *Secretary to the Government of Bengal.*

CALCUTTA,

The.....22nd.............*of*......March,.......*193* 8

Sanyal's entry into Bengal Presidency was also restricted by authorities after being suspected of illegal activities.

-2-

No.1180D /38Pol. 14th March1938.

To

R.T.Peel, Esquire, M.C.,

Secretary P and J.Department, India Office

Dear Sir,

It is understood that one Sachindra Nath Sanyal a notorious ex-convict of the Kakori Conspiracy case,has been in correspondence with Messrs. Victor Gollancz Ltd., London, with a view to the publication of a book entitled "Prison Life In India." The resultsof Sanyal's negotiations with Messrs. Victor Gollancz are not known nor whether he has decided to publish his book in India or in England

2. Should this book be pueblised , theGovernment of Indi would be glad to receive a copy by air mail to enable them to arrive at a decision as to its fintess for circulation in India before copies can arrive by sea mail.

Yours sincerely,

Sd J.A.Thorne.
Secy.

INDIA OFFICE WHITEHALL S.W.I.

16th Jan.1939.

P.& J.(S) 257/38

DearThorne,

Will you please refer to your demi-official letter of the 14th March 1938 No.1180, /D/38, Political relating to the proposed publication of a book by Sachindra Nath Sanyal entitled "Prison life in India. Up to the present we have heard

When colonial intelligence found out that Sanyal was in talks to print Prison Life in India, *a translation of* Bandi Jeevan, *in Britain, they sent a letter to Secretary India Office in London to ensure that it was not published. No copy of that English translation survives.*

Rash Behari Bose
79, Sanchome, Onden, Shibuya-ku,
Tokyo, Japan.
Phone: (36) 0404. Dated 8/11/38

My dear Sachi,
I thank you for your kindness in sending to me your Hindi book, just published. I offer you hearty congratulations. I hope you all are hale and hearty. It is getting colder here daily, and by the end of the next month snow will be falling. I hope you are carefully noting the world events, particularly in Europe and Asia. A new world order is being created now and this tendency will go on for some time, till the present injustice is completely done away with. Please read carefully the speech of the Japanese Premier delivered on the 3rd instant. It lays particular stress on the creation of a New Asia on the principle of Asia for the Asiatics. The whiteman's influence in Asia is destined to be doomed for ever, and the Indian leaders should take immediate cognisance of this fact.
With love

Yours affly
R. B. Bose

Letter from Rashbehari Bose upon receipt of the Hindi edition of Bandi Jeevan *in Japan.*

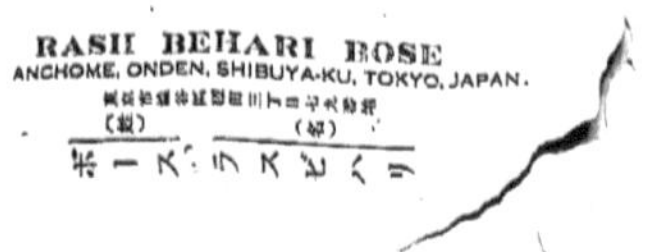
RASH BEHARI BOSE
ANCHOME, ONDEN, SHIBUYA-KU, TOKYO, JAPAN.

TELEPHONE: AOYAMA (30) 0404.

TOKYO, 17/7/ 1938

My dear Birla Maharajji,

I have never had the pleasure of your darshan, but I know your name for al long time, and I appreciate your services to the cause of Hinduism and Indianism. You are a pillar to Hindu Society and your philanthrophic activities are known throughout India. I bow my head to you for your noble activities for the cause of Bharatmata.

The object of this letter is to introduce to you Mr. Sachindra Nath Sanyal. He is working for the cause of Indian freedom for the last thirty years. He has suffered imprisonments for long periods. It was only last year that he was released from prison after the Congress Ministry came into power in the United Provinces. He wants to devote his whole life to the cause of Indianism. I shall therefore be much obliged if you could kindly see him and give him necessary advice and help.

With love and respects,

Yours affectionately,

Rash Behari Bose

Letter of introduction from Rashbehari Bose to G.D. Birla.

शहीद शचीन्द्रनाथ सान्याल स्मृति ग्रंथ
Shaheed Shachindra Nath Sanyal
Memmorial Souvenir
९०वाँ जन्म दिवस समारोह
90th Birthday Anniversary Celebaration
NEW DELHI, June 3, 1983

The memorial pamphlet of an event in 1983 on Sanyal's ninetieth birth anniversary that was attended by many surviving revolutionaries.

> Coming straight from Andamans. An interview is requested in connection with the cases of Bhai Parmanand and other political prisoners.
>
> —Sachindra Nath Sanyal

Pandit Malviya and Dr Ganesh Prasad came out as soon as they received the slip. We sat and talked in a small room. It was fortunate for me that Dr Ganesh Prasad had recognized me; in fact, he must have recognized me the moment he saw my name on the slip. He was full of praise while describing me to Pandit Malviya. I realized that he remembered even the smallest instance and incident from my student days. And while he was praising me, I was silently laughing. And with good reason too.

I had joined the Queen's College after clearing the entrance exam. Dr Ganesh Prasad used to teach mathematics. I was his student. Amongst all my teachers, he was the only one whose students failed several times. He used to pile so much work on the students that if they did all the tasks he assigned them, no other subject could be studied. In school, I used to score 100 per cent in my maths exams, but in college, once I became active in the national movement and the secret conspiracies of the revolutionary group, I could not devote my attention to college and studies. In the beginning, I used to be able to finish Dr Ganesh Nath's assignments and was counted amongst the bright boys who were made to sit on the front bench, closest to the professor. But over time, my work slackened, and I was shifted to the second bench and then the third.

When Dr Ganesh Nath was thoroughly dissatisfied with a student, he would be shunted to the last bench and treated as invisible. He used to call such a student a non-entity. He did not like his students to read anything other than the textbooks prescribed in the course. Hence, they read novels only on the sly. Eventually, I became a non-entity in Dr Ganesh Nath's class. One day, I deliberately brought an English book into the classroom and kept it on top of the course books to see if he would say anything or not. This was a collection of speeches given by Swami Abhedanand of the Ram Krishna Mission in America, published under the title *India and Her People*. Dr Ganesh Nath walked by my bench, saw the book, picked it up, leafed through it and put it back. I had wanted to see if he would berate me. This is what our relationship in the classroom was like, but here he was, praising me to high heaven to Pandit Malviya. But then, there was a reason for that too. While studying in college, entirely on our own merit and effort, we had started a school. When the school had reached the middle level, one year we had invited Dr Ganesh Nath as the chief guest for the annual function. Since then, I was no longer a non-entity.

Pandit Malviya heard me out. Then he told me to write everything down and send it to him by registered post. I did just that as soon as I reached Gorakhpur. I received the acknowledgement slip indicating that he had received the letter. But Pandit Malviya did not utter a word in favour of the release of political prisoners.

Jitendra Mukherjee and my brothers believed that Pandit Jawaharlal Nehru was the rising star in the United Provinces these days. They were of the opinion that if he were to raise the issue of political prisoners, then something could be achieved.

I stayed in Banaras for two days and then left for Gorakhpur. My oldest brother Bhupendra Nath was with me. Along with a life term in the Cellular Jail for my part in the Banaras Conspiracy Case, my sentence had also included an order to confiscate all my property. The house in Banaras belonged to my paternal grandmother. After my sentence, the police had taken possession of the house and they had also taken everything that was inside the house, even the bedding. In the name of guarding confiscated property, the policemen had also been using everything that was in the house. At the time of my arrest, my mother, my grandmother, my maternal aunt, her adoptive daughter and my youngest brother had been living in this house. They had no place to go to once the police took over the house. Then my maternal uncle had taken them to Gorakhpur, and that is where they were when I came back from the Andamans. My grandmother had gone to live with my paternal uncle.

I went to meet Pandit Jawaharlal Nehru once, in Allahabad. I drew his attention to the subject of political prisoners, and especially the terrible situation of the prisoners in the Cellular Jail who were serving long sentences. After hearing me out, Pandit Nehru stood up and said, 'Here we are making arrangements to go to jail, and you are asking us to release others.' I was left staring at him askance and wondering what to say. Had Pandit Nehru been from my party, he would have understood the importance of my request. Maybe this was the thought: why request the government for anything if one had to anyway pick a fight with the government? Nonetheless, this conversation left me feeling very disheartened.

In September 1920, a special session of Congress was held in Calcutta. All the political leaders were focussed on Mahatma Gandhi's motion for non-cooperation, and we could not achieve anything there. I took along the other released political prisoners and went to Lala Lajpat Rai. We requested him to chair the All India Political Sufferers' Conference and he accepted. Under his chairmanship, the conference was held in the hall of the Indian Association. Barrister B.C. Chatterjee and other revolutionaries of yore from Calcutta were very helpful in organizing the conference.

Many people made speeches. Some were moving, and some were dry. The late Mr Shyam Sundar Chakravarty got carried away and gave the longest speech, but his speech was anything but poignant. In fact, while speaking, he would keep falling on the chairperson, forgetting that there was someone seated there! Pandit Madan Mohan Malviya's speech disappointed those who had come to support the revolutionaries. J.N. Rai, B.C. Chatterjee and other barristers from Calcutta rebutted Pandit Malviya in this regard. But I have never in my life heard another orator equal the speech given by the late Annie Besant in that meeting. It was poignant and energetic. That day, I understood the meaning of eloquence. It was a scene I can never forget. A white stone statue seemed to have come to life and only the lips moved; occasionally there would be some movement of the hands and head. Goddess Saraswati seemed to speaking through Ms Besant. A current seemed to run through the entire hall. Pandit Malviya was embarrassed. From the chairman's seat, he ended up saying that some of these political prisoners were of such stature that even the governor was not fit to tie their shoelaces. After the meeting ended, Pandit Malviya issued an apology, trying to cover up his earlier statements by saying that he had actually meant this and that. In any case, this was how some publicity was achieved for the cause of the political prisoners.

By a series of coincidences, I ended up in the Subjects Committee of the Congress held in Nagpur that same year. Political temperatures were running high, thanks to Mahatma Gandhi's Non-Cooperation Movement. When the gauntlet had been thrown to the government, how could we petition them to release the political prisoners? I requested Bipin Chandra Pal to do something about the issue. On my insistence, he readied a proposal and got it passed in the Subjects Committee. Subsequently, Mr Pal put forth the proposal in the Nagpur Congress, and I seconded the motion. This was the first occasion on which I gave a speech in a public meeting. There must have been about 20,000 delegates. I was the first Bengali to give a speech in Hindi at the annual gathering. On the dais, I was seated next to Shri Narayan Damodar Savarkar, younger brother of the then president of the Hindu Mahasabha, Barrister Vinayak Damodar Savarkar. When I returned to my seat after the speech, Dr Savarkar told me that people had started weeping while I was speaking.

I don't remember the entire text of my speech now, but the gist of it was: 'This Congress sends its message of hope and sympathy to all political prisoners incarcerated in the different jails of India and in the distant Andamans Islands.' Mr Bipin Chandra Pal and I had drafted this proposal, and it was passed with the help of Mr Deshbandhu Chittaranjan Das. Mr Vijay Raghav Acharya, who presided over the session, had allotted me a mere five minutes to talk. As soon as I had returned from the Andamans, I had written a letter to Dr Savarkar exhorting him to advocate for the release of political prisoners. After that, Dr Savarkar and I went to meet Surendra Nath Banerjee. Mr Banerjee's first reaction was to accuse us of badmouthing him. We assured him that we believed nobody else had worked as much as he had for the political prisoners. And this was the truth. What is said from the heart has an effect. Mr Banerjee then listened to our petition. It must be noted here that we had gone to meet Mr Banerjee primarily to speak about Damodar Savarkar.

In the end, my efforts to bring about the release of the political prisoners were inconsequential. The British government released whomsoever they wished to. The main reason the issue did not get enough attention was because it was eclipsed by Gandhi ji's Satyagraha. Yet the cause of political independence had not yet made its mark on the Indian psyche, and that is why people were mostly indifferent to those who had lain down their lives for the cause of the revolution. During Aurobindo's and Tilak's times, however, the question of independence had become the centre of the lives of all workers in the national movement. That is why the Bengal revolutionary movement could not be squashed even by 30 years of oppression. Ultimately, the governor of Bengal, the viceroy of India and the British ministers had to accept that they could not suppress the struggle without the support and participation of the people of Bengal.

In Banaras, Jitendra Mukherjee and I went to meet the district collector after our meeting with Pandit Malviya. I have mentioned earlier that my release certificate stipulated that I should meet the collector and inform him of my return from the Andamans. I did the needful. The collector said that I should inform the police superintendent of my return. I felt insulted but, nonetheless, made my way to the office of the superintendent. The latter was not there but the assistant superintendent was. I told him that it did not matter to me whether his superior was there or not, as I had done my duty and informed them. He noted my name and address, and as a result, I was put under surveillance.

As far as I remember, I stayed in Banaras for only a day after my return from the Andamans. The next day, I left for Gorakhpur with my younger brother Bhupendra. I stayed there for a couple of months or so. I spent this time relaxing and recuperating. But I was constantly worried about wasting my life. I would look for opportunities to begin anew. I wanted to go to Calcutta but didn't have the money. There was a magazine called *Swadesh*, which was published from Gorakhpur, and I got an introduction to the editor, Mr Dashrath Dwivedi. I hinted at my situation to him one day and asked for help to go to Calcutta. He offered me hope but help did not materialize. I also went to Allahabad to meet Pandit Nehru and sent a registered letter to Pandit Malviya about the condition of political prisoners in the Andamans. I have already told you about the outcome of all this effort.

One day, I had gone to Banaras for some reason. There, I met two old companions, Mr Priya Nath Bhattacharya and Mr Suresh Chandra Bhattacharya. I proposed some organizational work to them. Within a few days, my brother received intimation from the CID deputy inspector-general, Mr Bigen, which mentioned my efforts to revive the party. I was surprised. Later, I came to know that Priya Nath Bhattacharya had given a confession letter to the police. I never met Priya Nath again.

Chapter 5

MR SANDERS AND BARRISTER CHATTERJEE

Out of four brothers, three of us had been arrested in the Banaras Conspiracy Case. Jitendra had been given a two-year sentence. The court had acquitted my other brother, Rabindra, but he was later put under house arrest in his house in Gorakhpur. When I came back from my stint in the Andamans, Jitendra had finished his intermediate, cleared the entrance and either was about to begin his bachelor's course or had already left; I am not sure of which it was. I was in the first year of my BSc when I went to the Andamans. After my release, I wanted to finish my studies. I wanted to at least do a BA course, but my mother and my brother were not keen on that; they agreed when I insisted. I felt that going to college would give me the opportunity to meet and recruit youngsters, although at the back of my mind was also the thought that a degree might come in useful later to get a job.

A relative of mine on my mother's side had received a letter from Mr Sanders, the deputy inspector-general in Faizabad, saying that he should send me to meet him once I got back from the Andamans. I think it is important to talk a bit about Mr Sanders before I move forward. The Banaras Conspiracy Case was investigated under his aegis. He was also responsible for the prosecution of the Mainpuri Conspiracy Case. My mother had sent a mercy petition to the government after I was sentenced. The government had rejected it, but when the Emperor had announced in December 1919 that political prisoners would be released, Mr Sanders told Mr B.C. Chatterjee to ask my mother to send in the mercy petition then, and he would recommend it. Mr Chatterjee had also gone to him to appeal in the Mainpuri case.

Mr Sanders tried his personal best to acquit some of the people implicated in these cases who were absconding. He told everyone that if the absconders surrendered, he would arrange for their release. And that is how most of the arrested were let off on various conditions. One of the accused, Pandit Devi Narayan, met with Mr Sanders but did not accept his conditions. Mr Sanders told him that he would not arrest him at that point because he had come to meet him of his own free will. He hadn't been caught by the police, so he could go wherever he wished. Mr Sanders said that he would give him enough time to leave but suggested that it was better for Devi Narayan to accept the conditions he had put forward.

In the end, it was decided that Pandit Devi Narayan would stay at his own place, but the police would not arrest him; meanwhile, Mr Sanders would consult his superiors about the possibility of releasing Devi Narayan without conditions. Mr Sanders then gave him a letter with instructions that the police were not to arrest him. After this, Devi Narayan was neither arrested nor ordered to surrender. In the history of modern India, this is probably an exceptional case; I don't think any English officer ever behaved so empathetically. But it is also a fact that in the Chauri Chaura case, the atrocity committed was ordered by Mr Sanders. In that incident, the aggressive reaction of the people had triggered the police. In that moment, both sides had probably become agitated and lost control.

It was this Mr Sanders that I had to meet after my return from the Andamans. On making enquiries after returning from Gorakhpur, I found that Mr Sanders was no longer with the secret police but was now a deputy inspector-general with the regular police in Faizabad. An old friend of mine, Acharya Narendra Dev, lived in Faizabad. I decided to kill two birds with one stone and meet both of them.

In Faizabad, I went to meet Mr Sanders. I had to wait in a room for about 10 minutes. The conversation I overheard was so civilized that no one could have guessed that the deputy inspector-general was investigating a dacoity in the adjoining room. When Mr Sanders met me, he was very polite; he shook hands and asked me to sit next to him. We had been tugging the rope on one end and they on the other, he said to me, and now that the tug of war was over, what did I intend to do? He suggested that I try my hand at farming and offered to help in any way that he could. I told him, 'I wish to study. If you could please help me get me admission in a college, it would be very helpful.' I realized that this didn't go down too well with Mr Sanders. But, to me, all he said was, 'If I can help in securing college admission, I will. But I have no power over college authorities.' I said, 'It will be impossible for me to get admission to a college if the police put a spanner in the works.' To this, Mr Sanders replied, 'I will ensure that the police do not present any problem in your admission.' I did realize that college admission was not going to be easy for me. I went off to meet Narendra Dev ji. I knew him from my college days at Queen's in 1910 and 1911.

I wanted to leave Gorakhpur for various reasons. When my brother Jitendra finished his BA, he was advised to pursue an MA, but he was not interested. Luckily, he got a job as a principal in the Anglo-Bengali Middle School in Allahabad. As far as I remember, he worked there for a year. As for me, I had taken admission in Muir College, Allahabad, but two days later, the principal summoned me to his office and told me that I could not be admitted to the college. I gave Mr Sanders's reference but to no avail. Naturally, this made me sad, but I was also happy because now I didn't have to take the exams! It would have been very embarrassing if I were to fail those exams. I went to meet Dr Tara Chand, the principal of Kayastha Pathshala, who was Lala Har Dayal's contemporary and also related to him. The combination of subjects that I wanted was not available at Kayastha Pathshala. I did take admission but left in a matter of days, the reason being that I had lost all interest in resuming my studies if I could not learn subjects of my choice. It is possible that I was also scared of failing the exams.

It was around this time that I seriously started working on reorganizing the revolutionary party. I have already mentioned that on my return from the Andamans, my old companion Mr Jitendra Chandra Mukherjee had come to meet me in Calcutta. I knew that he would not join the revolutionary party. His younger brother Dhirendra Chandra Mukherjee studied in Allahabad. He had passed his BSc with flying colours and was now studying philosophy for his Masters. He was interested in politics. In Allahabad, Dhirendra came to meet me. Just as a shopkeeper rejoices at the sight of a customer or an eagle at the sight of a small bird, I too rejoiced at the sight of this young man. I soon realized that Dhirendra was not as interested in an armed revolutionary movement as he was in the non-violent Non-Cooperation Movement. Nonetheless, I did not lose hope. I will speak about him at length later. On this occasion, however, I felt as frustrated as a shopkeeper who is unable to make a sale to a promising customer or as the eagle losing easy prey. Disappointed, I went back to Gorakhpur.

I had been living a kind of a student life before I went to the Andamans. There was no worry about earning a living. I ate at home and did whatever I wanted. After returning from the Andamans, I felt I had grown up, and a new sense of responsibility seemed to weigh on me. I felt that I should make arrangements for my own food and other expenses. I was around 28 years old at this time, and I had never, until then, prepared myself for earning a living. On the one hand, I was faced with the problem of a livelihood, and on the other hand, I wanted to dedicate my life to the nation. This was quite a dilemma that I faced on my return from the Andamans.

In those days, thousands of prisoners were being released in Bengal. Everyone had the same dilemma. Mr B.C. Chatterjee had collected some money to help those who were facing this problem. A big house had been taken on rent. After their release, prisoners would come to this house where arrangements had been made for two meals a day per person. People could stay here for 15 days to a month, courtesy Mr Chatterjee and the Young Men's Christian Association. They also helped the ex-prisoners find jobs and livelihoods. Having read about this in a newspaper, I presented myself at this house which was on Beniapukur Lane. Here, I met many political prisoners from Bengal but did not feel any excitement. I looked around to see how they lived and spoke with them to learn what they thought, but with most of them, I was left wondering why and how they ended up as political prisoners. I also met many of my old jailmates and realized that most of them were facing the same dilemma as I. Besides, all my erstwhile companions had not yet been released. Hence, meeting those who had been did not make me happy. Most of them had been party workers but none of them were close to me.

Just as a river gushing along its course finds its flow obstructed by villages and other human settlements in its path, similarly, our revolutionary zeal had been dammed for some time. When the time is right, the force of water can break a dam and cause a flood, which, in turn, displaces people and renders them homeless. Similarly, the revolutionaries, too, were floundering in the world after having been released. They were looking for some source of support, for sustenance.

I have rarely seen such intelligent thinkers, powerful writers or capable leaders as Barindra or Upendra Nath, who were the previous helmsmen of the revolutionary movement. As I have mentioned before, one day in the Cellular Jail, screwing up his eyes and face with contempt, Virendra had commented, 'Bengal is still following the road that I showed them. Even today the revolutionaries in Bengal haven't been able to chart a new path.' This was true to a large extent.

I would like to mention here something that Mr B.C. Chatterjee said to me when I got back from the Andamans. As I have mentioned before, in a letter written from the Cellular Jail, I had said that if the British government really gave Indians the opportunity to choose what was best for them, there would be no need for Indians to opt for the path of violence. Mr Chatterjee said to me, 'The British government will definitely give us this chance, and, therefore, it is your duty to work with the Montagu–Chelmsford Reforms and give up your underground conspiracy programmes. It is with this hope and trust that the government has released you.'

In reply, I said, 'Vinayak Damodar Savarkar had also

expressed similar sentiments in one of his letters, so why was he not released as well? If what you say is true, then Savarkar, too, would have been freed. I think there are two reasons why I was released and Savarkar was not. One is that there was tremendous pressure from the populace in Bengal to release prisoners like me. That is a big factor in the release of political prisoners. But Maharashtra did not have a movement as strong as that of Bengal. The second reason is that after the arrest of Savarkar and his companions, the revolutionary movement in Maharashtra had died. The government was, therefore, scared; if Savarkar was released, they believed it may give a new lease of life to the revolutionary movement in the state. Moreover, an important fact was that Savarkar had killed an Englishman in England. The British government was extremely upset with this crime. They had made it a policy that political prisoners who were accused of murder or dacoity would not be released. And that is why Savarkar could not be released.' To this, Mr Chatterjee had replied, 'The fact is that the British do not trust the Marathas an inch. The government believes that the Bengalis will do what they say but they do not think the Marathas will.'

I felt a little embarrassed to hear this and amused too. Embarrassed, because I felt Mr Chatterjee was giving Maharashtra too much credit in the political scheme of things and underestimating the Bengalis. This did not seem judicious to me. I was amused because Mr Chatterjee actually believed that the British government would allow us to achieve our goals. I knew for certain that the government would never give us any such opportunity and that we would have to take the path of revolution again. Mr Chatterjee also remarked that if the British government gave us the chance to take our country to the heights of progress that they had achieved in their own, we would be able to move forward without an armed revolution.

This time, when I was staying at the Beniapukur house, I had a conversation with Mr Chatterjee, who kept suggesting to me that we should have a permanent address that would serve as our centre. We could then use it to the optimum with the opportunities of political reform that came our way. It is important to understand the general political ambience of the country to understand Mr Chatterjee's mindset. It is also important to understand the circumstances of the revolutionary mindset.

Chapter 6

THE MONTAGU–CHELMSFORD REFORMS AND NON-COOPERATION

While in jail, we could see that there were three points of view amongst our leaders regarding the Montagu–Chelmsford Reforms. Soft leaders like Madan Mohan Malviya wanted these reforms that promised self-governance to be accepted without any conditions or demands. Another set of leaders wanted to reject the reforms outright. A third category of leaders believed that we should take advantage of the reforms, but they also warned against complacency and wanted a political movement that worked towards complete independence. The political prisoners in jail were in constant competition to prove that their respective native states were the most aggressive, which is to say that they would reject the Montagu–Chelmsford Reforms with greatest alacrity. As revolutionaries we sometimes forgot that it was one thing to reject these reforms and another to use them for our benefit.

This question came back to us when we got back from the Andamans as well. B.C. Chatterjee was one of those who understood the importance of a revolutionary movement but did not want to reject the reforms outright. Mahatma Gandhi was once a moderate, but, with time, he seemed to be giving up that policy. However, it is also possible that Gandhi hasn't been able to completely give up the moderate mindset even today. On the other hand, although C.R. Das was not an extremist, he empathized with the revolutionaries. He was sympathetic not just because of the sacrifice that he saw the revolutionaries make for the country, but also from a political understanding. He believed that all political movements in India were supported and strengthened by the revolutionary movement. C.R. Das and Tilak were of the same thinking. The former had entered the political arena only recently. It was while arguing the Alipore Bomb case for Mr Aurobindo Ghosh that he had developed certain revolutionary sentiments.

Tilak and Das did not wish to reject the Montagu–Chelmsford Reforms but did not want to accept them in their entirety either. Mr Motilal was a moderate, but pressure from his son was continuously increasing to change his views. At this moment, Indian politics stood at a critical fork owing to the different views of its political leadership. Mahatma Gandhi was not revolutionary in nature then; nor is he now. But he wields the strongest influence on Indian politics because of his prodigious personality.

It was decided under Mahatma Gandhi's leadership that the Montagu–Chelmsford Reforms would be entirely rejected. However, most of the revolutionaries in Bengal believed that the reforms should be utilized as far as possible. B.C. Chatterjee was also of this opinion. But the released political prisoners were not consulted, and no policy decision was taken. Moreover, many influential revolutionaries were still in jail. The political leadership of the country was essentially moving into Mahatma Gandhi's hands. The revolutionaries did not like this; neither did C.R. Das, Tilak, Lajpat Rai and other leaders of the old Garam Dal.

To understand the revolutionary movement that I created in North India, it is imperative to understand the political climate of that time as well as certain characteristics that defined the revolutionary movement after 1920. It must be noted that the revolutionary movement in India was not being run by just one organization. I somehow took charge of the revolutionary movement after 1920; hence, it is important to talk about the organizations that I worked with and what they were about. It is also essential to note that there were divisions in this underground movement and these differences were primarily caused by shortcomings in human nature. I hope that talking of this will also teach us something.

Here I would like to make a short detour to an earlier time of my life. My dear father passed away in 1908 in Calcutta. I shifted to Banaras in 1909. I was already a member of the famous Anushilan Samiti[36] in Calcutta, and when I moved to Banaras, I established a branch there. The history of the Anushilan Samiti is not important here; it is enough to mention that it had two branches. One had its headquarters in Dhaka and the other was based in Calcutta. I was affiliated to the Calcutta branch. When I set up the branch in Banaras, the Bengal government declared it illegal as per the judgment in the Alipore Conspiracy. Therefore, we had to change the name of the organization in Banaras. It was now called Yuvak Sammelan (Youth Convention). In my heart I wanted to maintain a connection with Calcutta's Anushilan Samiti, but circumstances did not allow that.

After the failure of efforts by Barindra and others, those who remained in the organization shifted their base to the French quarters in Chandernagore near Calcutta. And it is from this centre that the most popular leader of the movement, Mr Rashbehari Bose, emerged. He moved first to Dehradun and later successfully established a group in Punjab.

Pulin Behari Das was the founder-president of the Dhaka

Anushilan Samiti. He was sentenced to seven years in the Cellular Jail. The leaders who took his place in Dhaka started to liaison and work with the group from Chandernagore. Mr Shirish Chandra Ghose and Motilal Roy were the leaders of the Chandernagore group at this time. The Dhaka Anushilan Samiti did work with Motilal Roy, but the leaders of that group kept the organization completely independent. The Chandernagore group was not very influential in Calcutta. But Rashbehari, more or less singlehandedly, set up the organization in Punjab.

It was by coincidence that I joined the Chandernagore group. I got in touch with them through some members of the Dhaka Anushilan Samiti, and, since I lived in the western region, I was allotted to Rashbehari. He was an able and efficient leader. Because there was a bomb-making centre in Chandernagore, Rashbehari had a very close relationship with the Dhaka Anushilan Samiti. Through him, I later met and got to know the important party workers of the Dhaka unit. The understanding between the Chandernagore group and the Dhaka Samiti was that the latter would not send any of its men independently to North India, as the entire responsibility for northern region rested with Rashbehari.

The most prominent workers of the Dhaka Anushilan Samiti at the time were Mr Pratul Chandra Ganguli, Mr Trailokya Nath, Mr Narendra Nath Sen, Mr Ramesh Chandra Acharya, Mr Ramesh Chandra Chaudhary and Mr Nalini Kishore Guha. I knew all of them well except for Narendra Sen. I had a good working relationship with the Dhaka Anushilan Samiti till I was arrested and went to the Andamans. The leaders of the Dhaka group had even shared some of their secrets with me after Rashbehari left for Japan. But I also had a feeling that they were only beginning to confide in me slowly, and there was more to come. The group from North India and the Dhaka Anushilan Samiti were slowly moving towards greater cooperation. And in this situation, I had got arrested. Now, after my return from the Andamans, I did not want to make any plans without first consulting the Dhaka Samiti.

I had, without success, tried to unite the different revolutionary groups in Bengal before my arrest. When I came back from the Andamans, I wanted all the revolutionary groups in India to get together and form a powerful organization. I met many revolutionary leaders of Bengal while I lived in the Beniapukur house. Among the prominent figures of other groups whom I knew well, were Mr Jadugopal Mukherjee, Mr Bipin Chandra Ganguli, Mr Manoranjan Gupta and Mr Arun Chandra Guha. They had been working under Bengal's well-known revolutionary leader Mr Jatindra Nath Mukherjee. I met all of them after my release from the Andamans.

On the one hand, Mahatma Gandhi was making preparations for his Satyagraha movement, and on the other, these leaders in Bengal were trying to incite revolutionary feelings through their writings and working towards a new rebellion. However, no noteworthy leader emerged in Bengal after Mr Aurobindo in the open revolutionary movement. C.R. Das, Bipin Chandra Pal, Byomkesh Chakravarty, and to a certain extent B.C. Chatterjee and Shyam Sundar Chatterjee, also participated in the movement. There was also Tilak in Maharashtra and Lala Lajpat Rai in Punjab. Mr Motilal Nehru's affiliation had also started to tilt towards the Garam Dal (Hot Faction) owing to pressure from his son. Madan Mohan Malviya was counted amongst the Naram Dal (Soft Faction).

Mahatma Gandhi had reached India before my arrest. He had appealed to the revolutionaries that the country would benefit immensely if they gave up the path of underground revolution and joined him. Gandhi had a special place in Indian politics after the Satyagraha movement of 1919. Motilal Nehru was also inclined towards the Mahatma after the Jallianwala Bagh incident. Neither C.R. Das nor Motilal Nehru was a match to the personality of Mahatma Gandhi. If there was any leader who could rival his charisma, it was either Lokmanya Tilak or Lala Lajpat Rai. Bipin Chandra Pal's influence was lessening. His arrest on his return from England and the weakness of character that he exhibited on that arrest put an end to his leadership. C.R. Das showed certain qualities that were slowly coming to the fore.

He was not only a well-known barrister but also a large-hearted man. While he earned lakhs of rupees, he spent a substantial part of that money to help the poor and the needy. In fact, his father had left behind him a debt of 12,000 rupees. C.R. Das, with honesty and integrity, slowly paid off that debt once he finished his studies abroad and came back to India. He was a man of strong character as well as one who empathized with others' pain; he was also just and had the determination which ensured that plans were turned into action. As I have mentioned before, it was through his defence of Mr Aurobindo in the Alipore Bomb case that the revolutionary party got to know Mr Das. Had he wanted, Mr B.C. Chatterjee, too, could have become a powerful leader in Bengal in 1920. Unlike Mr Das, however, Mr Chatterjee never went into politics. Hence, it was the former who took charge of the revolutionary movement in Bengal after Mr Aurobindo.

The important leaders of the open nationalist movement in Bengal were not critical of the Indian revolutionary movement. They secretly condoned the use of arms for the revolutionary cause and, though they condemned violence publicly, they were never abusive of our methods. It was rather clear that their sympathy lay with the revolutionary group. And sometimes, when a revolutionary was hanged, these leaders would, in their statements, maintain and respect the dignity of valour in a way that would serve to bolster the spirit of the revolutionary movement.

There was no open political movement in the other states of India that was worth mentioning. Thanks to the efforts of the late Lala Lajpat Rai, other than Bengal, Punjab was the only enlightened state. Maharashtra was far ahead of all other states in industrial development. There had been adequate political awareness in this region, but no good leader emerged in Bombay after Lokmanya Tilak. Tilak was in jail for six years in Burma, and during this time, Maharashtra and Gujarat did not participate in any significant way in the political movements of the country. Pandit Jawaharlal Nehru had not yet made his appearance in the United Provinces. There had been no political movement in Bihar, nor had Bihar produced any notable leader. As a result, it was the most backward state in India. Madras was not much better than Bihar in this respect. Thanks to the revolutionary movement, which the common people referred to as the 'Bomb Party', there had been some awakening of political consciousness in other parts of the country. Before I went to the Andamans, I had, in some villages of the United Provinces, heard the name of Mr Aurobindo. But India's nationalist movement did a 180-degree turn with Mahatma Gandhi appearing on the scene.

The World War, too, had changed things all over the world. The common man in India could remain unaffected by these political developments. But the most far-reaching change came about when Mahatma Gandhi jumped into the political fray with his new political programme. Mahatma Gandhi understood the allure of the revolutionaries of India. He understood that if the political leaders of the country did not emulate their courage and sacrifice, their work would have no effect on either the Indian public or the British government. The draconian Rowlatt Act had been specifically enacted to suppress the revolutionary movement. The Mahatma launched a strong movement against this act. He had tested his strength in Champaran, Bihar, before he launched this movement. Gandhi had begun his first active but peaceful agitation here, and the state that was considered the most backward was organized to oppose the British Empire under the Mahatma's leadership.

In his autobiography, Mahatma Gandhi has accepted that he had not gone to Punjab before starting the Satyagraha movement in 1919. And because he had not campaigned at all in that state, he had no hope of his movement receiving any mass support in that region. Gandhi had not campaigned for his programme in the United Provinces either. I remember that before I went to the Andamans, Motilal Nehru had organized a meeting about the Mahatma's movement in South Africa. There was little enthusiasm about this event and not many people had attended the meeting. But after the World War, when Gandhi entered the political scene with the unique principle of Satyagraha, he was warmly welcomed, and the echo of it was heard throughout the country. Mahatma Gandhi says that he had not expected such a response. It was as if the entire nation had been waiting for this man, for his capable leadership to unleash its latent power. Had a leader like Gandhi not emerged, there would not be the kind of political awareness we see today in the country.

However, it must be said that the Indian masses had woken up just before the start of Mahatma Gandhi's movement. And this awakening was taking violent and radical forms against the British government. Even a leader as charismatic as the Mahatma would have had to accept defeat if he had gone against the mood of the people. This is also mentioned in Gandhi's autobiography. When he had sent his men to help the British government in Champaran, the people had not supported him—so much so that the Mahatma's emissaries had not been able to find transport to travel from one place to another. In other words, the people had already woken up. Gandhi took advantage of this awakening but he also did the freedom movement abundant good. Other leaders could not do the same. And that is what is special about Mahatma Gandhi.

The Jallianwala Bagh massacre in Amritsar was a consequence of the large-scale Satyagraha movement of 1919. The entire civilized world was stupefied. The English had a treaty with the Americans. A large number of political prisoners were released then. And that is when I had come back from the Andamans. Many of these prisoners left politics and embraced domesticity. But there were many who continued to believe that India could gain independence only by means of an armed revolution. I met members of various revolutionary groups while I was living in the Beniapukur house. But several leaders were still in jail. The state of the movement was like that of some huge town that had been destroyed by a raging fire or a typhoon. Just as one starts from scratch after a devastating earthquake, we began to rebuild the revolutionary movement.

Chapter 7

THE JAMSHEDPUR LABOUR ASSOCIATION

I started work on reorganizing the revolutionary group only after Mahatma Gandhi's Satyagraha had ended in 1920. I would like to describe some of the problems that I faced in this endeavour. As I have mentioned earlier, like many other freed political prisoners, I, too, was confronted with the dilemma of how to earn a livelihood. At one time, I considered the idea of opening a bookstore. It would be useful to carry out revolutionary work as well, I thought. But it was too expensive a project, and so I gave up the idea. Then I thought of starting a printing press. That would help in campaigning for the cause as well. But one would need at least 10,000 rupees to set up a press, and in the end, this idea, too, was abandoned. Then I thought of opening a general merchant's shop, which maybe could be set up for a couple of thousand rupees. Mother had some money left over from father's earnings. She and all my brothers were pressurizing me to take up some form of employment. Besides, Mr Sanders had written to my maternal uncle that I should be occupied in work, which would not give me time and opportunity for other activities. That is why he was keen that I should acquire some land and take to farming. I refused to do this. In the end, I decided to open a shop. But where to set it up? If the location was not appropriate, the whole enterprise would be pointless.

I traipsed all over Calcutta hunting for the right place to set up shop. We would be out from morning till night and bone-weary at the end of the day. One day, I was so frustrated that I wished I was a woman and then there would have been at least one way to earn money—that of the women I had seen sitting in the windows of red-light areas of Calcutta. I wanted to cry. I wondered how revolutionaries survived in other countries. I read many books to find answers to this question, but in vain. Tolstoy has written somewhere that if you are looking for something in a book, you will find everything but the information you are looking for, and that the main reason a book is written for is always the least mentioned in it. I read many books written by revolutionaries, but I did not find out how they survived. However, in a book by Mr Kropotkin, he mentions that apparently the revolutionaries in Russia were in the same dire straits as us!

While I was looking for work in Calcutta, my mother had come to Bengal to look for a bride for me. Sometimes I went to various relatives' houses with her. And in one such visit to a distant relative's place, it was decided that we would start a brick kiln in a place called Kalna in the Bardhaman district of Bengal, close to Calcutta. For some months, I was busy setting up the business. On the face of it, I was working, but in my heart I was weeping.

I started writing *Bandi Jeevan: Life in Chains* when I was working in Kalna. I would work all day and write till midnight. There was hardly any time to read. I used to try and meet the youngsters in the area as well. Sometimes I had to travel to Calcutta for work, and there, I would see small groups of young men collecting donations from shopkeepers to help those affected by floods. My heart would sing on seeing the youth serve the country thus. I would compare myself with them and feel extremely sorry for myself. I would think about what I had wanted to do for the nation and wonder what I was doing now. Their dedication made me want to cry, but it was not possible to thus give way to my emotions in a tram. What would people say on seeing my tears? I would discreetly wipe my eyes and try to be stoic.

The Calcutta Congress session had taken place before I set up the brick kiln. While I was occupied with the business in Kalna, however, there was not much happening in the Congress either. The brick business shuts down during monsoons. I had invested in the business and could not leave till I recovered the sum, although I had made up my mind to get out of it. I got married before I gave up the business. The hard work and the new living expenses were an added strain. In the end, I ended up selling my share to some relatives and I suffered a loss of 1,000 rupees.

After I left the brick business, I worked with BN Railway (The Bengal Nagpur Railway was one of the companies which pioneered development of the railways in eastern and central India. It was succeeded first by Eastern Railway and subsequently by South-Eastern Railway) on a salary of 50 rupees. I don't want to talk of my experience with this job, not here anyway. It would suffice to say that one day, I even contemplated suicide. Meanwhile, a man from Nagpur came to meet me. The chairman of the Jamshedpur Labour Association, Mr S.N. Haldar, had sent him. Mr C.R. Das's wife happened to be Mr Haldar's sister. The association was disintegrating, and Mr Haldar wanted me to help in salvaging it. I was told I would receive a monthly salary of 150 rupees. This offer came as a much-needed blessing. The head clerk at BN Railway tried to tell me that a job with the railways offered stability, which would be completely lacking at the Labour Association.

Therefore, it would not be prudent for me to leave my job, he advised, and I should reconsider my decision. But I did not want a stable job, and I happily accepted the offer, left the railways and went to work at Jamshedpur. There were 75,000 workers in Jamshedpur. I worked there for nine months. In those months, I learnt a lot about the Labour Association. I attended the Nagpur session of the Congress while I was working in Jamshedpur. There I met many revolutionaries from all over the country. I have already mentioned all that was done for the political prisoners at this convention.

Mahatma Gandhi's Satyagraha had been successful, but I will not write about it here. While the agitation was going on, I was working in Jamshedpur. It was when Gandhi's movement started to lose steam that I decided that it was time to start work on re-establishing the revolutionary party. I tried to resign from my job at Jamshedpur twice, but my resignation was turned down both times by the working committee of the labour union. I did not feel it was right to continue to accept 150 rupees every month from the union. It was not possible to work towards reorganizing the revolutionary party while I was involved with the work at the Labour Association. It was not possible to do justice to the work of the union either if one did not invest one's heart and soul, dedicating both day and night to it. And if one is taking a monthly remuneration, there was more reason to give it your all.

The Jamshedpur Labour Association had made great progress ever since I took on its work. Before I went there, there were practically no contributions to the fund. After I began work, my salary of 150 rupees came from the contributions. I had also appointed an accountant and a clerk at 50 rupees a month. Even after these expenditures, I had still managed to collect more than 1,000 rupees in union funds.

In view of all this, my monthly renumeration was hardly unearned, but I still thought the right thing to do was to quit working for the Labour Association, once I had decided to throw my energies into the movement again. Had I found somebody who could take over the work of rebuilding the revolutionary party, I would not have quit the union. There was no dearth of revolutionaries in Bengal then. So why did I have to take this step?

As I mentioned earlier, there was an organization that was working towards a revolution to liberate India. The Dhaka Anushilan Samiti did not support me in my endeavours after my return from the Andamans. Their attitude had changed from what it was during Rashbehari's time. The leaders of the Dhaka Samiti did not discuss with me their plans in these new circumstances. Mr Pulin Behari Das was the most senior leader in the Dhaka group. After the release of the political prisoners, the leadership of the Samiti had been in his hands. I had served time in the Cellular Jail with him in the Andamans. I could not fathom how he had become the leader of the group as he was not extraordinary in any sense—he was neither an intellectual nor a visionary. He had done his graduation, but he was not an intelligent man. He was not in the least interested in debating social and political issues or in reading books on these topics. He was not involved in any confrontation with the jail authorities in the Andamans, not even once. When the political prisoners would go on a hunger strike or protest against the authorities in other ways to safeguard their self-respect, Pulin Babu would simply stay away from trouble.

It is understandable that not everybody is ready to deal with all hardships, and it is wrong to expect them to do so, but a person who does not support the fighters and the heroes may still empathize and be a kindred-spirit. But Pulin Behari did not fall even in this category. I realized through my ability to recognize human nature that Pulin Behari did not have any leadership qualities. Moreover, he lacked the ability to have a logical discussion on any subject. He would not change an opinion he had formed despite any counterargument. He simply could not understand another point of view, one that may be different from his. And that is why I had decided, while in the Andamans, that I would not be able to work with him in any capacity after my release. All I can say is that I did not have an iota of respect for him.

The Dhaka Anushilan Samiti began work under the leadership of Pulin Behari after his release, although other leaders of the Samiti were not keen on this choice. Meanwhile, Mahatma Gandhi's Satyagraha was going strong. Deshbandhu Das also decided to throw in his lot with the Satyagrahis. He asked Pulin Behari, a couple of other revolutionary leaders and me to join him. At that time, I was completely stuck with the brick kiln business, and, therefore, despite wanting to with all my heart, I could not participate. Pulin Behari did not believe in Satyagraha. He did not join Mr Das either. In those days, I thought many a time of leaving the business and household responsibilities to embrace the political life. At times, I feel that I made a huge mistake by not doing so. Later, on hearing the speech I made in Hindi at the Nagpur session of the Congress, Mr Das had suggested that I should join hands with him and make the Labour Association a branch of the Congress movement. But a friend of Mr Das, a lawyer by the name of Mr Nishith Sen, told me in as many words that if I was not financially self-sufficient, I would not be able to establish myself in the political arena. I mentioned Mr Das's proposal to him, but Mr Sen did not change his opinion. In the end, I accepted Mr Sen's logic and continued to work as an organizing secretary with the Labour Association in Jamshedpur.

Meanwhile, other revolutionary leaders from Bengal, like Mr Surendra Nath Ghose, Mr Bipin Behari Ganguli and others, merged their groups with Mr Deshbandhu's Satyagraha movement. As I have mentioned earlier, the Anushilan Samiti had two centres—one in Dhaka and the other in Calcutta. The members of the Calcutta Samiti joined other revolutionary groups in the city and, eventually, this branch ceased to exist. Mr Jadugopal Mukherjee was a veteran of the Calcutta Anushilan Samiti. I, too, had been a member of this group. I had met Mr Jadugopal before I went to the Andamans and requested him to reorganize the Samiti. Sadly, he did not heed my request. Hence, I kept working on my own in Banaras. Later, when I was working with the Jamshedpur Labour organization after my release, Mr Jadugopal asked me to join his party. Since I had associated closely with the Dhaka Anushilan Samiti before I went to the Andamans, I thought it only prudent that I should meet the Dhaka people and see if they wanted to collaborate with me or not. Some of the leaders of the Dhaka Samiti had also been released, but unfortunately, I did not get along with them. Many leaders were still behind bars, and I decided to wait for their release. But now I realize that not meeting Mr Jadugopal was a huge mistake on my part.

There was something else that I was unaware of. Pulin Behari did not support C.R. Das; in fact, he had got together with groups opposed to Mr Das and was campaigning against the Satyagraha movement. Barrister S.R. Das was close to C.R. Das but he was a government advocate at that time. Along with his cronies who favoured the government, he wanted to start a campaign against the Non-Cooperation Movement, just like the Aman Sabha (Peace Committee) did in the United Provinces. The Dhaka Samiti had received a large donation from S.R. Das. This money was used to publish a weekly newsletter called *Shankh* and handbills called *Haq Katha*. I did not know that the weekly newsletter was printed with money contributed by opposers of the national movement. I used to write for this newsletter. I had just started on a biography of Lenin and had written four chapters. One day, while talking to Jadugopal in Calcutta, I came to know who funded these publications. I never had a good relationship with the Dhaka Samiti and my respect for them lessened now.

I had not found any leader of the Dhaka Samiti to be of the same calibre as Barindra, Upendra or Hem Chandra. The sole advantage that the Dhaka Samiti had was that it was organized and more or less united. The other revolutionary groups in Bengal were plagued by factionalism. The smaller groups were intent on maintaining their individuality and that is why many of them were weak. But the leaders of these groups were far more capable and stronger than those of the Dhaka Samiti. I empathized with the leaders of the other groups in Bengal. However, I was waiting for a leader of the Dhaka Samiti, Trailokyanath Chakraborty, to be released. Therefore, I did not join any revolutionary group in Bengal. Soon, I made up my mind to independently start working to set up a revolutionary group in the United Provinces and Punjab. I would decide later about which group to ally with in Bengal.

It is true that the Dhaka Samiti had managed to organize itself with donations from people in favour with the government, but it was facing a lot of flak in Bengal for opposing the national movement, and this caused unrest amongst its members. Amidst all this confusion, there was another rumour—that Pulin Behari had passed on a list of people from Bengal to S.R. Das, indicating that they were involved in once again preparing for a revolutionary movement. Pulin Behari had to leave the Dhaka Samiti after this story began circulating. He had already died politically. This time he was politically cremated.

The released political prisoners started flooding the monthly and weekly magazines in Bengal with articles on the revolutionary movement. The people of Bengal supported these revolutionaries. Both the educated and the illiterate wanted the revolutionaries to succeed. Some judges expressed this solidarity in their verdicts on political matters. Before I left for the Andamans, there was a case presented to Sir Ashutosh where four young men were charged with bomb-making. Mr Ashutosh charged one of the four and let off the other three. Later, he said that had he acquitted all four, the government would have appealed, and then all four would have been sentenced. That is why he had convicted one of the accused. There were other judges who displayed their empathy in a similar fashion. Even Bengalis working in government jobs were sympathetic to the revolutionary cause. In fact, the English monthly *Hindu Review* carried an article which said, 'The government employees also rejoice at every terrorist act of the revolutionaries.'

And then Mahatma Gandhi launched the non-violent struggle, which dealt a big blow to the revolutionary movement. In Gandhi's Satyagraha model, the biggest achievement was being sent to jail. There is no doubt that India's mass movement gained momentum and reached its peak under the leadership of the Mahatma. It gave people the courage and desire to oppose the British government. The day

Mahatma Gandhi decided to participate in the struggle for Indian independence, it became accepted that to participate in the national movement entailed going to jail, enduring hardships and giving all your time to the welfare of the nation. Before this, it was only the revolutionary groups that demanded daring, selfless sacrifice and complete dedication in the service of the country. Among the leaders of the mass movement, before Mahatma Gandhi appeared on the national scene, there were two types of mindsets. One group lacked confidence and only knew how to plead with the government. They believed that nothing would be achieved by threats or disobedience, and they did not trust or rely on the masses. They were known as the liberals.

The other set of leaders held the opposite view. They strongly believed that no nation in the world had been able to gain freedom by begging for it. Therefore, they wanted the movement to follow a path that demanded valour, sacrifice and intelligence. These leaders were known as extremists in our country. They had expressed their objective of a free India with such clarity, and in such heartfelt and touching words, that their vision appealed to everybody and made the youth of India impatient for a chance to sacrifice their lives for the liberation of the country. It was this objective that had led to the establishment of the revolutionary movement, which, in 40 years of unspeakable pain, has not been silenced but could never turn into a mass movement. When at last the mass movement in India under the leadership of Tilak, Aurobindo, Lajpat and Bipin Chandra was moving swiftly along the path of a revolution, Aurobindo suddenly left politics. Tilak languished in jail for six years, Lajpat went abroad and Bipin Chandra was alone and weakened.

It was in such a situation that Mahatma Gandhi appeared

on the political horizon. A new current of rebellion now coursed through the veins of the people. And with him came other strong leaders of the national movement in India. These leaders had not been heard of till then. What was Babu Rajendra Prasad's identity before he joined Mahatma Gandhi? Who knew Pandit Jawaharlal in 1919? In those days, Subhas Chandra Bose was just a student abroad. Motilal Nehru was counted as soft even amongst the liberals. When Tilak came to Allahabad, people would think of ways to prevent his being accorded a rousing welcome. With Gandhi's rise in national politics, on one hand, the feeling of rebellion started to take root with the common people, and on the other hand, there was also rise of a group of new leaders. The rise of such leaders even with the clout that Mahatma Gandhi enjoyed is important.

To participate in the revolutionary movement meant either to be hanged or to be sentenced for life to the Cellular Jail in the Andamans, which was as good as being buried alive. There aren't many men willing to bear such misery. But participating in Mahatma Gandhi's movement meant only a bit of hardship and a bit of sacrifice. That is why a large number of people participated in his Satyagraha. However, some young men like me did not understand how his movement could gain complete independence for India. We did not understand how we would capture political power if large numbers of people went to jail. And that is why we had decided that it was imperative to prepare for an armed rebellion. However, Mahatma Gandhi's Non-Cooperation Movement was very strong at that time, and most of the young men were participating in it. Gandhi had declared that we would achieve self-rule within a year. But a revolutionary movement requires extensive preparations and there are two important requisites—one is a political awareness in the masses and the second is an ambience where the revolutionaries are not under constant government surveillance over a long enough period of time so that they can prepare. If people went to jail in large numbers but without doing anything to inspire rebellion among the Indian soldiers in the British forces, then what good would going to jail do! And it would not suffice to merely inspire feelings of rebellion. A large-scale uprising requires a lot of planned organization. Who will organize and when? Keeping all these things in mind, I preferred to continue to work with the Labour Association in Jamshedpur while Mahatma Gandhi's Non-Cooperation Movement was at its peak.

The first cycle of the Satyagraha movement came to an end when Mahatma Gandhi's Bardoli programme was put off and he was arrested. I wanted to leave the Labour Association and start work on the revolutionary movement before Mahatma Gandhi's arrest. As I have mentioned before, I sent in my resignation twice to the office bearers of the union, but they rejected it. They did not want me to dissociate from the Association. However, I did not insist on leaving the Association till Gandhi was arrested. After this, I decided that it was imperative to not waste any more time and pick up the threads for resuming a revolutionary movement. I realized that work of the Labour Association was also important, but as far as I was concerned, the need of the hour was to organize an armed revolution. My understanding was that the labour movement too could be a part of a country-wide armed revolutionary movement, but the nation was not going to be liberated through a labour movement alone.

Looking at the situation in Bengal, I concluded that I would have to work alone in North India, that is, in the United Provinces and Punjab. Then, for the third time, I sent my resignation to the office bearers of the Labour Association in Jamshedpur and insisted that it be accepted because it was imperative for me to go to the United Provinces. This time they yielded to my insistence and accepted my resignation. I left Jamshedpur and went to Allahabad. That is the day I actually began work anew for the revolution in North India, and it was the beginning of a new chapter in my life.

Chapter 8

REORGANIZING THE REVOLUTIONARY GROUP (1)

I left Jamshedpur and went to Allahabad in 1921. I was already married by then. The day I left for Banaras for my wedding, certain old companions of mine had made comments insinuating that in getting married, I was being derelict in my duty to the greater cause. Their cruel words had hurt me tremendously. When I came back from Jamshedpur, I looked for them. The people who had taken over the work of the revolutionary group in the United Provinces after the Banaras Conspiracy were also the ones who had raised objections to my marriage. Yet their unkind words had also given me a ray of hope—that I would find people for my work when I began it. They joined me when I asked them to work with me on my return from Jamshedpur. No representative of the Dhaka Anushilan Samiti had so far come to the United Provinces.

Within a month of having returned from the Andamans, I had come to Banaras from Gorakhpur and searched for my old companions. It was then that I met and spoke to a couple of them, Mr Suresh Chandra Bhattacharya and Mr Priya Nath Bhattacharya, about resurrecting the party. I was not aware then that Priya Nath had given a long statement to the police. I have already mentioned that the conversation I had with Suresh within a month of my return from the Andamans had already reached the police. The chief of the secret service in the United Provinces wrote a semi-official letter to my brother, telling him that I was talking of restarting the organization and that I should be warned. At the time, my brother and the chief's wife both happened to be in the Oxford Hostel in Allahabad. My brother was doing his master's. I think Mr Biden's wife was either an undergraduate or a post-graduate at the university; I cannot be sure. In 1921–22, Mr Biden must have been the A2DIG, CID. The A2DIG is the chief of the political cell of the secret service. The day the revolutionaries seize all the papers of the secret service is when it will be known who the first to begin work on the reorganization of the revolutionary groups after the World War in the United Provinces was. As far as I remember, it was I.

After the Congress session in Nagpur in 1920, I had travelled to Agra, Allahabad, Banaras, Lucknow and other places with Mr Pratul Chandra Ganguly, an important leader of the Dhaka Anushilan Samiti. The Samiti had, even then, not sent a single representative to the United Provinces, but I had started putting together people, two at a time, in the United Provinces. And just as Pratul Ganguly did not confide in me, I too did not confide in him. And, therefore, it is possible that he thought I had not started any revolutionary work in the region.

While working for the Labour Association in Jamshedpur, I was also trying to arrange finances for restarting the work of the revolution. A couple of people who were disillusioned with the Dhaka Anushilan Samiti had approached me, but they did not seem resolute. When I left Jamshedpur for Allahabad, I had managed to collect some money for the movement. It was my good fortune that many rich people contributed to my cause in North India. I met with important Congress leaders in Allahabad. I got to know many party workers as well. I went to various hostels and tried to meet the youth. A couple of Congress leaders showed some interest, but it did not go beyond that.

After the Banaras Conspiracy Case, there was another case in Mainpuri. It is true that after the Banaras case, many young men were inspired to go the way of a revolution, but the Mainpuri Conspiracy had no connection with our earlier group. In Allahabad, I wanted to meet the people who had survived the Mainpuri case. After searching for a while, I got to know about one of the leaders, Mr Dev Narayan. I met him and, later, he came home for a meal. I also met him in Agra afterwards. He told me a lot of details about the Mainpuri case. A resident of Shahjahanpur, Mr Ram Prasad Bismil, was a noteworthy person in the Mainpuri case. Mr Dev Narayan told me that he and Mr Ram Prasad did not get along at all. This created a dilemma for me. I had to decide which of the two to admit in my party. I came to believe that if I took one, the other would not support me.

I told Mr Dev Narayan to move to Agra, and he accepted. He tried hard to convince me that I should now be part of an open movement rather than an underground revolutionary organization. And then he told me certain things about Ram Prasad that I am loath to repeat here. Listening to him, I was hesitant to include the other man in my group. But then I thought that if the two of them are such sworn enemies, it would not be right to take all that Mr Dev Narayan said at face value and believe him blindly. As far as an open movement was concerned, I, too, wanted that, so I accepted his suggestion. I felt good after speaking to Mr Dev Narayan. He was a serious, intelligent man. It is our country's misfortune that very few such serious and intelligent men participated in the revolutionary movement. I don't know if it was fortunate or unfortunate that Mr Dev Narayan did not fulfil his promise. It had been decided that he would leave his village and go to Agra to establish a centre there; had that happened, it would have been a proud moment for our movement.

The phrase '*Satyam bruyatpriyambruyat/Na bruyatsatyamapriyam*' (Truth, if spoken correctly, is always soft and soothing, while fabrication and lies, spoken anyhow, always end in unsettling ways) has no place in history. But I do not want to write anything that can harm the revolutionary movement. It is important to mention here that because the revolutionary movement was a secretive underground movement, there was every danger of the wrong kind of people joining it. If a revolutionary movement is not helmed by competent people, this lack of able and agile leadership may ruin the lives of many promising young men. I knew of many such small, useless and incapable revolutionary groups in Bengal. And I did not want that to happen in the United Provinces—a mushrooming of small parties headed by incapable leaders. However, when I started work in the United Provinces after coming back from the Andamans, no other group was working there.

There was a special session of the Congress in September–October 1920 in Calcutta. On this occasion, Mr B.C. Chatterjee introduced me to a freed political prisoner who had been convicted in the Mainpuri case. His name was Chandra Dhar Johri. The spark and enthusiasm I saw in his eyes that day convinced me that this man put his heart and soul into any task he undertook. To be honest, it was an almost fanatical zeal that I saw in Mr Johri, but unfortunately, I never got a chance to meet him again. I don't remember whether he was arrested in the movement of 1921 or not. It is likely that he was, and that is probably why I never met him again. The poor man had been released on certain conditions, and one of them was that if he participated in any movement against the government again, he would have to go back to jail and complete his earlier sentence. And, therefore, when Mr Johri took part in the Satyagraha, the district collector summoned him to his office and told him that since he had violated the conditions of his release, he was to be sent to jail directly to serve the rest of his sentence. This must have been in 1921, and all the hopes I had of recruiting him to help in our cause died away.

I was not a student and had never lived in Allahabad before this. Therefore, I did not know the young people in that city. In my opinion, the success of a revolutionary movement is highly dependent on the youth. I also believed that only young men from the middle class could lead the revolutionary movement. It is true that when the fight is declared, the workers and the farmers who join in will be the actual soldiers. But soldiers can't lead themselves. History is witness that often, during war or armed conflict, the army generals have become the rulers and martial rule is imposed instead of democracy. This can only be avoided if the people have the power to rule themselves. After reading the history of revolutionary movements around the world, I have concluded that the future social leaders of India shall emerge from its educated middle class.

After Mahatma Gandhi's successful movement, I was even more convinced that the Indian people were ready for a revolution, and their preparedness was inversely proportional to the availability of good and able leaders. The other thing was that Gandhi and his band of followers—that is to say, the other leaders of the movement—were not making an effort to secure complete independence for India. In fact, they thought that was just a foolish dream. They did not really believe that independence was even an issue worth talking about. These illustrious popular leaders believed that the young men who dreamt of liberating India had strayed from the path of reason and harboured delusions of grandeur. Mahatma Gandhi and his companions say, 'What is the use of shouting "Freedom! Freedom!"? What have those who shout thus achieved till date? Why don't they do what they think they can? They only make noise unnecessarily.' But the young men who wanted to bring to the mainstream the question of complete independence believed that there weren't leaders in the open movement who could do what was required to achieve this goal. This was the main difference between the revolutionaries and the Congress leaders, and this difference of opinion was the main reason that the two paths never met. Anyway, I do not wish to comment on the revolutionary path right now, and I think it is enough to say that after I came back from Jamshedpur, I only wanted to work with the youth.

There was no easy way for me to make acquaintance with the youth of Allahabad. I, therefore, started going to various hostels every day. I didn't know anybody, but when I would spy a group of two or three young men standing together, I would make my way there and stand close by. I would listen to their conversations, and if they talked about politics, I would surreptitiously join in. It is indeed sad that in all the days that I tried to overhear these conversations, I did not find a single group of young men who talked about politics, not to mention social or literary issues. Their conversations were so pathetic that it seemed insulting to even stand there, let alone listen to them. In the biggest hostels, I must have seen only a magazine or two, if any. The few youngsters who had any calibre at all would be busy with their studies or with sports. Our country saw a huge movement in 1920–21, but it did not touch a single chord in the hearts of the youth of the country.

I felt despondent. I would, in between, make trips to Banaras and Kanpur. Mr Suresh Chandra Bhattacharya worked in Kanpur at Pratap Press for some time and then in the *Vartman* office. An old colleague, Mr Surendra Nath Mukherjee, was in Banaras. Through him, I met a young man called Rajendra Nath Lahiri. There was another acquaintance who had said hurtful things when I got married. He had also started working with me. Let us call him Tarak Nath. As far as I remember, I met Mr Ram Dulare Trivedi in Kanpur through Mr Suresh, who introduced me to two other gentlemen—Mr Veerbhadra Tiwari and Mr Mannilal Awasthi. The latter, a graduate from Allahabad University, was then a principal in a national school. Rajendra Lahiri was doing his graduation. I started mingling with Congress workers in Allahabad and that is how I met two young men, Mr Banwari Lal and Mr Narendra Nath Banerjee whom the Congress men referred to as Nodu. Through Narendra Nath, I made the acquaintance of a senior person from the Thakur family in Aligarh who also joined us in our work. Through Mr Banwari Lal of Allahabad, we also found new recruits in Rae Bareilly, but it would not be prudent to mention their names. With help from the gentleman from Aligarh as well as Mannilal Awasthi, I managed to reach Fatehpur and other districts of Aligarh as well. If I remember correctly, it is thanks to him that I made the acquaintance of Mr Vishnu Sharan Dublish in Meerut. I don't remember whether it was through Mr Dublish that I met Mr Ram Dulare. However, it was Vishnu Sharan who introduced me to Mr Mahavir Tyagi. The latter gets the credit for taking me to Shahjahanpur, which led to my meeting Mr Ram Prasad Bismil and Mr Ashfaqullah Khan.

In 1922, I managed to spread my work over these eight

districts, although this task wasn't accomplished in a day. I think a representative of the Dhaka Anushilan Samiti reached Banaras towards the end of 1922. I am certain, at least, that no one from the Samiti was in the city when I had gone to Banaras in 1921 with Mr Pratul Ganguli after the Nagpur Congress session. Although Mr Ganguli knew some people who were studying in the Hindu College in Banaras, he did not introduce me to these students. My perception was that he did not wish to share information about his party with me. By 1922, my work had indeed picked up, but it was still only the skeleton of an organization that I had managed to put together. I am not sure, but I think it was in 1922 that I went to Lahore to meet Bhagat Singh. Using the methods I had employed in Allahabad, I had run into a very interesting young man in Fatehgarh. It was with his help that I met Bhagat Singh. There is a long story behind this incident which is as interesting as it is exciting.

I had gone to Calcutta two or three times before I moved to Allahabad from Jamshedpur, and several times after, I settled in Allahabad. I kept in touch with people from different revolutionary groups in Calcutta. Just as I was setting up an organization in the United Provinces, I wanted to set one up in Bengal too. Even while I had been in Jamshedpur, I had not been inattentive to this goal. I did not miss a single opportunity to recruit people for this purpose.

One day, in Calcutta, I saw a group of educated young men talking amongst themselves. I went and sat near them. It didn't take long to figure out that they were talking about politics. I slowly started to contribute to their conversation and got acquainted with them. One of the youngsters belonged to an affluent family. He had been a soldier in the British Army during the Great War and had travelled as far as Iraq and Mesopotamia. He had also been promoted in the ranks because of his abilities. When I met him, he was working at a senior post at the university and also studying at the engineering college. Through him, I met other young men in Bengal. I did not, however, mention to any member of the Dhaka Anushilan Samiti what I was doing or not doing. I had once told Mr Pratul Ganguli, leader of the Samiti, 'Listen! I don't know if I will carry on with this work in the future. If I decide to leave it all, I will give you all my resources (material and people), and if I decide to carry on then I will tell you accordingly. But you people are not willing to be open with me about working together in the future. How can we carry on like this? Cooperation is a two-way street. If you don't take me into your confidence, how can I work with you all?'

The problem I faced was that on the one hand, people from other revolutionary groups and parties considered me to be a part of Dhaka Anushilan Samiti, and on the other, the Samiti did not seem keen to work with me. A senior leader of the Samiti, Mr Ramesh Chandra Chaudhary, had once arrogantly declared, 'You people are not willing to learn anything about organization from us.' I now understood that I had to work alone. The Samiti did not want to share their information with me but did not want me to go my own way either. Their policy was to keep me in the dark and yet keep me in their group under some pretext or the other, telling me all the while that they had no objection to sharing any information with me and that I would learn everything by working with them over time. I did not like their contradictory behaviour and soon tried to avoid them as much as possible. I did not let them gauge that I was carrying on with my work.

Towards the end of 1922, I came to know that the Dhaka Anushilan Samiti had sent a representative to Banaras. Every time I went to Banaras, this gentleman, Mr Satish Chandra Singh, would come and try to talk to me. I had seen him in Calcutta quite often and knew him a bit. When I was in jail after the Banaras Conspiracy Case, Satish Chandra had come to Bihar to work there. He was not educated, and I cannot really comment on his political understanding, but he did have all the makings of a good soldier. However, a mere soldier cannot run an organization. With a heavy heart, I must admit that no revolutionary leader of the calibre of Barindra, Upendra and Hem Chandra has been seen in Bengal since their generation. The way these people led the revolutionary movement founded by Mr Aurobindo was never repeated. The leaders of the Dhaka Anushilan Samiti did not lack intelligence or courage. However, they could not understand that the revolutionary movement was a part of the national movement. The idea that forms the basis of the national movement is the construction of a new nation and a new civilization. They did not comprehend these things. The revolutionary leaders of Bengal knew very little of philosophy or history. Although they had started to read a bit while under detention, their reading was unorganized and chaotic. They would, for example, read a book by Bertrand Russell on China, but they read nothing by or on Sun Yat-Sen. They had no knowledge of the history of revolutions that had taken place in the world. Most of them showed no inclination to read and write even when they were in jail. I spent six months with many of them in Alipore Central Jail and I know them well.

An eminent leader today, Mr Manabendra Nath Roy was not considered an important figure in the movement when he used to work under the name of Narendra Nath Bhattacharya in Bengal. He was an underling to the renowned revolutionary from Bengal, Mr Jatindra Nath Mukherjee. Manabendra was talented, but that talent came to the fore only when he went to Europe and America. Jatindra Nath Mukherjee was no intellectual either, but he had astounding energy. Similarly, Rashbehari Bose was not a towering intellectual but he too had remarkable energy and charisma. Yet the prominent figures of the Dhaka Anushilan Samiti pale in comparison to the leaders of other revolutionary groups. Mr Bipin Chandra Ganguli, Mr Jadugopal Mukherjee, Mr Motilal Roy and Mr Shirish Chandra Ghosh had more pervasive influence and greater political insight.

There were many members of the Dhaka Anushilan Samiti who were far more hopeful and ingenious than the leaders of the Samiti, but they did not get an opportunity to grow or to lead. The Dhaka group did not have a programme that offered these young men the opportunity to hone their skills by contributing essays to monthly or weekly magazines and newsletters or by giving speeches from the dais. When a member had to be sent somewhere for the organization's work, the leaders of the Samiti would always send somebody who was a good foot-soldier but rather deficient from the cultural or intellectual point of view. As a result, they could never, on the basis of personality, impress and attract bright young men or renowned personalities to the cause. The reason was that the leaders of the Dhaka Anushilan Samiti did not understand that the revolutionary movement was but a small part of the larger national movement and needed to expand its boundaries in this way. Similarly, other revolutionary groups too lacked able leaders who had this broader vision; that is why they too did not fulfil their potential.

I never spoke to Mr Satish Chandra Singh about the organization of the party. If a person works with sincerity and dedication on something, he is bound to succeed. Hence,

Satish Chandra too had managed to put together a group of a few young men. The Dhaka Samiti leaders had sent him to Banaras without any consultations with me. I understood that the Samiti was looking to expand its organization in the United Provinces but did not want me in the picture. This widened the chasm that already existed between the Dhaka Samiti and me.

Around this time, I met an impressive young man, thanks to Suresh Chandra Bhattacharya. When I spoke to him, I understood that he was interested in literature. Later, I read some of his writings also. I have still not forgotten the effect that one of his essays had on me. It was titled 'Mother'. After I read the essay, I told the young man, 'You can be a pioneer amongst Hindi writers if you keep writing about literature. But you should learn in depth about English, Bengali and Hindi literature.' He did not know English at all. He used to write in *Aaj* under the pseudonym of 'Ugr' (radical). Today, I feel extremely proud that I had recognized the talent in this young man when it was nascent, for he has achieved a prominent place in Hindi literature. I had perceived his abilities when he had but stepped into the world of letters and nobody knew him. He had written the essay 'Mother' shortly after meeting us. It is sad that because of his poor knowledge of English, our relationship did not develop into a close bond. I am also saddened by the fact that he did not later develop an interest in English literature as I had suggested. There is no doubt that his writing was immensely powerful, but it could have reached more people if he had chosen to write in English. Yet I have no hesitation in affirming that our party benefitted tremendously from his writing, and for that, we shall be forever grateful. I will talk about this in detail at an appropriate place.

I did not get an opportunity to live in Banaras after I came back from the Andamans and, therefore, I could not set up an organization there, as it should have been. I had to live in Allahabad due to personal and worldly reasons. Amongst all the people I met in Banaras after my release, Mr Rajendra Nath Lahiri and Mr Bechan Ram Sharma deserve a special mention. Apart from them, most of the others who had joined the party left later. But fortunately, none of them turned traitor. I met some people in Allahabad through the National School; one of them was Mr Banwari Lal. Amongst the Congress workers, I made the acquaintance of Mr Keshav Dev Malviya. I had known his brother, Mr Kapil Dev Malviya, for a long time, and so we were family friends in a sense. Keshav Dev had often seen me visiting his brother, and one day, he came and met me. He agreed to work with me and introduced me to many young men.

One day, Keshav Dev suggested that we speak to a notable person in Kanpur about our work. This young man was Balkrishna Sharma. Keshav insisted that he would go to Kanpur and bring Balkrishna to meet me, and he did so one morning. We had a long conversation. In the end, I presented my scheme to them. There was a chance of another war being declared, I said, and if we were prepared, we could use that opportunity to try and fight for complete independence. But my proposal did not convince them. Balkrishna said that there was no chance of a war, and that it was not yet time to plan a revolution. My hopes were dashed to the ground.

Chapter 9

REORGANIZING THE REVOLUTIONARY GROUP (2)

I was at this time corresponding with Mr Rashbehari Bose. I would keep those letters with Keshav ji. All confidential letters for me came addressed to him. The groups led by Keshav ji, Banwari Lal ji and Narendra Nath Banerjee aka Nodu were moving forward with their plans separately. These groups were not acquainted with one another. The ones in Banaras did not know the ones in Allahabad. The groups in Allahabad did not know the groups in Aligarh or Fatehpur. I have already mentioned that with Banwari Lal's help, groups had been established in Rae Bareilly and Pratapgarh. Meanwhile the Congress had a session in Gaya towards the end of 1922. At that time, about 300-odd copies of *Bandi Jeevan* had been published. I went to Gaya via Calcutta with copies of the book. In Gaya, I met some people from Punjab. I also met some of the Sikh political prisoners who had been released from the Andamans; Bhai Pyara Singh was one of them. He embraced me warmly; we caught up on all the news and then got down to brass tacks. I felt that he was no longer interested in moving forward with the revolution. I came to know that Mr S. Dange had come to Gaya from Bombay and was talking to the leaders of various revolutionary groups from Bengal. Unfortunately, I did not get a chance to meet him.

However, I had another conversation with Pratul Ganguli. When the topic of Banaras came up, I told him that Mr Satish Chandra Singh was not the kind of person who was required in Banaras. It is possible that this remark of mine led to them recalling Satish Chandra from Banaras and sending Mr Jogesh Chandra Chatterjee in his stead. It has been 16 years now, and my memory fades. I do, however, remember clearly that in Gaya, I had met Suresh Chandra Bhattacharya, Sardar Pyara Singh and others from Punjab (whose names I do not wish to disclose as they have not been arrested), and some people from Bengal. We spoke of the plan of action for the future. Obviously, we did not sit together and talk for the policy for our group was that the lesser the groups from different states and regions knew each other the better it was.

Observing my attitude in Gaya, a relative of mine suspected that I was going to do something that would once again cause trouble. This person went home and informed my family that Sachindra was up to no good. Mr Suresh Chandra Bhattacharya supported me unreservedly at the Gaya Congress and afterwards, but it would have been wrong to ask him to carry out a dacoity or to shoot somebody as he was not the kind of man to do all that. If one does not understand the capabilities as well as the inhibitions of people, it is difficult to run an organization. And this is the reason that after our arrests as well as Bhagat Singh's, our group started to break up. I knew what work Suresh Chandra and others could do and what they could not. Suresh Babu was deeply interested in literature, and he was a thoughtful, principled and idealistic young man. He was aware of the dangers of being involved in revolutionary activities, but he never faltered in his support for us. I still have a copy of one of his letters from that time. His words are proof that he was pure-hearted and a man of lofty ideals.

I rented a small house in Allahabad after I came back from Gaya. Just as I had advised Bhagat Singh, I had also instructed the organizer of the Fatehgarh group, Mr Chheda Lal, to leave home and venture out. He resigned from his job and came to Allahabad. Banwari Lal, too, arrived in the city and stayed with Chheda Lal. Workers from different districts used to come and meet me in Allahabad. I would make arrangements for their stay in Chheda Lal's house, and that is how they all slowly started to get to know each other, although they were not allowed to ask each other's names or addresses. It was around this time that I met a sanyasi through Chheda Lal. We spoke at length in that house. The sanyasi claimed to belong to the Arya Samaj. However, he had a gang and their work was dacoity. He claimed that the policy in his group was to sell everything that was looted, and divide the money equally amongst the members. The sanyasi was now trying to set up a revolutionary group wherein the purpose of distributing the money from the loot was to be equipped to help each other in crisis. After listening to him, I politely told him that we did not want to have anything to do with such an organization. I told him that our revolutionary movement prided itself on its moral principles and that we were not soldiers who worked for rewards. We went into the field ready to sacrifice everything. Our work was to create a new movement based on good character and social work. Right now, our only goal was to renounce all worldly goals and to put together a team of youngsters who were completely dedicated to the cause. When we had such a team in place throughout the country, then and only then could we think of other tasks.

What amazed me was that the sanyasi argued hotly with me, claiming that their principles were more useful and viable than ours. He wanted us to join him to put together a massive revolutionary group. I was equally amazed to find that our friend Mr Chheda Lal agreed with the sanyasi to an extent. I did not say bluntly that we could have no truck with dacoits, but I did convey to the swami that our belief systems and principles were poles apart, and, therefore, we could not work together. In the end, he seemed to come to his senses and left, saying that we would not be able to achieve anything. I bid adieu to him with a modest smile. Thereafter, I spoke to Chheda Lal, explained to him the ideals of our revolutionary group and its raison d'être and told him categorically that we could have nothing to do with dacoits. I stressed the fact that we had jumped into the fray for a lofty cause, and we should never demean it by choosing such alliances and methods.

Around the same time, I came to know that another conspiracy was going to be initiated in the United Provinces, and I was going to be dragged into it. I was very surprised. I had been working on rebuilding the organization for barely a year and a conspiracy was already in the works! I began to suspect some of the people working with me of being involved in this new operation. One of the drawbacks of working in a secret organization is that you begin to suspect your own people at the drop of a hat. I doubted the news but was apprehensive too. I decided that it was better not to stay at home in such a situation. It was too much of a risk under the circumstances. I started staying with Chheda Lal and Banwari Lal, but would try and go home to eat my meals so that party expenditure would not increase unnecessarily.

I don't remember all this very clearly, but I think that just before this I had been caught up with family responsibilities and economic demands. I remembered what Mr Sanders had said to me when I had just got back from the Andamans: if I ever needed help, I should get in touch with him, and he would do what he could for me. I wrote him a letter. He was not with the CID at the time, but had been appointed a DIG with the regular police. He replied and told me to meet him in Banaras on a particular date. In those days, I was constantly tailed by the secret police. When I went out for party work, I would manage to give them the slip, but when my outing was for any other reason, I was not bothered by the fact that they followed me. I met Mr Sanders in Banaras. He wanted to know what sort of job and salary I was interested in, and asked me to tell him if there was any specific vacancy that I was interested in. He reiterated that he would help me in any way he could. I said that I did not know of anything specific so far. He told me he would inform me through a letter if he was able to find me a post.

A few days later, I received a letter from Mr Sanders, telling me that a good job was available and that it would entail a salary of about 100 rupees. The only condition was: I would have to undertake that I would not participate in any political movement as long as I was employed there. Mr Sanders had recommended that I be placed in a good department with ample scope for promotion. I understood that this was a good opportunity, and that Mr Sanders's proposal was fair, but my conscience did not allow me to accept such a condition. I had not accepted any conditions when I had been released from my life sentence in the Cellular Jail, and therefore it did not seem right to do so now. I wrote to Mr Sanders and said, 'I will forever be grateful for the kindness and magnanimity you have demonstrated, as a true Englishman would. But I am sorry to say that when I did not accept any condition even for my release from the Andamans, it would not be right for me to do so now. If I accept a government job, it would mean accepting the rules and laws of the government. I will not be able to accept this condition.' I did not receive any reply to this letter, and I did not expect to either. When I had fled from home, taking my children with me, I still had Mr Sanders's letter with me. But when I was arrested, the letter and several other important documents and books passed through many hands and were lost to me.

I am not very sure, but I think it was when I had been staying for some days with Chheda Lal and Banwari Lal that I realized that the threat from the police was now less serious, and so I let my guard down.

I had gone to Fatehgarh with Mr Chheda Lal for party work. We had to visit several towns and villages. It was the policy in our party to recruit and incorporate determined, self-aware and principled young men. When many such individuals come together, a vast organization comes into being. One day, we had been resting on the banks of the Ganga after we finished our rounds. In some time, we started to walk around to see if there was any place where an outsider could stay. That day, men and women belonging to the 'Saadh' community of Fatehgarh had gathered in large numbers on the banks of the river. Families were passing by on laden bullock carts. They seemed to be happy and carefree. Women were in the majority and most of them did not observe the purdah. They bathed in the river without hesitation and sat on the banks and ate their meals. They sat in small groups and shared their life experiences. Once in a while, some men and women would move from one group to another. I heard that the Saadh community was quite rich and that they were mostly businessmen. At the end of the day, some of them would go back in the bullock carts and some went home walking. They seemed to be returning from some fair.

While we were walking along the river bank, we were

searching with keen eyes to see whether, in this crowd of women, children and old people, there were young men too. That is to say, I was trying to ascertain if there were any young men who were educated and who could be of use to me. Then I suddenly spied, through an open door, a young man in a room reading a book. I was excited and walked into the room right away, followed by a couple of my companions. When he saw us, the young man kept his book aside and looked at us. From his expression, I could tell that he had been completely engrossed in his book. I glanced at the book and found that it was in English. I apologized to him and told him that we couldn't stop ourselves from coming in to see a young man so absorbed in his reading. With great humility, he invited us to take a seat. He was perfectly comfortable being alone but did not seem disillusioned or unhappy with human company. I picked up the book and saw that it was the latest on Indian history by Frederick Eden Pargiter. We began talking about Indian history. In the course of the conversation, it was revealed that the young man's sister Mrs Parvati Devi had been sentenced to two years' rigorous imprisonment in the Fatehgarh Central Jail on account of a seditious speech given during the Satyagraha. He was here to meet his sister.

We learnt that he was a teacher in Lajpat Rai's National College in Lahore. His name was Jaichandra Vidyalankar. He was a graduate from Gurukul, and he had written two books on Indian history, one of which—titled *Outline of Indian History*—had won the Mangla Prasad award. Talking of his sister led the conversation to politics and Satyagraha. It came out that Dr Kichlu had opened an ashram in Amritsar. The well-known revolutionary teacher from Bengal, Mr Jyotish Chandra Ghose, had also gone to the ashram but had not maintained a relationship with them afterwards. When I heard

Jyotish Babu's name, my heart skipped a beat. Jyotish had had a long conversation with Jaichandra and other students, and I figured they must have also spoken about the revolutionary movement. I thought it was nice that someone from Bengal had set up base in Punjab before I could. Only when I heard from Jaichandra that Jyotish had lost touch with the ashram did I realize that no organization work had been done there. I spoke with Jaichandra at great length about violence and non-violence, Mahatma Gandhi's policies and the Satyagraha. When the young man came to know that I had gone to the Andamans and spent four years there, he was very interested and wanted to know more. He said he would come to Allahabad from Fatehgarh. My book *Bandi Jeevan* had already been published, but I did not have a copy with me, and I wanted Jaichandra to read it. It was decided that we would carry on our conversation at the National College, Allahabad, where we would meet.

We met in Allahabad. Jaichandra was impressed by my book, and he joined our group. He invited me to Lahore, where I was hosted at his house. During that trip, I met some young men in Lahore, one of whom was Sardar Bhagat Singh. The youngsters in Lahore were all from Rawalpindi, Gujranwala, Gurdaspur or Hoshiarpur. They were students of the distinguished 'Tilak School of Politics'. I kept talking to these young men late into the night, one by one. I initiated them to the revolutionary path by telling them the history of armed revolution, how it was impossible for India to attain freedom without an armed revolution, and how armed revolution was a certainty and a necessity.

Mr Kedar Nath Sehgal was an old acquaintance of ours in Lahore. I went to meet him as well. This man dressed in black from head to toe, every day and all year. He had vowed that he would not wear white till India had won complete independence. I met other companions of yore at Kedar Nath's place. None of them, including Kedar Nath himself, came forward to work with us again. Mr Kedar Nath told me that he was somehow related to Mr Prithvi Singh of the first Lahore Conspiracy Case. And much as I wished to meet up with the latter, unfortunately, it did not happen.

There are many things I don't recall correctly, and I think I am mixing up the sequence of events that occurred in those days. Maybe if I could look at various communications of that time, I could put them in chronological order. I was in Amritsar during the Akali Satyagraha in Nabha. I had gone there right after I had met Jaichandra. The courage I saw in the Sikhs during the Satyagraha was not matched in any other region of the country. There was firing in Nabha every day, and groups of Sikhs—farmers, labourers, students, young men, old men, people from all walks of life from all over the state—would go there to face those bullets. I saw with my own eyes the kind of martial welcome they received when they came to Amritsar, and so many sisters, mothers and wives would come and meet them. The garlands they put around the necks of these men were woven with their hopes and love and blessings. Arrangements had been made in Amritsar for rations and provisions, and there was a hospital as well where many men injured in Nabha would come for succour. Their preparation lacked nothing other than arms. These Sikhs did not have the blessings of Mahatma Gandhi, and not a single important leader of the Congress was associated with this Sikh movement. But I must say one thing: the kind of efforts the Sikhs make for their own people, for a leader from their own community, they do not make in a pan-Indian movement involving other communities.

I had many conversations with a popular Sikh leader during this time, whose name I will not mention here. It will be revealed the day India gains freedom. This leader had come to me in confidence with a proposal. He told me that the Sikh movement had reached a stage where it seemed impossible for them to continue with it. Their farming had been adversely affected, their businesses had shut down and there seemed to be no possibility of any talks or settlement with the government. It was very difficult to say what the result of the Gurudwara Movement would be. In such a situation, I felt that if there was a spate of violent agitation and terrorist attacks, the government would feel pressurized to be heavy-handed in its dealings with the national movement as a whole. I assured him that if the Congress leaders did not raise any objections, we would do as he wanted, but we did not want our actions to have a negative effect on the public movement.

Another important incident which took place at this time was that Sardar Gurmukh Singh, convicted in the Lahore Conspiracy Case, managed to flee from jail. I had first met him in the Andamans. After my release, Gurmukh Singh had been transferred to a jail on the mainland. The last I had heard was that he was being transported from one jail to another in Madras. The courage of this Sikh was extraordinary; during one of these moves, he found an opportunity to jump into the dark from a moving train even though his legs were chained. The mad, boisterous Sardar Gurmukh Singh simply disappeared into the ocean of life, and the police were befuddled. How he later managed to get rid of his chains and where he went and how, I have recounted in my book *Vichar Vinimay* (Exchange of Thoughts). I will not repeat it here. Speaking to the popular leader from Lahore, I came to know that Gurmukh Singh was in Amritsar and I went to meet him.

I reached a small house in a narrow lane near the gurudwara. There were shops on the ground floor and Sardar Gurmukh Singh lived above them. The Akali leader whom I had befriended was also with me. I had last seen Gurmukh in the Andamans in 1920. Meeting him after all this time, while he was still an absconder, was somehow satisfying. On the one hand, the might of the Empire was being used to mercilessly crush the revolutionaries, and on the other hand, they carried on enthusiastically, with determination and dedication and utmost belief in their ideals, despite the many obstacles in their path, and often despite being unknown and helpless. The other thing that must not be forgotten is that the Akali movement was an open movement and not an armed revolution. Its leaders were hardly revolutionaries. At the same time, they did not stress on non-violence. The movement was being run fearlessly, given the circumstances, and the Akali leaders did not hesitate to express their support for the other movements in the country. These leaders never criticized or made disparaging remarks about the armed revolutionaries. However, in their conference, the Akalis announced that they did not believe that the time for a revolution had arrived, and, therefore, they were advising the young men who were involved in revolutionary activities to give them up. Their bravery and their courage were commendable, the Akalis said, but the time was not right. If we compare this mindset with that of the Congress leaders, the feeling one gets is that Mahatma Gandhi and his followers considered the revolutionaries to be their enemies and that of the country.

From the platform of the Congress party, and even from the seat of the chairperson, statements were made that created a cruel and strong sense of factionalism in the country. These leaders seemed to be very bitter towards the revolutionaries. They sometimes derided the revolutionary movement as being infantile, and at other times, they would rub balm on their own wounds by referring to it as fascist. Sometimes they would say that the revolutionary movement has taken the country back 50 years or that they make martyrs out of strong, innocent men. These criticisms were not motivated by a broader contemplative strategy or a historical impulse to safeguard the welfare of the nation. It is motivated purely by a deep sense of arrogance. The Congress leaders have neither accepted the idea of complete independence for India, nor even thought about it. At a time when every colonized country in the world is impatient to gain freedom, desperate for it, and willing to sacrifice everything for it, pursuing this goal with incredible courage and determination, the popular leaders of India are bitter and disparaging towards the revolutionaries who are trying to carve a path to freedom for their countrymen to the best of their abilities simply because the latter do not acknowledge their leadership. But the Akali leaders show empathy for the revolutionaries and support rebels like Sardar Gurmukh Singh by giving him sanctuary.

There was another prominent Akali leader in Sardar Gurmukh Singh's room. They were discussing whether terrorism would benefit the Akali movement or not. I knew that our party was not yet organized completely, but I also knew that we now had the capability to assassinate a few British officers. I was also aware that the revolutionary movement would suffer terribly by falling into terrorism. I understood above all that the country could not be liberated through terrorism. But we have been forced to take recourse to terrorism in order to attract the attention and sympathy of our fellow citizens as well as the help and support of leaders of the mass movements. I have forgotten to mention this aspect in my book *Vichar Vinimay*. One of the basic reasons for the Indian revolutionary movement's adoption of terrorism as a means to achieve its goals was the fact that many rich people contributed to the cause on the condition that cruel and oppressive Britishers would be assassinated. Barindra has openly admitted to this motivation.

In Gurmukh's room, it was decided that we would attack the viceroy of India with bombs and pistols. Sardar Gurmukh Singh was also involved in setting up a group based on the Bolshevik dogma in Punjab, but this unit was not in any way equipped to carry out an attack on the viceroy. As I have mentioned earlier, I had managed to put together a small group in the United Provinces. I promised these people that I would consult Deshbandhu C.R. Das and get back to them on whether I could take responsibility for planning an attack on the viceroy or not. I told the leaders of Punjab in no uncertain terms that we were not willing to do anything that would harm the people's movement. Some revolutionaries from Bengal had promised Mahatma Gandhi that they would not create any obstacles for his work for an entire year. I had also hoped that I could interest C.R. Das and other Congress leaders like him in the revolutionary movement, and, therefore, I did not want to commit to any terrorist conspiracies against his will. I knew that a few days ago there had been talks between C.R. Das and a representative of the British government about reaching a settlement on various political matters. The Akali leader and Gurmukh Singh supported my stand.

There was a discussion on where the attack on the viceroy should take place. My readers will be astonished to learn that the Sikh movement was so widespread and intense that senior

Sikh officers were willing to support the plan in every way. A Sikh officer who was present in Gurmukh Singh's room during this discussion told me that the attack could be carried out in Shimla itself and that we could obtain information about the itinerary of the viceroy down to the last hour. I knew a little of Shimla and the many paths that led in and out of it as I had lived there for a year. Arrangements were made for me to visit Shimla.

It would not be out of place to mention another thing here. I was shown a copy of a telegram. This was a telegram that was sent from a general in the army to a military officer in Nabha. It was written in code and I was asked to decipher it. I saw that there were columns of four-digit numbers in three rows. Sikh officers had copied these coded telegrams from the post office and given it to the rebels. I explained to them that it would take months to decode something like this; moreover, it would require someone who was an expert in cryptography, and I was not. I pointed out to them that the CID had still not been able to break our codes. The Akalis told me they had arranged for a whole file related to Nabha to disappear from the viceroy's office. This is what a people's movement based on community ties can do! The Sikhs who worked for the government were willing to do anything for their people. It is not only difficult but impossible to find such a commitment to community anywhere else in India.

After the Akali leader and the Sikh officer left, I had a long chat with Gurmukh Singh about the organization. I came to know that Gurmukh had been to Russia and that he had a base and network in Kabul as well. There was a special route to Kabul from Punjab, which Gurmukh Singh had used many times. He told me that he wanted to set up an organization that was based on the principles of the Bolsheviks. In my conversation with him, I also understood that the Sikhs no longer wished wish to work with communities other than their own. That was disheartening, but I understood that the poison of communalism had spread to the revolutionary movement too. I concluded that Sardar Gurmukh Singh would not work with me.

I returned to Lahore from Amritsar. I had already made arrangements for communicating with Gurmukh in the future. I told Jaichandra everything about Gurmukh Singh, but I remember clearly that I did not tell him about the plans to attack the viceroy. Around the same time, I spoke to Bhagat Singh and came to know that his father was preparing to get him married. I had only then realized that I had made a huge mistake by entering into a marriage. I explained to Bhagat Singh that the responsibilities of domestic life would prevent him from contributing substantially to the revolutionary movement. Bhagat Singh did not want to get married. It was my practice to test new recruits to the group to see how much they were willing to sacrifice. Only those who were willing to leave home and jump into the fray wholeheartedly were considered members of the group. Accordingly, I asked Bhagat Singh, 'Are you willing to leave home? If you get married, you will not want to do this work in the future. And if you stay at home, you will have to get married. I do not want you to get married, and, therefore, you must leave home and go where I ask you to.'

He agreed to leave home. I had wanted to meet Sardar Kishan Singh (Bhagat Singh's father) because I had had some contact with him earlier. But once it was decided that Bhagat Singh was going to leave home, I decided not to meet his father. I remember meeting Sardar Kishan Singh later in a house on the outskirts of Lahore, but I don't remember now why I had met him. On my instruction, Bhagat Singh left home and went to the United Provinces. Initial arrangements for his stay were made at Munnilal Awasthi's house.

Chapter 10

MEETING MOTILAL NEHRU, JAWAHARLAL NEHRU AND C.R. DAS

I have not been able to mention a lot of things that happened in Bengal. I went to Calcutta many times after I left Jamshedpur and moved to Allahabad. In fact, I went to Calcutta many times from Allahabad as well. I am yet to narrate that part of the story.

I had gone to Bengal with news from Punjab. I remember clearly that I met Deshbandhu C.R. Das many times and spoke to him about Punjab. I don't think there is any harm in detailing that today. It would also not be wrong to talk about the conversation I had with Pandit Jawaharlal Nehru, especially since Pandit Nehru has made several observations in his autobiography (*An Autobiography*) on the revolutionary movement. I had met Pandit Motilal Nehru and Jawaharlal Nehru in Allahabad after I left Jamshedpur. At that time, Motilal Nehru was occupied with setting up the Swaraj Party, and the Delhi session of the Congress had not yet taken place. I am not sure if the annual convention in Gaya had already taken place. I had very humbly and sincerely requested Motilal Nehru to think about restructuring the Congress party along the lines of Ireland's Sinn Féin or other political organizations in Europe. In these organizations, various types of men are recruited into the party, and diverse political viewpoints and sentiments are represented at their meetings. The basic requirement is an organization of men who are motivated and willing to make personal sacrifices for the welfare of the nation.

I had many thoughts, but before I could begin to enunciate them, Pandit Motilal Nehru started to laugh at my proposal. I did not have an opportunity to explain to Pandit Motilal that before the French Revolution, a lot of political clubs had been set up, especially in Paris. He did not even pay attention to what I had to say. Whenever he found some free time during the day, he would smile, look at me and ask, 'So, Mr Sanyal, any other brilliant suggestion?' To hide my embarrassment and discomfiture, I would reply, 'Everyone here is brilliant, so what brilliance can I display?' This was the extent of my conversation with Pandit Motilal Nehru. I had long conversations with Pandit Jawaharlal Nehru over a couple of days. Had our opinions been the same, I would not write this today. In that case, he would have been an associate, and to publish an associate's views for the enemy to read would be treachery. Moreover, Pandit Jawaharlal Nehru has expressed his views on the revolutionary movement in his autobiography, and as a national leader, he has also, from time to time, issued statements on the revolutionaries. I believe that in this context, the conversation I had with Jawaharlal Nehru, too, needs to be recorded in history.

I have mentioned that I met Pandit Jawaharlal on my return from the Andamans while looking for support and help for the release of political prisoners. That was when I made his acquaintance. After I was disillusioned with Pandit Motilal, I decided to have a long and clear conversation on these matters with Jawaharlal Nehru. When I expressed my wish, Pandit Jawaharlal gave me an appointment. When I went to Anand

Bhawan at the designated time, he was having his breakfast. Just as we got talking, Pandit ji was served some fruit. He asked me, 'Will you have something?' I declined with thanks. He spoke to me while he ate. We must have spoken for at least an hour and a half. I wanted to convince him of the need for a revolutionary movement and its potential for success.

At first, when I looked at Pandit Nehru's face during our conversation, I felt as if I was a rather misguided young man, a simpleton who had lost his way. It was if Jawaharlal Nehru was doing me a favour and wasting his time by listening to me. Something along the lines of, 'This poor chap is a lost soul and he wants to say something, so one will have to give him some time. What to do … If it has to be done, might as well do it at breakfast.' But as the conversation progressed, his indifference changed to interest and he responded with the seriousness that I wanted from him. He did not hide anything from me and answered my questions openly and clearly. According to him, in these modern times, it was impossible for the people of our land to carry out an armed revolution against the British regime. I gave him the examples of Russia and Germany and pointed out that armed revolutions had taken place in these countries in modern times. Pandit Nehru tried to explain to me that a secret underground movement would not be successful because we would find very few men to participate in it, and second, the few men that we would find would invariably have amongst them spies and traitors. It would not be possible for the organization to do any work because of these informers. We would come up with secret plans, and in no time, these would be exposed, and we would simply be sacrificing our lives on the hangman's noose or in jails; we would accomplish nothing by walking this path.

I accepted that a secret mission often spawned traitors

and the organization would be sabotaged many times because of them, and that we would be sacrificing our lives too. Nonetheless, I told Pandit Nehru that I believed the organization would get up and get going again and again, and would be stronger and more widespread every time. And the loss of lives at the hangman's noose and in the Cellular Jail would only motivate more and more people to participate in the movement, moved by the spirit of sacrifice. People will not think twice about giving up their lives, bravery and determination will increase, and a revolutionary zeal will take hold of the nation. I told him that the first conspiracy had been hatched in Bengal, but seeing its result Punjab was awakened and the wave of the revolution spread to that region as well. There were innumerable conspiracy cases, but consequently, the revolutionary group was only amplified and not diminished. The more numerous the hangings and the sentences to the Cellular Jail, the more the sense of the need for a revolution intensified in the country. Hence, the movement did not break down because of the betrayals and arrests and executions; in fact, it grew bigger.

As far as informers are concerned, it was only natural that their number would increase along with our activity. Since we are working on a small scale right now, they can't harm us much; but as our work grows, they will multiply and do everything they can to harm the country. During the American war of independence, even rebel generals had turned traitor and gone over to the British side. Pandit ji had asked me, 'How will you procure arms and armaments against the British? What can you do in the face of the training that the British Army receives? Do you have that kind of military training and education?' I accepted that this was one of the challenges we faced; we needed to send our people abroad to learn the art of warfare and acquire training in factories that manufacture arms and ammunition. And this could not be done openly. It had to be managed in a secretive manner, as part of a conspiracy. I don't feel that it is appropriate to write about what I told Jawaharlal Nehru with reference to our means of procuring arms.

Pandit ji was not convinced that we could obtain weapons or ammunition to match the might of the British Army. He argued, 'Even if you manage to procure the military training, how will you establish an army to match the British Army? And even if you could manage to smuggle in rifles and bullets, what will you do to combat machine guns, armoured tanks, artillery and airplanes?' I laughed and replied that in this respect there was no nation equal to Germany in the entire modern world. Yet the people of Germany had managed to break the German empire and its military might to establish a democracy. They, too, had had to face the German generals and their troops armed with machine guns, artillery and airplanes. But in the face of a revolt by the people, the Kaiser had to flee to Holland, and Hindenburg, too, had to accept defeat. The army that had fought the combined might of France, England, Italy and America, when it sided with the revolting masses, used its military technology and prowess against the Kaiser. Therefore, however big the British Army was, whatever its strength, it would not be able to combat a rebellion in its own ranks. If the Indian platoons sided with us, all its might would not be of any use to it.

But my argument did not win. Pandit Nehru was not convinced that an armed rebellion was possible in India. In the end, he extolled the policy of non-violence (ahimsa) and said that he believed in it and that was what humanity was. He believed the country would benefit only by walking on the path shown to us by Mahatma Gandhi. I think towards the end of the conversation, my impatience was obvious. Finally, I asked Pandit Nehru questions on the policy of non-violence that were personal and had nothing to do with the policies of the revolution. But he answered all my questions patiently and was not irritated with me at all. Maybe the reason was that these questions were important for personal growth and not totally unrelated to our broader topic.

In my conversation with Pandit Nehru, we also spoke about the relationship that our secret movement would have with the open movement. According to Nehru, there could not be an awakening in the masses without creating an open movement and no movement in India could be successful without an awakened people. However, the people could not be awakened or motivated with an underground movement. I accepted his argument to a large extent. But I still insisted that an open movement and a secret underground movement should be carried out simultaneously. One would be incomplete without the other. I spoke of the recent Bengal movement, telling Pandit ji that the moderate leaders in Bengal did, in soft tones, criticize the revolutionary movement, but they also insinuated that when the open movement failed, there would be such a bloody, armed rebellion in India that the situation in Ireland would seem tame in comparison. The moderate leaders conducted their movement in Bengal in such a way that the effect of the revolutionary movement on the British government would not be diminished in any way. There is no doubt that a mass movement is crucial. In Bengal too, the mass movement had gained momentum and become intense and purposeful, and that is why the revolutionary movement had gained wings there as well. The open movement in the United Provinces, Bihar and Madras had not been significantly strong.

Therefore, I requested Pandit Nehru that the mass movement be controlled in such a way in the future as to not harm the revolutionary movement. The two movements should be complementary to each other. I thought this to be fair.

I was hurt when Pandit Nehru said that this was not possible. The reason was that the mass movement under the leadership of Mahatma Gandhi was based on the principles of non-violence, thereby making it impossible for the two movements to co-opt each other. In fact, Pandit ji believed that revolutionary movement, by its very nature, would harm the non-violent Satyagraha if the former continued. That is why he would not like the work of our movement to be placed before the public ever. I categorically told Pandit Nehru that with such a hope, he was creating hopelessness because the revolutionaries would now do as they thought fit. For when the principles were so divergent, then the practice would surely differ! All Pandit Nehru said to this was that it should not be so.

We parted with adequate affection. I met Pandit Jawaharlal Nehru a few times after this incident. I had gifted him a copy of the first part of *Bandi Jeevan*. He read it and asked others to read it too. He told me that the language of the second part should be a little easier. I had many conversations with him in the Naini Jail as well. I will talk about that when I speak of life in jail.

I met other Congress leaders in Allahabad as well. A couple of those gentlemen empathized with the revolutionary movement, but they never helped us in any practical way. Other than Pandit Jawaharlal Nehru, among the leaders of the open movement in touch with the underground movement, Deshbandhu C.R. Das is the one I had the most serious conversations with. I don't remember when I first met C.R.

Das. My endeavour was to establish contact with leaders of the open movement so that respected people would empathize with the revolutionary movement, and, if possible, to enlist their support when need arose.

After having spoken to a leader of the Gurudwara Movement about this, I realized it was imperative for me to meet C.R. Das. I needed to understand whether the attack on the viceroy would impact the open movement. I did not want its leaders to blame us for having sabotaged their movement and I also wanted to ask C.R. Das for some financial assistance for the revolutionary movement. So I met him and spoke to him in absolute privacy.

Some of the revolutionaries from Bengal were already acquainted with Deshbandhu C.R. Das, but I was not. Reading Mr Subhas Chandra Bose's book, I found out that Mahatma Gandhi had met some revolutionaries from Bengal in 1921 through Deshbandhu, who had also been present at the meeting. These revolutionaries had promised the Mahatma that they would ensure that their activities would not pose an obstacle for his programme and that they would also contribute to the Congress movement to make it a success. As far as I knew, there was no representative of the Dhaka Anushilan Samiti at this meeting, and I guessed that those who attended from other revolutionary groups in Bengal probably did not take me into confidence because they thought me to be a member of the Samiti. I was at this time working with the Labour Association in Jamshedpur. As I have mentioned earlier, the Dhaka Anushilan Samiti, with support from the rivals of C.R. Das, opposed the Satyagraha. I was given this information by members of other groups in Bengal.

I decided to get acquainted with Deshbandhu Das on my return from Punjab. He already knew of me. My brother used to send applications for the release of political prisoners along with the letters that I wrote from the Andamans to all senior leaders of the national movement. Only C.R. Das and Akhil Chandra Niyogi had answered his pleas. The first time I personally met Deshbandhu was at the Nagpur session of the Congress. Some people at the convention believed that if he was to leave law and join politics, the ambience would change drastically. I was one of these people. However, Mr C.R. Das did not believe that even if he went into national politics, the people of Bengal would respond positively. He was not sure that they would quit their jobs and colleges. Amongst those who publicly urged C.R. Das to engage with national politics full-time at the Nagpur session were a lawyer from Bengal—Mr Girija Prasanna Sanyal—and I. At the time, there was tension between Mr Das and Mahatma Gandhi. Therefore, those who spoke in favour of Mr Das were not looked upon favourably by Gandhi.

It turned out that I was the only Bengali who had stood up in an open convention and spoken for the release of political prisoners. Moreover, I had spoken (and spoken well) in Hindi. Later, I heard that C.R. Das had expressed an interest in recruiting me to the labour division of the Bengal Congress. Unfortunately, I was stuck in Kalna with my brick business at the time and, therefore, could not fulfil my desire to work with Deshbandhu Das. Above all this, an important fact was that I used to write an essay titled 'Bandi Jeevan' for the monthly magazine *Narayan*, which was edited by C.R. Das. I had heard that he paid special attention to this essay. I knew this from Mr Hemant Kumar Das, who was a close confidante of Deshbandhu. After the Nagpur convention, Deshbandhu Das had invited some party workers for a meal. I was also included in this invitation. This is how I met him, and when

I expressed a wish to speak to him privately, he readily agreed.

I spoke to Mr C.R. Das two or three times. As far as I remember, the first conversation I had with him was the most significant, and we spoke about Punjab among other topics. When I reached his house, he greeted me with affection and took me to a room where we could speak privately. To begin with, I told him that it was well known that he magnanimously helped even those he disagreed with. I said that he probably did not agree with my principles, but I had worked up the courage to ask him for some help. Then I apprised Deshbandhu of my secret plan. I told him about the Akali leader from Punjab, and said that if he felt an attack on the viceroy would not harm the open movement and if he did not have any objection to it, we would like to carry out that attack. If he felt that this would damage the movement, then we would not undertake it. If we undertook this mission, our representative would go to Punjab and sacrifice himself for the Sikh cause, thereby winning the hearts of the Sikhs. Then our man would stand in court after the assassination of the viceroy, and in a demonstration of empathy with the Punjabis, say: 'When you try to use the might of your Empire to crush our national movement, it is for us to demonstrate that force cannot crush a national movement. Englishmen, if you think that the Sikhs are alone and do not have the support of the rest of India, then you are mistaken. It is to rid you of this illusion and prove to you that the Akalis are not alone that I have given my life.' Mr C.R. Das heard me out and became thoughtful. 'Give me till tomorrow morning,' he said. 'I will think about this and give you my reply. Meet me tomorrow.'

The Sikh leaders had also mentioned something other than the conspiracy to assassinate the viceroy. I shared this with Mr Das as well. The Sikhs told me that the British wanted to somehow incorporate Kashmir in British India and then declare it their colony. They were preparing to post a large number of British platoons in Kashmir. The Sikh leaders wanted to know how a movement could be started against this ploy. I told them that I would take no action without consulting Deshbandhu Das. They, too, wanted to apprise Mr Das of the Kashmir issue. Mr Das did not give much attention to this issue, however, and I don't remember now what he said to me about it. The next day, I reached his house in a state of great excitement. C.R. Das said to me, 'I did not sleep a wink. I thought about your question all day and night, and I concluded that it would not be right to mount an attack on the viceroy at present. On the other hand, in the event of my arrest, you people can carry out the mission.'

I understood everything that he was saying. What could I say in reply? I knew that working in politics meant you have to take advantage of all kinds of people. I was expecting financial help from Mr C.R. Das. Moreover, our organization was still nascent, and I did not want to get involved in something that would give the government a reason to focus on destroying us. Keeping this in mind, I conveyed my decision to the leaders of Punjab. They, too, had to bow to the circumstances.

I don't remember clearly if I had requested Deshbandhu Das for help while talking about the Punjab situation or after it. As far as I remember, I had spoken to him about this before my agreement with the Dhaka Anushilan Samiti. As far as financial assistance was concerned, Mr C.R. Das told me to find an avenue that he could help me through. After some thought, he told me that if we had somebody in Bada Bazaar, he would contribute to our cause in the form of a monthly salary for that person. He could also work for the Congress at the provincial committee level. Mr Das knew that

I was operating in the United Provinces and he must have wanted an acquaintance of mine to work for the Congress. The Congress workers in the bazaar were hardcore followers of Mahatma Gandhi; C.R. Das possibly wanted me to help him find somebody who was an influential man in Bada Bazaar and would be loyal to him. I introduced him to such a person. Mr Das promised to give me 300 rupees a month.

Unfortunately, I opposed C.R. Das over something in a pamphlet at the Gaya Congress. Mr Das had criticized the revolutionary movement from his position as chairman of the convention. He said, 'Had I been convinced that the revolutionary movement could succeed, I, too, would have participated in an armed revolution. I do not believe for a moment that the revolutionary movement can at all be successful and that is why I do not contribute to it.' To be political is to know if a movement is going to be successful or not before it is apparent. In my pamphlet, I wrote that the day people understood that the revolutionary movement was going to be successful, it would not matter to us if people like C.R. Das were with us or not. It is our duty to oppose even the biggest leaders when it comes to safeguarding our principles. We can all work together in the field, but as revolutionaries, we had vowed that there could be no compromise on principles. So, when Deshbandhu C.R. Das criticized the revolutionary movement from the seat of the chairperson of the session, we, too, were bound to respond to him. Sadly, this response annoyed him, and he refused to meet me again when I requested a meeting.

I think this falling out with Deshbandhu Das happened when I was in Calcutta after fleeing from the United Provinces. I realize now that I had turned an ally into an opponent because I was immature and did not yet understand the ways of the world. After my arrest, at the Bengal State Political Conference, there was criticism of the government's having sent thousands of young men to jail without trial. On that occasion, Mr Das had said in an open meeting that all political prisoners were not innocent, and, therefore, it would not be prudent or fair to demand everyone's release. There was strong disapproval of Mr Das's statement at the state conference. Despite the opposition, Mr Das had publicly asked if everyone believed that Sachindra Nath was innocent. There was a lot of altercation in the meeting about this statement, and Deshbandhu Das went on to say: '*if Sachindra Nath was indeed not innocent, then why were disclosures not made about it?*'

It is possible that he made these comments on the basis of information obtained from the secret service of the British government, which should have been shared, but since the others had no such information, they were not willing to back Mr Das and condemn me. Members of all parties spoke on my behalf against Mr Das. This is a good example of the mindset of our most distinguished leaders. The revolutionary movement was principally an underground movement. It was as easy to criticize it from the platform of an open movement as it was difficult for the revolutionaries to answer the criticism. They had to work undercover. All the great leaders of our nation have criticized the revolutionary movement. And if any revolutionary has tried to respond, they have tried their best to cut him down to size. There is one exception to this attitude, and that is Mahatma Gandhi. Gandhi had criticized the revolutionaries at the Belgaum Congress. I had written a riposte, and the Mahatma had published it on 12 February 1925, without any changes, in *Young India.* He had also printed his comment at the end. My heart is filled with respect for him even today.

I had once come to Calcutta for some work and got into a huge argument with Mr C.R. Das. There was another person in the room when this conversation took place. I think he was Ashwini Kumar Dutta's brother or nephew. I don't recall this incident very clearly, but what I do remember is that Mr Das got very agitated and was replying to me loudly and in sharp, derogatory language. Needless to say, agitation does not pay heed to logic. In the end, this other gentleman could not take it anymore and even he argued on my behalf with Mr Das. I distinctly remember one of my own rejoinders on that occasion. Deshbandhu Das was arguing vehemently in favour of non-violence, and, in the end, he said that mental strength was superior to physical strength, accusing the revolutionaries of focussing more on the latter. To this I had replied, 'You are misunderstanding us. You think to fire a pistol or a rifle only requires physical strength. You are forgetting that it takes more than that to pull a trigger. A wrestler, too, can fire a gun, but that does not make him a revolutionary. Can a person be part of a revolutionary movement without mental strength? A young man has less physical strength than a professional wrestler, but he will easily take up arms in a rebellion whereas a wrestler will not. Why do you attribute only physical strength to the act of pulling a trigger?'

Similarly, I remember another exchange we had in reference to financial aid. The debate was about how a revolutionary movement can be successful. When I had answered all his questions well, in the end, Mr Das had asked me, 'Very well, suppose everything else falls into place, how will you take the common man into confidence? There is no provision in your plans for people's participation. No revolution can succeed without the participation of the people.' To this, I replied, 'We don't see this as a problem. Let us assume that in the factories within a 10- or 12-mile radius of Calcutta, there are at least 10 (if not 11) lakh workers. It is not difficult to get the workers to strike if we put in about three months of work. In the event of such a huge strike, the army and the police will be called in. If, in such a situation, we have an adequate number of educated soldiers and enough arms and ammunition to back the agitated workers, it will not be difficult to start a revolution. Don't you think the people will support us in such circumstances?' I remember that he had no reply to this.

It would not be out of place to recount another such episode. Deshbandhu Das was so impressed and influenced by his conversations with me that, in an open meeting, he had warned the British government that they were making a huge mistake if they thought the revolutionary movement had been snuffed out. This movement was so serious and so widespread, he declared, that if the government ignored the will of the people, it would repent for it. This statement prompted the Bengal government to send a superintendent of the secret service, Mr Bhupendra Chatterjee, to meet Mr Das. The government wanted to know what the basis for the statement was and whether the situation was as tricky and delicate as it had been in 1915–16. Mr Chatterjee troubled Mr C.R. Das with many questions for a long time. I met Mr Das once after his meeting with Bhupendra Chatterjee, and he had recounted it all to me. All of Calcutta was talking about the government being made anxious by Deshbandhu's statement.

When Mr Das had made this statement, I had just reached an accord with the Dhaka Samiti. The leaders of the Samiti did not like my association with C.R. Das. According to them, his statement had alerted the government, and this would cause obstacles for us. I did not agree with them. I believed that this endorsement had strengthened the revolutionary movement and would help us; it was evidence of how the revolutionary movement was leaving its impact on the national movement. But the leaders of the Dhaka Anushilan Samiti did not accept my point of view.

Chapter 11

THE EXPANSION OF THE PARTY IN NORTH INDIA

I had to continuously tour the states of the United Provinces and Punjab for the work of the movement. And when I felt that I could leave the work in these states to other people, I took my family and, as a fugitive, went off to Calcutta. By then, the work towards a revolution had progressed considerably in Punjab and the United Provinces. Here, I will try and describe the expansion of the party in the region to the best of my ability.

I established 20–25 insurgency centres in the United Provinces and Punjab around the beginning of 1923. That year, I participated in the special session of the Congress in Delhi. I had no truck with the Dhaka Anushilan Samiti till then. After the Delhi convention, I named my organization 'Hindustan Republic Association' and formulated its aims and objectives. I had resources to figure out the laws.

While working for the labour movement in Jamshedpur, I was also engaged in collecting funds for the revolutionary movement. A rich gentleman had, luckily for me, promised to give 150 rupees every month to the cause. Even after my arrest, this great man continued to contribute the amount regularly. We could manage our railway expenditure, for instance, with this money. None of us had been involved in dacoity in

Punjab or the United Provinces before we made our pact with the Dhaka Anushilan Samiti. The gentleman who gave us a monthly contribution never asked us for accounts. We all worked together on trust. There were other people who helped us similarly.

Once, I was staying at Mr Vishnu Sharan Dublish's place at the Vaishya Orphanage in Meerut. Mr Dublish was the president of the orphanage. I was sitting under a tree on a charpoy one day when Thakur Todar Singh of Aligarh came to visit. He did not know me. There were a couple of copies of *Bandi Jeevan: A Life in Chains* lying on the charpoy. Mr Todar Singh picked up a copy and praised the author. Mr Dublish had already told me that Thakur Todar Singh was a rich landlord and a good man. He had also warned me to not introduce myself during his visit as it was possible that he may not be sympathetic to the revolutionary movement. Mr Dublish had gone inside the house for some work, and I sat outside on the charpoy talking to Todar Singh. When he asked about me, I introduced myself. I had figured that it would not be difficult to enlist his support for the cause. But Mr Dublish did not like this, and later, he made fun of me, saying: 'The moment Thakur Todar Singh said he would bow before the author of *Bandi Jeevan: A Life in Chains*, our dear Mr Sanyal jumped up and said here I am!' Even today, Mr Dublish likes to make fun of me over this incident, but it is not true that I had straightaway introduced myself to Todar Singh. While talking to him, I had realized that, with a little pressure, one could get him to contribute to the movement, and that is why I revealed my identity when he asked for an introduction. He invited me to a meal at his place and eventually agreed to employ one of my men as a teacher in a school he owned on a monthly salary of 40 rupees. It must be mentioned that Thakur Todar Singh was not favourably inclined to the revolutionary movement; he was an ardent follower of Mahatma Gandhi. But we had managed to secure financial aid from him. Unfortunately, the man I sent to Thakur Todar Singh's school did not work with us for long. After some months at the school, he left the revolutionary path. It was this man who had made harsh comments to me in Banaras on the occasion of my wedding. Thankfully, he informed me through a brief letter that he was leaving the revolutionary movement because he did not find himself fit for it. This happened before September 1923, and, therefore, we did not get much help from Thakur Todar Singh after all.

I must mention another incident from Meerut. This, too, happened before we had formed an alliance with the Dhaka Anushilan Samiti. I was to go to Lahore via Meerut. There were a few 500-rupee notes and some change in my wallet. I took out two 10-rupee notes and put the wallet in the upper pocket of my coat. I went to buy a ticket and there were only three or four men in the queue ahead of me, but when they left, there was some pushing and shoving for some reason. I did not understand that this was a ploy that pickpockets employed. I learnt about it later in the jail. When somebody pushes you, your attention is riveted on that person, and that is when the pickpocket strikes. When I finally reached the window after all the pushing and shoving and asked for a ticket to Lahore, the clerk at the window told me that there was still time for the train and tickets would only be sold later. I turned away, and while trying to put the notes back in my wallet, realized that it was missing. I was aghast; I lost my nerve and did not know what to do next.

I must have exclaimed that my wallet was missing because someone suggested that I should inform the police. If I was to go to the police, what name would I give them? If I gave them my real name and told them that I was staying at the Vaishya Orphanage, the police would later be able to connect Mr Dublish to me. Nonetheless, I went to the railway police station and a head constable quickly came with me to the ticket window. He asked the people standing around about who had been there, which tonga had gone where and whether anyone recognized the miscreants. We went back to the police station, and the policemen wanted to know whether they should write a report. They asked me where I was staying in Meerut, and I told them I was staying at the Vaishya Orphanage, but I also said that it was futile to write the report as I was unlikely to get the wallet back. I also told them that there were 500-rupee notes in the wallet, and if I got the money back, I would give half of it in reward. I did not file a report and came back to the ticket window, feeling like a fool. How was I going to go back? It was so difficult to manage funds!

After some contemplation, I thought it right to go back to Mr Dublish's place. I was even apprehensive that he and other companions of mine would suspect that I had defrauded them of the money. That would be catastrophic. But the other members of my group did not know where I got this money from. There were only two people other than me who knew about it. One, of course, was the person who gave it and the other was the person who sometimes delivered such contributions to me. There was nobody else who could question me about the money, and if I didn't talk about it none would know that I had lost the wallet. Even so, I was embarrassed and scared.

When I got back Mr Dublish came to me, laughed and asked what had happened. I had missed the train. I told him to pay the tonga driver and I then told him the whole tale. I narrated my tale of woe, and instead of becoming angry and disbelieving me, Mr Dublish felt sorry for me. He asked me to stay the night and he would arrange for some money. He also gave me a vest that had a pocket on the inside. The next day, he got me 200 rupees. Since that day, I have never kept my wallet in a coat or shirt pocket. This was the second time I had lost money to a pickpocket. The first time was at the Howrah station.

I would like to mention here another gentleman I met in Meerut. His name was Chaudhary Vijay Pal Singh. He had a lot of empathy for us but never managed to find an opportunity to help us. I had borrowed a book *The Soviet Constitution* from him. Before September 1923, I had tried to understand communism and the constitution of the Soviet Union by reading about it. To return to my narrative, I eventually developed a close friendship with Mr Dublish. His house was in the village of Mawana in the Meerut district. He insisted that I accompany him home on one of his trips, and said Hastinapur was very close to Mawana and a place worth visiting. Which Indian would not get excited at the idea of seeing Hastinapur? Indraprastha, Hastinapur and Delhi are three names woven together in the history of India. However, I have a very bad habit. When I go somewhere for work, I don't do anything else. This is a drawback. It is a flaw to not be able to see things in a wider perspective. I got so involved in my work in the United Provinces that I could not get away to Mawana for more than two days. I have still not been to Hastinapur. Some of my companions have visited the place, but I have not managed to find the time.

I have been to Meerut many times, and with Mr Dublish's help, I had managed to find a few more people in the city.

However, because of my arrest, the organization in Meerut could not establish itself. A member of the Arya Samaj used to visit the orphanage often. After some conversations, he agreed to work with us. He used to travel to Punjab frequently. But sadly, in my absence, this gentleman did not do any work. I was to go to Punjab from Meerut. After losing my money, I put it off. But it was inevitable; I finally went there via Banaras and Allahabad.

In Lahore, I used to stay at Professor Jaichandra Vidyalankar's house. This time, too, I stayed there. I don't remember whether it was on this visit or an earlier one that I found out Sardar Gurmukh Singh and others were setting up a separate organization and no longer wanted the Sikhs to get together with non-Sikhs to participate in the Indian revolutionary movement. In fact, Sardar Gurmukh Singh wanted our worthy companion Sardar Bhagat Singh to leave us and join them. Gurmukh Singh tried his best to convince Bhagat Singh not to get involved with Bengalis because that would only get him the hangman's noose and nothing else. But Bhagat Singh did not leave us. Whatever Gurmukh Singh said, he would relay it to us. I too kept meeting Gurmukh. He gave me a copy of the rules and regulations of his organization. From this I learnt that their organization was based on the Russian communist principles. I remember that I had several conversations about communism with Gurmukh Singh. But then, he wasn't a full-fledged Marxist because he was not convinced about materialism. If I'm not mistaken, I think he told me that there was no need to copy Russia's political system in its entirety.

A gentleman named Sardar Santosh Singh had just returned from Russia when I had gone to Punjab. He was detained in his village at that time, but I did find out that Santosh Singh was, in fact, the director, legislator and founder of Gurmukh

Singh's organization. I had started reading up on communism long before this, but I still did not understand it completely. My understanding improved a great deal after my conversations with Gurmukh Singh and then reading Vijay Pal Singh's book. I spoke to Jaichandra about Gurmukh Singh's organization, and we discussed whether and how the principles of communism should be included in our organization. Jaichandra also did not know much about communism at that time. However, we had slowly started thinking about this ideology. A revolutionary of an earlier generation from Bengal who was settled abroad, Mr Narendra Nath Bhattacharya, used to send articles to India on European communism. We managed to lay our hands on the weekly journal *Vanguard of Indian Independence* that he published, and we learnt more about this political philosophy.

We had been exposed to Russian communist principles through this trip to Punjab, and we also got to know young men from as far as Rawalpindi. This was mainly because of the teacher Jaichandra. Had he stayed on with our movement till the end, he would have probably earned greater fame and respect for participating in the national political movement than he did for his research in history. It is our misfortune that Jaichandra left the arena of nation-building and limited himself to historical research. Indeed, a professor in Paris, on reading an essay by Lenin, had said that Lenin would have made a good professor. Jaichandra is possibly content with the name he has earned in history, but I still regret his loss. I believe if he and other people like him had participated actively in the revolutionary movement, it would have influenced Indian polity very strongly.

The credit for the foundation of the revolutionary movement in Punjab goes to Jaichandra Vidyalankar because, alone, I would not have been able to achieve so much in such a short time. It is thanks to Jaichandra that I met the students from the Tilak School, a set of people whom I could send on extremely difficult missions to rough places. I don't think it would be wrong to speak here of a couple of important efforts the revolutionaries made at that time. As far as I know, I don't think any revolutionary group has dared to plan such operations, although Sardar Gurmukh Singh's group accomplished theirs successfully.

I have forgotten the name of the person who sent us to the area of Gilgit and Jamrud on the Kashmir border, not far from Peshawar. The idea was to integrate the Indian revolutionary movement from the outside through the borders. This person had spent many days near Gilgit under extremely difficult conditions. Through him, we found out that merchants from both India and China passed through Gilgit, though under very strict observation. One had to carry rations that would last for months to travel on that path. It was not impossible to arrange the import of arms and ammunition through this route if both money and brains were optimally used. At a time when we were contemplating ways of smuggling weapons into India from abroad in large quantities, this path seemed ideal. Had I not been arrested soon after that operation, I am sure the revolutionary movement would have taken a completely different trajectory. We had also inspected the route from Peshawar, and I am sure the British government is aware that it is not only natural but also possible for revolutionaries from abroad to come through the Peshawar route.

A special session of the Congress was held in Delhi in September 1923. All kinds of people would come from all the states on such occasions, and that is why the interstate organization of the Congress had progressed so well in the country. During the special convention in Delhi, I met and spoke to a professor from Karachi, Mr Gidwani; Mr Qureshi (former editor of Mahatma Gandhi's *Young India*); Mr Narayan Subbarao Hardikar from Maharashtra; Mr Yusuf Imam, a barrister from Mirzapur; Mr Shatrughan Singh, the diwan of Bundelkhand; and others. Professor Gidwani wanted to know to what extent Deshbandhu C.R. Das was involved with the revolutionary movement. I wanted to know what Mr Gidwani's views on the revolutionary movement were. After talking to him, I was convinced that Mr Gidwani did not believe in ahimsa as a principle. He did not have concrete views on violence or nonviolence as a policy. At the time, he was teaching at the National College. He was respected amongst the youth of his state and a vehement opposer of Deshbandhu Das. Professor Gidwani had once come to Nabha with Pandit Jawaharlal Nehru in connection with the Akali movement. They had been released a few days after their arrest and neither of them came back to Nabha to participate in the Satyagraha there.

The employees of the steam navigation companies of East Bengal and the Assam–Bengal railway workers had gone on strike. Mr Deshbandhu did not have much of a role in orchestrating these strikes, but once they began, he did everything he could to help them. The strikes were very successful.

As I have mentioned earlier, I spoke to Pandit Nehru before attending the Delhi session of the Congress. I had to take the place of Dr Ansari at the Delhi Congress and I met Pandit ji there. He was happy to see me and took me to a separate room to introduce me to Mr Qureshi. I noticed that these leaders were curious about the underground movement. Mr Qureshi seemed very serene to me. Although he was alert and interested, he did not speak much. I met him next when

I was in the witness box as an accused in the Kakori case and Mr Qureshi was amongst the onlookers.

The founder of the Hindustani Seva Dal, Dr Hardikar, was in America at one point, and he met some people from the Indian revolutionary movement there. One of them was Pingle. The readers of *A Life in Captivity* are, of course, very familiar with this name. After the failure of the Punjab revolution, when Rashbehari was picking up the threads and restarting work in Banaras, he had received a communication from Mr Hardikar. I was aware of this, and that is why I was keen to meet him at the Delhi Congress. Unfortunately, I did not feel content after meeting him. I realized that he wanted to leave his old ways of thinking. From 1916 till today (that is, 1926), Mr Hardikar has been serving the nation in his own way. He is a generous, intelligent and serious man. But if we were to compare the work done in 23 years by such a sagacious person to that of Sardar Bhagat Singh or Mr Jatindra Nath Das or Mr Suryakant Sen of the Chittagong Armory case and many other revolutionaries from Bengal, could we say that Mr Hardikar's influence on the national movement was more than that of the revolutionary movement? Mr Hardikar did not wish to establish an underground group or do it clandestinely. He wanted us to set up a massive army of volunteers with the help of the Congress leaders and under the auspices of the Congress, taking advantage of its reach. Today, he is also trying to do that, but he has not been successful.

The Indian revolutionary movement has never depended on Congress leadership. In fact, it has been the other way around, and the revolutionary movement has had a strong influence on the Congress movement. One could say that it was the revolutionary movement that impelled the Congress to make significant changes in its goals. When the sons of

India were travelling abroad and risking their lives to call for complete independence for India, when Mr M.N. Chatterjee, Mr Abdullah, Mr Mahindra Pratap and Rashbehari were working with all their heart and soul towards achieving India's freedom, the Congress leaders were merely aiming at provincial self-rule. The revolutionaries had tried to ensure that the Congress called for complete independence and made that its chief objective numerous times, but they failed every time. So many young men sacrificed their lives at the gallows, fighting for India's independence. Years passed; countless conspiracies were hatched and then exposed. In those years, there was no month that went by in which a political conspiracy case wasn't tried in some state or the other. Around 2,000 (or maybe 3,000) young men were jailed by the British without a trial for a term of five years or ten years. Did this have no effect on the leaders of the Congress?

In December 1929, the British government sent out a message for the revolutionaries through a manifesto. On the one hand, there were improvements in the laws of governance in India, on the other, draconian laws were made, based on the Rowlatt Committee's sedition report, to keep India securely within the clutches of the British. These laws were formulated mainly with the aim of crushing the Indian revolutionary movement. Mahatma Gandhi, when he first entered national consciousness, had begun his movement against these draconian laws. As a result, the revolutionary movement was not crushed. Mahatma Gandhi's movement also grew. Gandhi's Satyagraha began to protest the Rowlatt Act. Yet, as I have pointed out, the Congress's highest goal was to achieve provincial self-rule. At the Congress session in Ahmedabad, the revolutionaries tried their level best to change the Congress's demand, but Mahatma Gandhi won by a large majority. But in the end, the Congress did change its demand. So, would it be wrong to say that the revolutionary movement had a strong influence on the Congress movement?

We had a lot of exchanges with Mr Yusuf Imam of Mirzapur and Diwan Shatrughan Singh from Bundelkhand. We understood each other, but the sad fact is that in my absence, nobody contacted them for any work. Today, while communalism is spreading like wildfire, Yusuf Bhai remains a true nationalist. Both Mr Yusuf Imam and Diwan Shatrughan Singh participated wholeheartedly in the Congress movement. Like true patriots, they continue to serve the nation.

It is indeed unfortunate and sad that the leaders of the revolutionary movement did not get an opportunity to participate in the open movement. For this reason, perhaps the revolutionary movement did not influence the national movement as much as it should have done. This was one of my main motivations for wanting to participate in the open movement after my release from the Andamans. I had made an appeal to my countrymen at the Delhi session of the Congress for an Asian federation of oppressed sections of society, keeping in mind the objective of complete independence for India. This programme also called for setting up a volunteer organization of generous, determined patriots who understood the problems of the country. I had spelt out my programme clearly and made the appeal succinctly and in decorous English. Professor Jitendra Lal Banerjee is a well-known and powerful writer in English, and when he read the appeal, he wanted to know who had written it. Mr Bipin Chandra Ganguli, the well-known revolutionary leader, was with me. He told Mr Banerjee my name. I went with Mr Ganguli to get Mr Banerjee's signature on the appeal. I was at the Delhi session as a delegate, and my name was at the very end of this appeal. As far as I remember, Mr Bipin Chandra Ganguli's signature was at the very top. Many of the All India Congress Committee members had signed the appeal. This document was our first step towards creating an open movement. I was also hopeful that we could manage some funding through contacts made at the Delhi session. There can be no movement without money. Mr Ganguli was completely in favour, and he said that he wanted such a movement, but it would be difficult to procure the funds. He promised me that in all matters, other than that of money, he would help and support me completely.

I had also gone to Mr Subhas Chandra Bose with my appeal. He read it very seriously. I had quite a few debates on this subject with him. According to him, it was not yet time to start a campaign that diverged from the Congress campaign. He also said that it was not right for one person to be involved in an open movement as well as an underground movement. This was the first time I had spoken to Subhas Babu about the revolutionary movement. I wanted him to lead our movement. I had no objection to anybody else taking over the leadership of the group. In fact, if I could have convinced Subhas Babu to take over, I would have been the happiest person. I tried to explain all this to him, and he heard me out, but he did not give me a firm reply. All he kept saying was that it wasn't his time yet. In the end, it was decided that I should meet him again in Calcutta, and I did. I will talk about this meeting later. Ultimately, Subhas Babu did not sign my appeal.

I had also approached the leaders of the famous revolutionary group from Bengal, the Dhaka Anushilan Samiti. I had so far not been able to sort out my tangled relationship with the Samiti, and, therefore, I was not expecting its leaders to sign my appeal. I explained my objective in a few words, and they were hesitant. I, too, did not insist. Seeing their hesitation, I laconically told them not to sign if they didn't want to. My indifference got them thinking. They asked me to wait while they conferred with each other. A little later, some of them signed the appeal as representatives of the Samiti. I believed that the revolutionary leaders should participate in political programmes in an open manner. Mr Bipin Chandra Ganguli understood the importance of this, but the leaders of the Anushilan Samiti did not agree.

I had approached Deshbandhu with my appeal too. He looked at it and laughed, and asked why the programme did not include the issue of the entry of Congressmen into the legislative councils. I told him that we were all in favour of the programme for council entry, and if he agreed with what we had written, we could include that in the appeal. I knew that Mr Das would not sign. At that time, he was focussed only on one thing, and that was the council entry. Nothing else mattered to him.

A strange incident occurred which benefitted me. I did not have the money to get my appeal printed. A few of my companions were also staying in the Dharamshala (traditional inn) where I was lodged. I wrote the appeal in consultation with them, sitting in this very inn. One of them handed me a bundle of notes and said they had been found in such and such room. We decided that if we found the person to whom this money belonged, then we would return it, else we would use it for our work. I hoped that no one would come for the money and spent every moment of my stay fearing that someone would turn up. Fortunately, no one claimed the money, nor was there any talk in the inn about money being lost. The bundle contained 75 rupees. The appeal was printed at the Arya Samaj press in Delhi. The press charged us extra because of the paucity of time. But at least they printed it; no other press would have.

We tried to distribute the pamphlets in the Congress pavilion, but the volunteers there did not allow it. We managed to reach the head of the volunteers, Sardar Asaf Ali, with help from Mr Jitendra Lal Banerjee. Mr Asaf Ali promised us that he would get the volunteers to help distribute the appeal pamphlets. We had printed about 5,000 copies. We kept 300 with us and gave the rest to Mr Asaf Ali. We were later disappointed to find out that not a single copy had been distributed.

I had also sent copies of the appeal to various Indian newspapers, but not one of them printed it. I sent a few copies to Rashbehari in Japan and Mr Tarak Nath Das in America as well. A well-known paper in America, *The New Republic,* printed the appeal word for word along with a write-up by Mr Tarak Nath on the importance of the document. Rashbehari Bose sent me a copy of the newspaper from Japan. A copy of the appeal had also been sent to Mahatma Gandhi's *Young India.* This appeal generated no discussion in India.

We were taken aback by something that the novelist Mr Sarat Chandra Chatterjee said. Like us, he, too, was not a blind follower of Mahatma Gandhi. Actually, the majority of people in Bengal did not idolize Mahatma Gandhi, but we were thrilled when Mr Chatterjee's Samiti joined ours. Speaking of Mahatma Gandhi, he told us that the Satyagraha in Bardoli was not called off because of the violence in Chauri Chaura but because the farmers had already paid the ground rent for the year to the government. In fact, according to reports, the farmers in Bardoli had taken all their removable belongings out of their huts. A subdivisional officer in Gujarat had informed Mahatma Gandhi of this development, and the latter had sent one of his trusted people to Bardoli. He had also confirmed the SDO's report. This had left Mahatma Gandhi with no choice but to call off the Bardoli Satyagraha.

It is imperative to mention here two important events that occurred in the Delhi session of the Congress with regard to the revolutionary movement.

I had become well acquainted with Mr Purushottam Das Tandon of Allahabad before the Congress session. Mr Tandon was aware that we were involved in a secret underground movement. He was empathetic to our cause, although he was a conservative in his political views. But we never managed to use his support constructively. The Delhi Congress passed a resolution to the effect that Congressmen could become members of the legislative councils and participate in their proceedings. At the time, Mahatma Gandhi had distanced himself from political life because his Satyagraha had failed and all the effort had gone waste. There is always despondency when a movement fails. People were filled with hopelessness and had become low-spirited, all the more because the Mahatma had retreated from politics. Other leaders helmed the national movement during these days. When the movement once again picked up momentum, Mahatma Gandhi reappeared on the scene. Gandhi was against council participation at the time of the 1921 Satyagraha. Deshbandhu Das, Pandit Motilal Nehru and Lala Lajpat Rai were in favour of it. Pandit Jawaharlal Nehru, Mr Purushottam Tandon and others were against it.

The Das faction won the debate in the Delhi Congress. I had then put it to Mr Tandon that it was time to try and change the larger political goal of the Congress. He agreed with me. As far as I remember, Mr Rajendra Prasad had also supported Mr Tandon's proposal in the open session. Mr

Tandon proposed that it was time to change the Congress's demand from the British government. My name was mentioned as a supporter of this proposal. Before I could get a chance to speak, Maulana Abul Kalam had, for some time, ceded the chair of President to Mr Das. I was secretly happy about this opportunity. Unfortunately, Maulana Mohmmad Ali stood up to speak, and he spoke for an hour and a half or maybe two. Mr Das did not want to interrupt him. I did not get a chance to speak.

Mr Tandon was in favour of the demand for complete independence. But I am not aware of any efforts he made in his life towards achieving this aim. In the session that followed the Delhi session, he did not campaign for a change in the Congress's objectives. Yet, his position on violence and non-violence was no different from the principles of the revolutionaries or those of Mr Aurobindo and Lokmanya Tilak. Mr Tilak tried to link his philosophical beliefs to logic and Indian philosophy by writing *Gita Rahasya*. Mr Aurobindo spoke about his political and philosophical ideas for years in daily and weekly newsletters. There was a wave of armed revolution in the entire country and especially in Bengal. Like the Akali Sikhs, Aurobindo never condemned the revolutionary movement. In the open movement, he never bowed to the beliefs of the big leaders as far as the debate on violence and non-violence was concerned.

Deshbandhu Das also stuck to his beliefs like Tilak and Aurobindo, till a few days before his death. When Mr Ernest Day was erroneously shot down, having been mistaken for the Bengal police commissioner Tegart, the Bengal State Congress Committee passed a resolution in praise and appreciation of the revolutionary Gopi Mohan Saha. Mr Das was actively involved in the passing of this resolution. Mahatma

Gandhi was livid over this development, and, because of his disapproval, another proposal was brought forth in the All India Congress Committee that opposed the resolution of the Bengal State Committee. However, Mr Das stood resolute. Notwithstanding the fact that Mahatma Gandhi gained more votes, there was a large number of votes in favour of the resolution passed earlier that felicitated Gopi Mohan Saha. The Mahatma had won by the force of his personality, but he said that so many votes in favour of Mr Das proved that belief in ahimsa was still not strong. What is surprising is that the resolution in praise of Sardar Bhagat Singh was passed in the Karachi Congress on consultation with Mahatma Gandhi and with his help. What is even more surprising is that before going abroad for the Round Table Conference, the All India Congress Committee in Bombay passed a new resolution against the one that was passed in Karachi which had praised Bhagat Singh. The Karachi resolution was withdrawn. Therefore, whenever questions were raised on the Congress policy on violence and non-violence, Mr Tandon never spoke against Mahatma Gandhi.

In his personal life, Mr Tandon is a great and generous man. He was the managing director of a bank when Lala Lajpat Rai passed away. Lala Lajpat Rai had been the president of the Lok Sevak Sangh. On Mahatma Gandhi's urging, Mr Tandon quit his post at the bank and took over the responsibility of the Lok Sevak Sangh. In 1921, during the Satyagraha, he quit law and had to face a lot of economic hardship, but he never asked for help. Much before Mahatma Gandhi had come into the national movement, Mr Tandon followed the policy of ahimsa in his personal life. In Allahabad, he used to wear canvas shoes to court. After a lot of debate, it was he who had raised the question of complete independence during the Delhi session.

He always had a soft spot for the revolutionary movement. It is our misfortune that Mr Tandon did not actively participate in the movement.

I am writing about the distinguished leaders of the national movement so that my readers can understand their thought process. It is difficult to say what form the Indian revolutionary movement will take in the future, but there is no doubt that that historians will have to analyse the various aspects of the Indian national movement. I believe and hope that the history I record here will help the historians in the future. That is my motivation for writing this book.

Today, the Congress has accepted that complete independence is our aim, but there have been many debates over the years, and we must always remember that the first effort for establishing this objective as the ultimate goal of the national movement was made in the Delhi session.

Chapter 12

REVOLUTIONARY GROUP AND COMMUNISTS

I want to mention another important event here. Around this time, I met a person in Delhi who must have been about 30 years of age. His name was Qutbuddin Ahmad. He introduced himself and told me that he was Mr Manvendra Nath Roy's man. I was thrilled to know this. Qutbuddin said warmly, 'I have been wanting to meet you for a long time. Manvendra Roy has called you to Moscow. An International Communist Congress is to be held there. Roy Sahib wants you to be there. I have come to Delhi to especially meet you.' I said, 'I am not all that familiar with communism.' Qutbuddin said, 'I have been instructed to explain everything to you.'

I had already learnt much about communism, but Qutbuddin's offer was a bonus. I had a long conversation with him. It is from him that I first grasped the importance of the basic tenets of this worldview. This was an important milestone in my life.

Qutbuddin explained to me that communism was based on the tenet of creating a world where property was not in private hands but controlled by society. As soon as I heard this, I thought of the *sanyasa ashram* in the Hindu tradition, and I said that the achievement of this goal depended on the final evolution of humankind. Without the ultimate evolution of man, would property ever belong to the society and not stay in individual hands? Qutbuddin said that a social structure could be created through a revolution that would transfer property from individual ownership to be held in common by society, and the eventual progress of all mankind was possible through education. This was a completely new concept for me. I was left astounded for a while and I felt that maybe Qutbuddin was right. For a moment I wondered about the sanyasa ashram and wondered if it was possible to achieve in such a natural and easy way through communism what for Hinduism is the definitive journey and evolution of a lifetime? But this was just a fleeting doubt. Soon, I understood that after a revolution of the kind that Qutbuddin described, humankind would be able to reach what in the Hindu tradition is the final destination. I wanted to learn more about this ideology. I took another appointment with Qutbuddin, met him and had a long conversation about communism.

We spoke at length in Queen's Garden in Delhi.[37] Qutbuddin tried to give me a historical perspective from the ancient times till today. He drew on the ideas of H.G. Wells about the matriarchal societies of the past, in which life was driven by the wishes and decisions of women. Men were acquiescent to women in those communities and the women ruled. According to Qutbuddin, the rules and laws of society are not eternal—they depend on the needs and desires of whomsoever is in power and controls the strings of governance. Hence, the progress of the society also depended on the powers that be. Only if the people in power wish it can all men prosper and a just society be established. An individual can prosper only if they have the support of those in power. If we wait for individual progress, then society will come to a standstill. The basic cause for all the misery in the world today is that all avenues for wealth creation are concentrated in a few hands; societies run on their whims and desires. They control political power too. On the one hand there is affluence, and on the other, countless people are crying out in distress and being crushed by poverty. Even in democracies, where everyone is equal in theory, the capitalists have a free rein, and the rich manage to buy votes with their money. A true democracy can only come into being when there is no difference between rich and poor. This inequality can only be eradicated when wealth does not rest in individual hands but is held in common. This can only be achieved by a revolution and in no other way. There is no just society without economic equality.

I listened to everything Qutbuddin said serenely and with attention. I had read so many histories of revolutionary movements and so many accounts of societal change, but I had not yet learnt to look at history from the economic viewpoint. I was amazed and fascinated by the economic principles of communism that Qutbuddin explained to me. I was ashamed and embarrassed that I had not been aware of these basic principles that underpin the world. We debated for hours on questions of history and the strange movement of economics, and from there we moved on to materialism, non-duality and theology. I was as thrilled to have met and spoken to Qutbuddin as I was astounded and impressed by the new ideology that I had been introduced to. So, now I was faced with a new dilemma in life. Earlier in my life, I had been dealing with the conundrum of knowledge versus action in theology. Then I wrestled restlessly with the question of violence and non-violence and had to face a lot of hardships when there was a severe clash between Gandhi's path of Satyagraha and the path of armed revolution. And now, in the end, I was drowning in these new concepts of materialism, the economic analysis of history in communism and the latest political and philosophical conception of the state apparatus. This created a unique problem for me.

I could not disprove the noble principle in the idea that wealth should not be in individual hands but held in common by society. But when I spoke to Qutbuddin in Delhi, I did not understand true wealth is control over the means of generating wealth. For the first time, I felt that I was not capable of being a follower of this prodigious ideology. The idea of becoming a communist evoked images of a sanyasi for me, and I did not think myself apt for it. I also could not accept that all development in society could be dependent on the economic structure. When I tried to explain the basics of theology to Qutbuddin, he accepted that they had value from the philosophical point of view and they may be useful too, but these philosophical musings were immaterial to our discussion because of communism's anti-religion attitude. Today, when I remember all this, I wonder if Qutbuddin was, in fact, not so familiar with theology. Or maybe, seeing my strong leanings towards theology, he had shown his tolerance towards philosophy so that he could reel me in towards his way of thinking, trying to show me that philosophy and religion were two different things.

I had to concede to a large extent the truth in Qutbuddin's statement that religion had been responsible for a lot of injustice in the world. But I was not willing to accept to any degree the notion that religion in itself was not virtuous just because it had been used to perpetrate injustices. It is neither logical nor historically accurate to say that because it has been misused, religion cannot be used for any good. And it is not logical to analyse history through a purely economic perspective. In short, I was exposed to a new inspiration when I came in touch with communism. But the principles of communism had elements that I did not accept then, and after a long time of studying them in detail, am unable to embrace even now. I do not think of materialism as the ultimate truth from the point of view of logic, philosophy and human consciousness. No comprehensive new ideology can be born through such a principle alone.

The special Congress session in Delhi was important for the revolutionary movement. The first attempt to change the objective of the Congress was made in this session. Communism had a strong influence on politics in North India. The advent of this worldview was a very important development in the history of the Indian revolutionary movement. However, the communists did not have any organization in India till the Delhi session of the Congress. Even in the Kanpur Bolshevik Conspiracy Case in 1924, hardly any people were involved. There was no political group in those days which was as organized and widespread as our revolutionary network in India. A group based on the principles of communism was being set up under the leadership of Sardar Gurmukh Singh and Sardar Santosh Singh, but their efforts were limited to Punjab. Communism did not seem to have any influence on the other revolutionary groups in Bengal. In the history of the Indian revolutionary movement, the group that I had set up in northern India was the first to accept certain tenets of this ideology.

There were aspects of this worldview that we had not accepted, not because we did not understand them, but because we did not find them practical and resourceful. In hindsight, recent developments in the modern history of Europe seem to prove our decision right. Those who are eager to accept an ideology from the previous century, unchanged, without thinking of the contexts of space and time that we inhabit, forget that communism has not been able to triumph in Europe and America even after decades of effort and dissemination of ideas and that the European communists have had to change some of their policies. Today, the slogans call for a united front rather than struggle. It is important to note that progressive groups in England, France and America have refused to collaborate with the communists. The efforts of the communists to establish a United Front in Europe have failed.

I went to Kanpur from Delhi via Agra and Mathura. In Kanpur, I stayed with a gentleman named Mr Satyabhakt. He is a well-known writer in Hindi. I was very keen to learn more about the principles of communism from him, as he wanted to establish a group based on the ideology in the United Provinces. One of the basic tenets of communism is that success can only be achieved through a revolution. While we were revolutionaries in practice, Mr Satyabhakt did not want to tread on the path of a revolution. However, he had good books on communism, which I read. My understanding of this ideology was helped tremendously by a book titled *The ABC of Communism*, written by Nikolai Bukharin and Evgenii Preobazhensky. Among the books and material that I read, the ones worth mentioning are Vladimir Lenin's *The Proletarian Revolution* and *The State and Revolution*, 'From Utopia to Science' and the Fourth and Sixth Reports of the World Congress of the Communist International. I also got the opportunity to read several newsletters edited by Manvendra Rai. Thus, by 1924, my understanding of the principles of communism had grown. I had many conversations and debates with Mr Satyabhakt. We discussed, dissected and criticized materialism, subjectivism and the materialist interpretation of history and the class struggle.

After my conversation with Sardar Gurmukh Singh of Punjab, I felt it was important to prepare a written manifesto for my group. I got to work on it as soon as I reached Kanpur. It is important to write in detail about this because there are various perceptions in India about the revolutionary movement. Many prominent and distinguished leaders take this revolutionary movement very lightly. As for the Indian people, they perceive the revolution as nothing more than the intermittent shooting of British officers or policemen and the collection of money through dacoities in rich people's homes. Our countrymen have not understood till today that the effort to liberate India through a revolution is based on a logical and historical perspective. The reason for this misunderstanding is that, in truth, most Indians don't want to do anything to free the country. No Indian leader has the mindset of Giuseppe Mazzini, Giuseppe Maria Garibaldi, Eamon de Valera and other revolutionary leaders of Europe. Otherwise, they would have been able to understand the revolutionary movement. Second, the revolutionaries never propagated their ideology among the people. They did not try to attract the masses to their cause by participating in a public movement and giving fiery motivational speeches.

It was during my stay at the Andamans that I realized that the revolutionary movement in India needed to create a literature that could only come into being if the educated section of society participated in it. But unfortunately for India, people with an intellectual or literary bent of mind did not participate in the movement and, therefore, it did not produce the literature it should have. For a revolution to succeed, it is of primary importance to set down in writing its goals and ideals in the form of political literature that has the power to motivate. The Indian revolutionary movement was sadly deficient in this respect. It has been 20 years since the last Satyagraha and there has been no literature in the interim. What we have produced in terms of writings is only 1 per cent of what movements in Europe, America or China have produced. The numerous books, booklets and magazines which have been published on the communist movement have created a revolution in the world. In many monarchies, a single booklet by a communist is considered more lethal than a machine gun. Yet, biographies were written in Bengali in the latter half of the nineteenth century of Mazzini, Garibaldi and other European revolutionaries. There is no equivalent today to the literature written at the beginning of the twentieth century by Bankim, Rabindranath, Navin Chandra, Sarat Chandra and others. There had been a burst of production in the historical disquisition and scientific research, in poetry and in art—that is to say, in every sphere of national consciousness. When the first conspiracy case was tried in the Calcutta High Court, the judges were informed that the language of the *Jugantar* newspaper was so pristine that it was impossible to translate it. The power of Milton's verse, the lustre in Burke's style, the elegance of Marley's language—it was as if all these qualities came together in the language used in *Jugantar*. There is nothing equivalent in Hindi.

During Napoleon's time, Germany was severely divided. In a hundred miles, you could travel through 30 independent regions. One attack by Napoleon gave rise to nationalism. German literature too had demonstrated a great awakening then. In contrast, the discussion and writing on the national movement in India has been disappointing, to say the least. There has been no literature other than the autobiographies of

Mahatma Gandhi and Pandit Jawaharlal Nehru, not to mention a couple of books by Subhas Chandra Bose. This state of affairs is rather dismal. These thoughts had ingrained themselves in my mind while I was in the Cellular Jail. I still regret the fact that I could not produce some of this literature myself. The problem was that I was so involved with working towards a revolution that I could not find the opportunity or leisure to turn my efforts in this direction.

I wanted to write an exhaustive account of the usefulness and necessity of the revolutionary movement. I wanted to reply to every denunciation ever published of our movement, calling it a futile activity by insignificant and indiscreet people. Unfortunately, to write such an account demands a lot of time, which I do not have. If I sit down to write such a book, then the work of the organization suffers, and if I am devoted to the work of the organization, then I have no time left to write. The revolutionary group working in India during Rashbehari's time did not have any manifesto. The Indian revolutionary group in the United States and Canada was known as the Ghadar Party. All the parties in Bengal had different names. As I have mentioned before, I named the group that I had established 'Hindustan Republican Association'. And I did manage to write the manifesto for my group even in the circumstances I have just described. I think that this manifesto has an importance in the history of the Indian revolutionary movement. It is now in the hands of the police. But the decision in the Kakori Conspiracy Case cited several excerpts from the manifesto.

I will try and provide an introduction to this manifesto by citing some portions here, and my readers can see the strong principles and ideology that the Indian revolutionary movement was based on. The aims, resources and structure of the organization are mentioned below:

NAME

The group shall be called 'The Hindustan Republican Association'.

AIMS

The stated objective of the HRA is the establishment of a Federal Republic of the United States of India by means of an organized and armed revolution. The provisions and the form of this democracy will be announced by the representatives of the people when they are able to practically implement their objectives. The democratic federation will be based on universal suffrage and will work towards abolition of all systems which make any kind of exploitation of man by man possible.

ORGANIZATION

Governing Committee: The group will be governed by a central committee. The central committee will have a representative from every province of India. All decisions will be unanimous. The committee will have complete powers. The central committee will be informed of all the tasks in various provinces. The main task of the committee will be to coordinate the work in the provinces and ensure that it is carried out within the guidelines of the group. All tasks carried out abroad will be conducted under the aegis of this central committee.

Provincial Organization: There will be a working committee comprising five representatives of the five departments in each province. The committee will be responsible for all tasks. All decisions of the committee will be unanimous.

The Five Departments:

1. Publicity work
2. Mass contact
3. Financial collection and terrorism
4. Acquisition and secure storage of arms and ammunition
5. Establishing contacts abroad

1. *Publicity Work*
    a) Through public and secret newsletters and pamphlets
    b) Through personal dialogues
    c) Through public meetings
    d) Disseminating our message in an organized manner at religious gatherings
    e) Through magic lantern shows

2. *Mass Contact*: Will be carried out by the district in-charge
3. *Funds*: These will be collected through voluntary contributions, but force can be used when required. The group will be duty-bound to appropriately avenge the extreme oppression caused by the foreign government.
4. *Arms*: The endeavour will be to ensure that every member of the group receives a weapon, but these arms will be kept safely in the different centres and they will be used with the discretion of the provincial committee. The arms cannot be moved without the permission and knowledge of the leader of this division and the district organizer.

5. *Foreign Division*: This division will be under the direct control and direction of the central committee.

The District Organizers and Their Duties

The district organizer will be responsible for the activities of the members of the district unit. The organizers will try their best to establish branches of the group in every part of the district. Every organizer will stay in close contact with all public programmes and organizations for successful mass contact. They will divide their teams into small groups and ensure that these groups do not know each other. As far as possible the organizers of the different districts will not be acquainted with one another. They will not follow each other's work nor acquaint themselves with the others' names or faces. No district organizer will have the right to leave his station without informing his superior.

Qualifications of District Organizers

1. Every district organizer should be capable of leading a group of people with different natures and behaviour.
2. The district organizer should be able to understand the contemporary political, social and economic problems and to understand how they affect the motherland.
3. Every district organizer should have an understanding of the Indian culture and traditions, as also knowledge of the history of India.
4. Every district organizer should be aware of the contribution that India can make to human civilization. Our ancient civilization has shown us

that it is India alone that can balance the spiritual and the material in the human condition.

5. It is imperative that the district organizers be generous and brave, as without these qualities all their abilities are pointless.

Responsibility of Provincial and Central Committees

It is incumbent on the members of these committees to ensure that all members of the organization are steeped in the ideology of the group and are competent. Otherwise, it will spell doom for the organization.

MANIFESTO

All work in the organization will be carried out on two levels, one public and the other secret.

The Public Programme

1. To honour different organizations like libraries, palaestras, volunteer groups and so on.
2. To establish an organization of farmers and workers. Competent persons from these divisions should be sent to factories, railways and coal mines so that they can influence workers and impress upon them the fact that workers are not mere tools and that the revolution will benefit the working class. The farmers must also be organized like the industrial working class.
3. Every province should publish a weekly magazine or newsletter and propagate ideas of democracy and freedom.
4. Booklets should be published to spread awareness of what is happening in countries abroad and the

ideologies that dominate the political discourse there.

5. Our organization should hold sway over the Congress and other public organizations, and take advantage of it.

The Underground Programme

1. A secret printing press should be set up to publish material that cannot be made public.
2. Arrangements should be made to distribute such literature.
3. Branches of the organization should be established in all districts across the country.
4. Funds are to be collected in every way possible.
5. People who can handle arms and ammunitions and lead an army should be sent abroad for training in military and scientific fields.
6. Attempts are to be made to acquire arms from abroad and to manufacture them in the country as well.
7. Close contact should be maintained with Indian revolutionaries abroad, and work should be carried out in coordination with them.
8. Recruitment of our members into the British Army must be ensured.
9. Acts of revenge must be committed on and off to attract the masses' empathy for our cause.

About the Members

1. Members will devote all their time to the organization and be ready to sacrifice their lives if required. Only such members will be recruited by the district organizers of all provinces.

2. All members will obey the orders of the district organizer.
3. Every member will strive to hone their skills. The success of the organization depends on how enterprising, talented and dedicated its members are. No member should forget this.
4. The conduct of each member should be above board so as to not malign the name of the organization.
5. No member of this organization can become a member of another organization without the permission of the district organizer.
6. No member will go anywhere without informing the district organizer.
7. Every member will strive to not make obvious to the public or to the police their connection with the revolutionary movement.
8. It is imperative for the members to keep in mind that their private conduct or a single mistake can destroy the organization.
9. No member will hide from the district organizer any detail of public work.
10. Treachery will result in the expulsion of the member or a death sentence. The provincial committee will have the right to decide the punishment.

If anybody was to read the guidelines and the manifesto of the Hindustan Republican Association and the Hindustan Democratic Federation, they would surely understand that it was based on the principles of democracy and socialism. This was not an imaginary movement. These brave young men of India willingly gave up the comfort of a home life, the love of parents and the affection of siblings, and all the attractions of the world to go to the gallows or spend entire lifetimes in the Cellular Jail in order to turn their goals into reality.

A revolution had taken place in Russia. The embers of communism had ignited dissatisfaction in the biggest empires and unsettled their rulers. They had touched all the shores of Europe and America, lighting fires that were growing more powerful by the day. Keeping in mind all these developments, even if we look critically at the revolutionary movement in North India, it can hardly be said that the movement was an infantile project fuelled by the madness of some short-sighted young men or the frenzied and futile activity of a few desperate volunteer workers. If the argument is that the merit of a movement cannot be judged on the basis of the high-sounding words it uses to cite its founding principles, then the only answer can be that every new ideology in the world has begun at the level of thought and language before it is realized as action and event. And here in India, the revolutionaries, in the face of extreme opposition from the world's biggest empire, have succeeded through their sacrifices in animating the dormant and despondent minds of their countrymen.

Mahatma Gandhi had no role to play in the freedom movement from the end of the Satyagraha in 1921 till 1930. During this decade, it was only the revolutionary movement that was announcing to the world, in no uncertain terms, that the young men of India were willing to sacrifice their lives for the liberation of the country. The impact of the movement on the great leaders of India is very evident when one reads the speech given in 1929 by the chairperson of the Lahore Congress, Pandit Jawaharlal Nehru. If I am not mistaken, Pandit Nehru had been bold enough to say that the youth of this country, through the revolutionary movement, had kept the national cause alive.

It may be true that all members of our organization did not understand our manifesto in its entirety. Two insights were essential to this understanding. Those who do not care for Indian culture and perceive its importance in the progress of humankind cannot understand this manifesto; those who accept communism to be impeccable and infallible have also not wholly understood it. The two are related: those who have not understood the essence of the Indian civilization cannot possibly understand the shortcomings of communism. Many will feel that communism has not been integrated in its wholeness in this document and conclude that it is because the writers of the manifesto have not understood the ideology. Just as on the one hand, Pandit Nehru has called the revolutionaries fascists, on the other hand the new Marxists criticize the manifesto because it does not mention the class struggle.

My companion Mr Manmatha Nath Gupta, for instance, belongs to the second school of critics. In many of his articles, he has remarked that while Mr Sanyal has incorporated elements of communism in the manifesto he has written for the Hindustan Republican Association, he has not understood the issue of class struggle. Mr Manmatha Nath calls himself a comrade and therefore it is only right that I address him as a comrade. Comrade Manmatha Nath believes that there is no mention of class interests or their conflict in our manifesto and, therefore, he concludes that the writer of the manifesto has no understanding of this idea.

Mr Manmatha Nath never spoke about this before the arrests happened. And that is because he did not understand the manifesto well enough. In fact, it is not possible to understand the merits of this manifesto either without understanding communism. Mr Manmatha Nath himself was not well versed in this regard, although it is possible that his understanding of this ideology may evolve in the future.

In my defence, I would like to say two things to the reader. The materialist interpretation of history plays an important part in the communist ideology, and the issue of class struggle is inherent in this interpretation. Anybody who does not accept this is not a true communist. I have read these principles with much attention and given them serious thought, but I have not been able to imbibe them. However, I had accepted that in a democratic and free India the rights and interests of the workers and farmers should be protected. History is witness that it is with help from the farmers and workers that all successful revolutions have been carried out. Therefore, in nation building after a revolution, the welfare of these classes should be looked after. But to achieve this end, it is not essential to move forward through the path of class struggle or to subscribe to the materialist interpretation of history.

When I was arrested, a small piece of paper was found on me where I had noted the drawbacks of a materialist interpretation of history. This piece of paper is an exhibit in the Kakori Conspiracy Case. I am also writing a book disproving the materialist view of history. In my book *Vichar Vinimay* (Exchange of Thoughts), in an essay titled 'Vyakti, Samaj Aur Marxvaad' ('Individual, Society and Marxism'), I have critiqued certain aspects of the materialist perspective in 23 pages. I have also requested some communist friends to write a rejoinder, but so far, no one has responded. I will also argue that certain portions of my manifesto to show that there is a consciousness of class in the document. Look at the second guideline of the public programme. It is evident that one of the primary goals of the revolution is to safeguard the interests of the farmers and workers. I do not wish to carry out here a criticism of the theory of class struggle as I have written a long essay on this subject in *Pratap*, a weekly magazine published from Kanpur. The essay is titled 'Change in the Communist Approach'. I do not think this is the right place to carry out a critique of the communist ideology in the history of the revolutionary movement; that requires a separate book. It will suffice to say that the manifesto of our organization incorporated many principles of the communist ideology, and if we rejected some tenets, it was done after much thought and deliberation.

A notable point is that even though the manifesto draws on the communist worldview and incorporates socialist principles, the name of our organization makes no reference to communism or socialism. It would be a mistake for people to assume that this was because we did not comprehend these ideologies. In fact, I had wanted to emulate Sardar Gurmukh Singh's group and append the word 'socialist' to the name of our organization, but decided not to do it on the advice of my friend, the teacher Jaichandra. Justifiably, we were apprehensive that the many rich people contributing to our cause would withdraw their patronage on encountering the term in our manifesto. After our arrests, Sardar Bhagat Singh added the word 'socialist' to the name of our organization. But no other changes were made to the manifesto. The document clearly mentions as a goal the construction of a society where exploitation of man by man will be impossible. It very clearly states that in the India of the future, all factories and industries like railways and coal mines will not be in private hands but will belong to the state. The manufacture of airplanes and ships too will be in the hands of the state. From all this, it is quite evident that communist ideas underpin many of our policies.

If one reads the second guideline of the public programme in our manifesto, there can be no doubt that class consciousness as outlined in the communist ideology is ever present in our outlook. The guideline emphasizes the importance of spreading awareness among farmers and workers in factories, railways and coal mines, and to organize them as part of the movement. I would like to draw the readers' attention to one line in particular: 'Workers are not mere tools, and the revolution will be for the benefit of the working class.' It encapsulates the communist spirit completely. Apart from this, the manifesto released by our organization mentions other priorities which make clear the communist approach: for example, the vision of a free judicial system in independent India, not to mention universal suffrage. Instead of competitive markets, we envisage co-operatives because that is the way to welfare.

At the same time, the revolutionary group is more international than national, and both traditional and modern in its outlook. It will pursue paths shown by the ancient sages of India as well as the Russian Bolsheviks of the twentieth century. It would not be out of place to mention here that some of our friends turn up their noses at the mention of ancient sages and say that it is stupidity to mention them in the same breath as modern Russia. As if universalism is the product of the Russian Bolsheviks, as if there was no concept of world unity or salvation in ancient India! Readers can decide for themselves who is stupid.

Pandit Jawaharlal Nehru's statement that Indian revolutionaries were fascists is also way off the mark. I think this is the right place to offer my criticism of the same.

Chapter 13

THE SUPPORT OF THE DHAKA ANUSHILAN SAMITI

After the special session of the Congress in Delhi, Mr Jogesh Chatterjee of the Dhaka Anushilan Samiti approached me several times on the instruction of the leaders of the Samiti and expressed a keen desire to work with me. The leaders of the Anushilan Samiti did not want me to work on my own, but neither did they want me to have the status in the Bengal revolutionary movement that I had in Punjab and the United Provinces. Around the same time, Mr Jadugopal too wanted me to work with his group. At that time, Mr Jatindra Mukherjee, Mr Narendra Nath Bhattacharya (who is today known as Manvendra Nath Roy) and Mr Jadugopal were working together. The latter asked me to stay in Calcutta and take charge of the working class there. Then I received a proposal from a well-known bookseller to take charge of his shop in Calcutta. I had accepted all the proposals, but in the end, the bookseller was hesitant to hand the shop over to me. I understood what he was feeling. He feared that I would land in trouble with my political activities and ruin his business in the bargain.

I did not go to Calcutta. A few days later, an acquaintance of mine from Dhaka, Mr Govind Chandrakar, came to meet me. We had been together in the Cellular Jail. He had to abscond while he was participating in a revolutionary task. The police had finally caught up with him and a companion of his and surrounded their house. There had been no escape for them. They had picked up arms and escaped from the place, firing at the police. The police had returned fire, and Govind and his companion had been badly wounded. But by the grace of God, Govind Babu is alive today. There is a lead bullet inside his body even now. Maybe because of that and the rigours of prison, his body shows signs of leprosy. I was very happy to meet my old friend. He told me that a senior leader of the Dhaka Anushilan Samiti, Mr Trailokya Nath Chakravarty, wanted to meet me. Govind Babu had come to Allahabad from Dhaka to take me there and told me that I would not have to bear the travel expense to and from Dhaka. I, too, was interested in meeting Trailokya Nath, and I had never been to Dhaka before this. As far as I remember, I went from Allahabad to Calcutta by train and from there to Goalundo, and then on to Narayanganj by steamer. Then I took another train from Narayanganj to Dhaka.

I would like to recount an incident that took place on the train between Calcutta and Goalundo. I was lying on one side of the berth, and there was a person on the other side. Between the two of us was a partition of about one-and-a-half feet in height. The two people on the berth could not see each other because of the partition. After a while, I saw a hand and a leg hanging over this partition. I did not like this—who would like a shoe hanging over one's body? But this was a train ride, and since it wasn't touching me or about to touch me, what could I say? In some time, there was more of the leg hanging over the partition and the hand was almost touching my head. I got very angry. I assumed this was someone in deep sleep, and with my leg managed to push the unruly limbs back to the other side. But the action was repeated. This time I sat up and saw that it was a short Japanese man who was doing all this very deliberately. I felt bad and wished I had behaved more politely. He was a foreigner and an Asian, after all. Besides, I was curious about the Japanese. The Bengali passengers were all laughing, just like me, and were also curious.

I don't remember now if that Japanese man spoke English or not. Anyway, I told him that it was night, and that he should sleep and let me sleep. I also explained that I was being courteous because he was a foreigner. The Japanese man kept laughing. We lay down and he was up to his old tricks again. His shoe was touching my body and his hand was on my head. I commented aloud to my Bengali co-passengers on how this foreigner was unabashedly teasing me. Would we be as bold when we travel abroad? When I could not get him to stop with polite requests, I gave him tit for tat. I put my leg over his dangling leg and my arm over his arm. I started to behave exactly like him. When finally I started to pull at his hair, he retreated. I suppose the Japanese man may have played this trick to see how regressive we could be. As for me, I was wondering if he would go back to Japan and badmouth us Indians.

We reached Goalundo at dawn. I had never been there before. Besides the land required for the railway line, there was only water all around; the train seemed to have stopped in the middle of the ocean. Near the spot where the train had stopped, a couple of huts were visible in the water. One was the ticket house and the other was the office of the goods storehouse. On the western railway, just as you get hot *poori*s at every other station, in Bengal, you can get Bengali sweets. At Goalundo, we got onto a steamer.

The house we stayed at in Dhaka was a place where many revolutionaries took refuge and were trying to print counterfeit currency. I was aware of this because I had earlier got into heated debates about funds with the leaders of the Anushilan Samiti, and I had maintained that we could not be successful in producing counterfeit notes while we lived in this country. If we wanted to do this, I had argued, we should go abroad and learn the art using modern technology and scientific methods. I was in favour of other kinds of violence. I was hopeful when I saw that efforts were on for printing the currency, and at the same time, I was jealous too that they might beat us all at it. But when I saw some half-done samples of the notes, I was not convinced that they would succeed. In the end, I was proved right. They did manage to print the currency, but it was useless.

I had many conversations with Mr Trailokya Nath Chakravarty. He accepted the legitimacy of my complaints against the Samiti and promised that I would not find opportunity for such discontent in the future. I was satisfied with his assurances. He is a simple and genuine person, and his actions match his words. The strength with which he had supported me in the Andamans had been exemplary, and no other leader of the Anushilan Samiti had shown the same solidarity. I felt I was now ready to work with the Samiti.

It was finally decided that my organization would work with the Dhaka Anushilan Samiti, and after the merger of the two groups, no aspect of their work would be kept from me. Mr Trailokya sent with me a letter for Mr Jogesh. It said that he was to henceforth work under Mr Sachindra Nath. I went back to the United Provinces with the letter. Jogesh was very happy when I gave him the letter. I, too, wanted an experienced worker and was very happy to have him work with me. I never found his conduct unsatisfactory in any way. He was always good-natured and would happily do whatever I asked of him. He never gave me the impression of belonging to another group. Even when I had differences of opinion with the other leaders of the Anushilan Samiti, Jogesh Babu continue to follow my directions. I trusted him implicitly and entrusted to him the entire work of the United Provinces.

The now-released Mr Rajendra Nath Lahiri was more educated than Jogesh. He was also a close friend who had been working with me for a long time. But since he was not as experienced, I saw fit to entrust the responsibility to Jogesh rather than to Rajendra. The responsibility for Punjab had been entrusted to Jaichandra Vidyalankar. I had not yet introduced Jogesh to Jaichandra or many other members of the group. However, he met those who had come to the United Provinces from Punjab for work. When I brought the letter from Mr Trailokya, I had decided that Jogesh would leave Banaras and move to Kanpur. Rajendra was in Banaras, but I did not have a trustworthy person in Kanpur.

Sardar Bhagat Singh was already settled in Kanpur at the time. He had come to the United Provinces long before I joined the Anushilan Samiti. Bhagat Singh was very capable but lacked experience. To return to my narrative, that is how Jogesh Babu and Bhagat Singh both came to be in Kanpur and got to know each other. Mr Raj Kumar, Mr Vijay Kumar and Mr Batukeshwar had not yet joined our group. Mr Suresh Chandra Bhattacharya was also in Kanpur, but he worked for our group rather half-heartedly. Work picked up in Kanpur after Mr Jogesh reached the city. I was in Allahabad; Rajendra was in Banaras; and Jogesh in Kanpur. We did not have a trusted person in Lucknow. Hence, the people in Allahabad and Kanpur were managing things in Lucknow. Slowly, I introduced Jogesh to all the workers of the United Provinces. Jogesh had a few friends in Banaras—Mr Manmatha Nath

Gupta, Mr Sachindra Nath Bakshi, Mr Pranvesh Chatterjee, and the late Chandrashekhar Azad.

When Jogesh went to Kanpur, his companions in Banaras worked under Rajendra. Till my arrest, Jogesh worked with me quite smoothly. I never suspected that he hid anything from me or that he had discriminated in any way within the group. But his companions did not behave fairly with Rajendra. I came to know of it later. Till we were both arrested, we were completely dependent on each other. It is also true that with every passing day, Jogesh felt that the movement in the United Provinces was far more successful and productive than the one in Bengal. History today has proved that the contribution of the revolutionary group in North India is far greater than that of the Dhaka Anushilan Samiti. Jogesh was so impressed with the programme in North India that he would go on fund-raising trips to Bengal and bring the money he collected to the United Provinces. As far as I remember, the leaders in Bengal did not know of this; otherwise, they would surely have taken a share.

Jogesh's conduct never gave me cause to think that he regarded me as a member of a separate group or that his own loyalties were with another group. In fact, the leaders of the Anushilan Samiti always said that Sanyal was part of their group. I would confide in Jogesh everything about the programme in North India that I did not even reveal to the leaders in Bengal. This was partly because I was working with Jogesh continuously, and it was necessary to share information with him. Second, I did not have many opportunities to meet the Bengal leaders. Third, it is true that there was a spirit of competition between our group and the Samiti. Fourth, the leaders of the Dhaka group did not share everything with me. But slowly, we were starting to understand each other, and a feeling of camaraderie was growing between us.

I wanted us to reach Russia and Western Europe through Kashmir and Kabul, with the help of the Punjab branch, to arrange for supplies of arms and ammunition via this route. I did not mention any of this to Jogesh or the other leaders of Bengal. These programmes are in the works even today. I think it would not be appropriate to go into further details, but I have mentioned this to give the reader an idea of my relationship with Jogesh. I had been very keen to find an experienced worker so that I would not have to go from one place to the other. When I found Jogesh, I was satisfied that I could stay in one place and control the revolutionary movement from there.

I had managed to lay the foundation of the revolutionary movement in Punjab and the United Provinces. Our organization was now present in every big city of the United Provinces. We had capable and reliable workers in Punjab.

I have already mentioned that I went to Kanpur from Delhi. The first Bolshevik Conspiracy Case was being tried in Kanpur. I have also mentioned that I was going to be arrested in this case. A moderate leader in the United Provinces had warned me before the prosecution began that I would most probably be arrested in this connection. Hence, I was very careful about going out. In those days, I had to roam around in Punjab and the United Provinces almost as a fugitive. A lot of revolutionary leaders were being arrested in Bengal under Regulation 3 after the special session of the Congress in Delhi. Mr Satyendra Chandra Mitra and Mr Subhas Chandra Bose were amongst them. I was already alert, and after the arrests in Bengal, I had made up my mind to flee, else I knew I would not be spared.

Chapter 14

GIVING UP HOME AND HEARTH

I have already mentioned that I got married after I returned from the Andamans. By the time I had to flee from the police, I had two children. The biggest question before me was where I should leave my wife and two children when I run away. We were four brothers, and I was the eldest. The brother next to me in age was also married and taught at St Andrew's College, Gorakhpur. He was also arrested along with me in the Banaras Conspiracy Case, and had been kept under house arrest in Gorakhpur after the court ordered his release. The third brother was not yet married and worked in the Indian Press. My mother was alive then. My mother's sister lived with her. My youngest brother was in college. My brother, the professor, was very unhappy with me. He did not want me to be part of any political activity. It did not help matters that my political views were not 'normal'. Intelligent people did not get involved in such politics, in his opinion. He, Rabindra Nath Sanyal, would angrily tell me, 'I will lose my job because of you. You are on your own trip and you refuse to listen. Don't you have any sense of responsibility towards us? If Jitendra and I lose our jobs, we won't be able to pay the house rent. You are a married man. You have children, and you are not a bit bothered about what will happen to them!'

My mother, too, would get angry with me, but I couldn't blame her. She had been widowed around the age of 32, and she had had a difficult life. I had gone to the Cellular Jail when I was 22 years of age. I had not wanted a normal domestic life when I got back. My mother had hoped that marriage would tame me, but she had been disappointed in that too. She was unhappy to see her hopes dashed and kept worrying about the future. If it was a matter of a few days, it would have been tolerable, but only one who suffers familial unhappiness all year round can understand what misery it can be. If I was to leave my wife and children with my mother and brothers and flee, I would be creating a burden for them. It would also mean that I would never meet my family again. History has shown that when absconders come back to the family after running all over the world, that is where they are caught. When I got married, I had told my brothers that I was going to devote my life to the revolutionary movement and asked them to look after my family if the need arose. It would be their way of serving the nation. If I was willing to put my life in danger, then surely my brothers could look after my family! My second brother, Jitendra Nath, happily came forward to do the needful.

After I entrusted the responsibility for the United Provinces to Jogesh, I decided to go underground. The police in the state knew me well but the Punjab police did not. Whenever I looked at my wife, I would feel guilty about having dragged someone's daughter into such a mess. If I were to flee forever, her life would be ruined. I would look at my son and think that I would be depriving him of a father's love. I found the idea of being forever bereft of the love of my brothers and the affection of my wife and children unbearable. The idea of 'forever' unsettled me. But I couldn't also take my wife and children and hide in either Punjab or the United Provinces as most of the policemen recognized me. And if I went to small towns, avoiding the big ones, I would attract a lot of attention for being a Bengali. I could not, therefore, go underground in North India with my wife and children. I had nonetheless decided to keep my children with me at all costs and, therefore, I decided to flee to Bengal. But my aim was not to run away to save my life. If I was to carry on my revolutionary activities while on the run, I would need the support of the organization. It would be easier if I lived as a fugitive but stayed away from all revolutionary and political movements while trying to simply eke out a living. But with the might of the British Empire being channelled to look for me, if I continued to carry out dangerous revolutionary activities, I would be easily tracked down.

It was, therefore, essential for me to figure out my lodging arrangements and other support systems before I went on the run with my family. I went to Bengal and made all the arrangements. I thought it might be easier for me to find refuge in the French settlement of Chandernagore near Calcutta. I spoke to a gentleman from Chandernagore, who was not a member of the Anushilan Samiti but worked for *Aatmshakti*, a Bengali weekly magazine, and was associated with the revolutionary movement. It was while I was trying to bring together many revolutionary groups in Bengal that I had met this gentleman. His name was Narendra Nath Banerjee. He was very supportive of my plan to move to Chandernagore and requested me expressly to live in his house. Meanwhile, I had requested mother to give me 1,000 or 2,000 rupees from the money my father had left behind so that I would be less burdened for some time. My mother said that I would waste the money, and so she would give me a monthly stipend instead. I agreed and told her that she would need to send me at least 25 rupees a month. She agreed. It was a difficult endeavour to live like a fugitive with a wife and children on just 25 rupees a month. But I could not depend on the revolutionary group for financial support. I had jumped into a dark ocean of uncertainty, taking my family with me.

I knew deep in my heart that sooner or later I would have to give up home and hearth. To flee implies leaving your family in the long run and being separated from them for an unknown time, hiding in God knows which hellhole to escape the clutches of the police. The thought of this separation was making me anxious day by day. We brothers were close to each other. I remember that Rabindra Nath had got a boil on his cheek when I was about five years old and I had been very upset because they had to make an incision to drain the boil. I had said that I would never allow it. I remember that my mother had tried to calm me by saying that another brother of mine studied in Calcutta and he had to regularly make such incisions but there was nothing to worry about. Another incident I remember is when, one day, a friend of my father's had picked up my youngest brother. We did not know this gentleman well and my middle brother had started shouting and pulling at my youngest brother's feet to get him down from the man's arms. These bonds of affection from childhood have prevailed till today.

When I was lying helpless in a British jail, languishing in a solitary cell for countless days, these loving brothers of mine had uncomplainingly looked after my children. Everyone is willing to share your sorrow for a short time, but there are few who would take on the responsibility of your brother's family and bear the burden for 12 or 13 years. Why would I not be anxious and unhappy to be separated from such brothers? And what can I say about the love of a mother? Whose mother is not loving? And which child does not love their mother? I was filled with sadness at the thought of being separated from such a family. I knew I would have to leave home one day, but I kept putting off the day. I had decided to take my children with me, but I did not know how to leave my poor mother. If I was not able cut off these familial ties, I would have to quit politics.

I took solace in the thought that my mother had four sons, and if one were to leave, she would still have three with her. One day my mother was staying on the banks of the Sangam during the Ardh Kumbha (known as Kalpvaas). There were saints and sages all over the riverbank. Tens of thousands of people thronged the riverbank for a glimpse of the sadhus—naked, semi naked, smeared with sandal paste, dressed in a variety of clothes, fair, dark, of all categories. I was one of these thousands. My mother would roam independently with her group, seeking blessings from various sages. It was there, on the banks of the Sangam, that I met a very serene sanyasi. Without my saying anything, he seemed to read my mind and provide me with answers to the many questions in my head. It is not important to detail that here.

A visit to this sanyasi can convince those who doubt the power of yoga, for he is still alive. His name is Paramhans Swami Jayendra Puri. These days he lives in the Shivpur Ashram near Banaras. When I was preparing to go underground, my mother had managed to reach him before I did and told him of her worries—how her son had taken to the prohibited path to serve the nation: 'He does not listen, try as I might. He had been sent off to the Cellular Jail once, but by God's grace got out in four or five years. Now he wants to do the same thing again. I have not been able to talk sense into him. You are a mahatma, and if you were to say something, he would surely listen. I am very unhappy; I am not at peace even for a minute. I am a widow and my dear son is my support.' The sanyasi told her to bring her son to him. Mother knew that I visited sages and had special warmth for them. One day, she offered to take me to a highly learned sage. I went along happily, only to find that she had taken me to the same sage that I used to go to! I was also accompanied by my wife and my son, who was little more than a year old. My mother pointed to me and said to the sanyasi, 'This is the son I told you about.' He told her that I had already visited him and he asked me to sit with him.

After a while he said to my mother, 'My child! When you have four sons, then you should give one away. If one of the four wishes to lead a life for a cause, you have no right to stop him.' Tears welled up in mother's eyes, yet she was laughing because she knew now that mine was the path of duty. I was not doing anything wrong or untoward. My mother's simultaneous feelings of sadness, anger, love and pride were transformed at once into both joy and grief with the few words uttered by the sage. She looked at me with tearful eyes and laughed, and I felt victorious and happy. My eyes turned to the great man, and without saying a word, I offered him my gratitude and surrendered to him.

The sage turned to me and said, 'Child! According to the Hindu Shastra, if you are married, you cannot undertake any course of duty without your wife's permission.' I knew this. Even if a person wishes to become an ascetic, he must not only take permission from his parents but also his life partner and other well-wishers. I replied, 'The very first time that I got a chance to talk to my wife, I had asked for her permission for what I intended to do. I am willing today to accept that if she does not permit it, I will not go down the path that I wish to.' Swami ji turned to her and asked, 'Child, do you give your husband permission to do this?' That poor young soul, trembling and smiling, with her eyes lowered, docilely nodded her head to say yes. A few tears rolled down her cheeks. The sanyasi was agitated. He laughed and said to me, 'No, my dear son! This girl is too young. Her permission while crying is not acceptable.' I told him that I would ask her again and said, 'I promise that if she does not give me her express consent, I will not take up the challenge.'

As I write about this incident, my heart swells with joy and pride. Even today, in our country, there are sages and saints who understand the blistering path that rebels like me take. And we can't be proud enough of this deep and impalpable empathy that is inherent in our society. However dangerous and difficult the path of duty may be, our sanyasis still do not shy away from acknowledging its worth and support revolutionaries like me with all their heart. A wife is so highly regarded in our society. She is not a material possession but a partner, the other half without whom, according to the Hindu tradition, a man is incomplete. A man truly comes into his own in society only when he has a wife. In a Hindu society, no auspicious act can be undertaken without the presence of the wife. Today, we forget how important a woman's status is in a society that requires a man to seek her permission to become a sanyasi. There is so much noise about women's rights in Western society. As if the rights of men and women are separate and independent of each other! In our social concept, a family is made of a man and a woman coming together as husband and wife, and that is why men and women have the same rights in our society. The word '*sahadharmini*' (wife or companion on the path of virtue) is more embracing even than the word 'comrade'. The word implies that a wife cannot possibly be a partner in crime, while a comrade can be. In Hindu society, the relationship between mother and son is deeper than in Western society. In the West, a son leaves home to live separately with his wife and children once he gets married. In the Hindu system, mother, father, brother, sister, wife and child all live together, and the family is a singular unit. Men and women are not separate entities. But this is not the place to talk about social science. I was writing about the past and got carried away by nostalgia. I hope my readers will forgive me.

The Kumbh Mela in Prayag was held in February 1924. I fled from Allahabad in June. All the people close to me were present in the house at that time—my maternal uncle, my maternal aunt, her adoptive daughter, all three of my brothers, my brother's wife and my own wife. My brother Rabindra Nath was in Allahabad, too, as he had vacations. Whenever we brothers met, the first week was invariably spent in heated debates. Mother would be screaming for us to come and eat while we would be busy arguing and debating. How could a morsel of food go down our throats without dissecting all social and political issues? My brother Rabindra Nath was in favour of sweeping social reforms, and I favoured the old traditions. Rabindra preferred that there be complete freedom for men and women to interact in society, whereas I was opposed to it and still am. Rabindra favoured coeducation, and I opposed it. Interestingly, in the political sphere, I was in favour of extreme revolution, while he was in favour of gradual reforms. A battle was inevitable in such a scenario. For a week, we would ignore each other because we knew any more debate would lead to a fight. But the next year when we met again the debates would begin anew, and there would be no peace for a week. While we debated, the neighbours thought we were fighting!

Rabindra Nath knew that I was moving ahead on a difficult and treacherous path in politics. One day, we started our old debate again. There were five of us in one big room. My mother and my maternal uncle also participated in the discussion. My wife was sitting at a distance and listening to our debate. As is normal, the conversation began lightly and slowly turned serious. My mother was an educated, sensible lady. She held clear and independent views on political and social issues. She did not spare you in an argument on account of maternal affection. Although Rabindra Nath had done an MA in history, his political views were not balanced or clear. He would often cross the line of truth in excitement. In this debate, my maternal uncle supported Rabindra Nath. All three of them were trying to deter me from walking the dark, destructive path of a revolutionary. But they could not win at the intellectual level.

Although I concede that a thinking mind is not everything for a human being. Not all intelligence is based on thought. A person's education, feelings, customs and upbringing—all these put together define a person's path of duty. The path of a revolutionary was not just an intellectual decision. Our desires are shaped by our nature, and with intellect, we support that propensity. The intellect is only a tool. We decide our duty based on our fundamental inclinations. It is still not known where these tendencies come from or how they develop. If it is the environment that nurtures propensity, then what is it in the environment that causes it to change and develop? Many powerful people have gone against the prevailing environment and changed their circumstances as well as those of society. Mahatma Gandhi has changed India's political environment by pursuing Tolstoy's example. Why did Mahatma Gandhi emulate Tolstoy and not the nihilistic anarchists or the Bolshevik? Why did Pandit Jawaharlal Nehru follow Mahatma Gandhi and not the revolutionaries of the world? Who has the answers to these questions? Are not personal likes, dislikes, feelings and upbringing an important influence in these matters? Despite living in the same sociopolitical environment, the communists, the socialists, the followers of Gandhi, Muslims, the Hindu Mahasabha people, and the revolutionary Congressmen want to walk different paths. The answer to all these palpable questions is not simple.

Did my brother Rabindra Nath know that I had chosen the historic path taken by many well-known and respected revolutionaries? His manner and tone while arguing with me created the doubt that he really did not understand my choice. During the debate, there was a moment when the question arose as to whether what I was doing was right or wrong. When Rabindra Nath said that I was moving forward on the wrong path, I asked mother what she thought. She smiled gently and said, 'No. I don't think so. I cannot say that the path you have chosen is wrong. But I know that it is unbearable for me. I can still conjure up the terrible scene described by the woman who brought me news of your first arrest. A strip of cloth was wrapped around your neck, she said, and both your hands were cuffed as you were being taken to the police station.' This was after my arrest in 1915. My mother's face clouded over while speaking of the incident.

Our conversation till then had been happy and playful; all of us were teasing each other with gentle humour. Suddenly everyone became serious. Mother addressed me by name and asked, 'Are you not afraid? Do the scenes from the Cellular Jail not haunt you?' I replied, 'Of course I clearly remember those scenes, and I get upset. I am also scared. My hair stands on edge when I think of the prison food and the terrible behaviour of the jail authorities. But the truth is that the path I have chosen does not foretell a good end for me. Yet how can I turn away from what I perceive to be my duty? If India is to be liberated, many young men like me must bear such torture and this is the only path that will lead our country to freedom. There is no other way.'

My answer and mother's silent support put an end to the discussion. Mother's comment seemed to have shaken us all. Just as a tree soaked in rainwater sheds droplets of water when shaken, all of us brothers started crying. Weeping, I told them that the arrangements for my departure were in place. I would not delay unnecessarily. In that moment, no one knew who should console whom. The boisterousness of the previous hour had disappeared. Affection and love had taken the form of tears. We all seemed to have come closer to each other. I could not imagine what my young wife was going through. She sat with our child on her lap, still, intently listening to what we were saying. I don't know if she was cursing her destiny or seeing new meaning in it. There is no doubt that she feared her uncertain future. The day had arrived to take my family, children included, and walk alone the known-unknown, certain-uncertain path. Who knew where we would end up and in what condition? I was brave enough to take my small children and young wife on the path of my revolt against the British rule! Since the way ahead was uncertain, I requested my aunt's adopted daughter to accompany us for a few days. Everybody at home agreed with the idea. Neetu Didi was willing to go with us.

We had to slip past the eyes of the police, get to the railway station with all our luggage and the children without them noticing us. There was strict surveillance at the railway station. And there was no man the police would recognize more easily than me in Allahabad! My brothers were about to leave for the station with my children. I was still at home. Mother's forbearance was at the end of its tether. She was trembling more than she was crying. Her lips and her chin quivered; her brows were pulled together and the tears would not stop flowing. When she picked up one of the children at the door as they were going to get into the car, she started to cry uncontrollably. My two-year-old son was looking at her, perplexed. Even the Buddha did not have to witness such a scene when he left.

I went separately to the station. My uncle and brothers put my family on the train. I came into the carriage from another side and met them in the train when it was about to leave. I think it was about 10 o' clock.

If I felt any guilt at all about the choice I had made, it was over leaving these loved ones. To flee was not weakness or cowardice for me. Many people had told me that the uncertainty of a fugitive life was so overwhelming that they ended up surrendering to the police. I never felt this burden. On the contrary, when I boarded the train, I felt an extraordinary jolt of energy. For one thing, I had successfully fooled the police again; this in itself was a small victory. My readers should not think, however, that this was just a game of hide and seek with the police. If caught, we would lose our lives. Many of our countrymen still think of the revolutionary life as a kind of game. But the British government took us so seriously that they spent a fortune in trying to stop us. There are many instances of the government having spent thousands of rupees following a young man on mere suspicion. The misfortune of the revolutionaries was that they were unsuccessful in the long run; otherwise, their critics would have been quiet and embarrassed today. Even today Indians are not enamoured of the idea of independence. They are still not impatient for freedom. However, I had started long ago on the path of revolution, happily and with an indomitable spirit.

Chapter 15

IN BENGAL ONCE AGAIN

I sent another telegram to Mr Narendra Nath Banerjee in Chandernagore once I reached Mirzapur. He knew I was coming but not the day and time that I would reach. Had I sent the telegram from Allahabad, it would have attracted the police's attention. However, they were least likely to pay attention to some passenger sending a telegram from the Mirzapur station. But something else happened. Some people just don't have any luck, try as they might to take all precautions. And I was one of those unlucky ones. The journey had been smooth, but when the train approached Chandernagore, I was rather anxious. My ticket was for Calcutta; that was for a reason. The stop at Chandernagore was very brief, and I had a lot of luggage. I looked around, craning my neck to see if Narendra Nath had come to the station. I could not spot him, and I became extremely nervous. Nonetheless, I had to get off the train. My co-passengers helped us with the luggage and, thereafter, I stood helplessly on the platform, wondering where to get help from. I had left home and come here with my family, but it was beginning to look as if I would have no place to stay. It had been decided that I would stay at Narendra Nath's house and pay him a token amount as rent. I had seen the house too.

I was getting the coolies to gather the luggage while looking around furtively. I feared attracting the attention of the police. In the meantime, the station emptied and only a group of two or three people were left there. They seemed to be waiting for someone. After a while, they came towards me, and I, too, approached them. They asked me where I was coming from and where I was going. I told them I was going to a friend's house. I gave them Narendra Nath Banerjee's name and address, and introduced myself as well. They were surprised when I told them all this and laughed. 'We got your telegram. One of our acquaintances is called Sachindra Nath; he lives in Mirzapur. And one of us is called Narendra Nath. There are two people of that name in our locality. We thought our acquaintance was coming and that is why we came to the station. But we will go back and inform your friend that you have arrived. You come by carriage and we will go by bicycle.'

There was a ray of hope, and I felt a little stronger. Narendra Nath lived rather far from the railway station. After a carriage ride of about an hour, I saw Narendra Nath on the road, a good way from his house, waiting for us. He didn't seem happy to see us, and I immediately got worried. My worry was not unfounded. Narendra Nath nervously said to us, 'It is not possible for you to stay in my house. Agents of the British government have made an agreement with the authorities in Chandernagore. It is not safe for a fugitive to live in Chandernagore now. We are required to inform the police if we have guests from outside. My family is not willing for you to stay with us now.' My mouth was dry. I did not have the courage to look at my wife and children, but I did not let my fear and anger show on my face. I requested my friend to give us refuge, so I would have time to make arrangements, for a couple of days. He was too scared to give in to my entreaties. He did not even want to stand there with us any longer. His attitude and behaviour made me angry, disgusted and offended. I did not even want to look at Narendra Nath anymore. I told the driver to turn around.

Where was I to go now? My wife was rather angry with me and said, 'You are about to embark on such an important task with the support of these people?' What could I say! I was just looking at her and wondering how angry she must be. I said, 'Don't worry. I will just make other arrangements.' But I knew that was easier said than done. There were revolutionaries from 1914 in Chandernagore. I had not gone to them so as to avoid police attention. I was aware of the political situation in Chandernagore. Yet Narendra Nath had not said anything to me, and I assumed he had thought about everything before he agreed to let me stay in his house. The readers can judge for themselves how criminal it was on his part to throw me into the deep end of the ocean in such a callous manner.

My erstwhile revolutionary companions lived far from Narendra Nath's locality. It had taken us an hour to reach Narendra Nath's place, and it took us another hour to reach the other locality. And with us were a two-year-old son and a three-month-old daughter both distraught with hunger. We did not have milk. The mother took care of feeding the little girl, but the boy was crying for food. My wife said, 'I don't mind being your partner when it comes to your work, but I can't bear to see my children like this. What shall I feed them? It's been two hours and there is no arrangement for our stay. Your companions are such that they did not think twice about endangering such small children. What are you thinking of, working with such people? You have no experience in any of these matters, and you are dragging us all over the place.' There was no end to the nastiness of the British government on the one hand, and on the other, there was pain of treachery by companions such as Narendra Nath. The cherry on the cake were my wife's words. My dear readers can understand what I must have been feeling. How much patience, confidence, determination and dedication are required for revolutionaries to manage to do their work in such contrary situations!

I went finally to the house of Mr Shirish Chandra Ghose, an acquaintance of the famous revolutionary Rashbehari Bose. My son cried all the way. All he said when he was hungry was '*doodh dao*', which means 'give milk'. When I saw no alternative, I gave him a *rosogulla* (a dessert popular in Bengal made from ball-shaped dumplings of cottage cheese). He gulped it down in no time. We were worried that it might not agree with him, but after having one rosogulla and some of the sugar syrup, the child quietened down. We felt better too. Then we saw Mr Shirish. He greeted us with joy and excitement. I felt as happy as one does on seeing an oasis in the middle of a desert.

It would be appropriate to mention some things about Mr Shirish Chandra Ghose here. He was one of the few remaining revolutionaries from the group that had been arrested in the very first bomb conspiracy case in India, which came to be known as the Alipore Bomb case and was heard in 1908. Aurobindo Ghose, as well as Barindra Kumar Ghose, Upendra Nath Ghose and Hem Chandra Das, had belonged to the group. Mr Motilal Rai and Mr Shirish Chandra Ghose had kept the group functioning after that. Rashbehari Bose, who is now living in Japan and will surely be hanged if he risks coming to India, is very close to Mr Shirish Chandra. The latter had been in solitary confinement for many years during the World War. He was released when all the prisoners were released at the end of the War. He had accepted certain conditions put forth by the police before his release. He had agreed to not participate in any revolutionary movement in the future.

I have already mentioned the conversation I had with him on my return from the Andamans. I was scared that he may be hesitant to help me. But when I arrived in Chandernagore as a fugitive, he came forward happily to help me. Mr Shirish Chandra was a bachelor, but there were women in his house—his sister-in-law, an aunt and others. He did not get nervous at all on seeing me with my family. Patiently, he entrusted my wife and children to the women of the house. I felt as a man must feel when he touches land after swimming long in the sea. The children got their milk and I was able to breathe again.

In theory, Chandernagore is French territory, but the British government controls the governor here. Nonetheless, the revolutionaries do get a respite of sorts here. The British police cannot arrest them directly or do so without the help of the French police. The spies of the British government roam around freely in Chandernagore, but they must approach the French police to make any arrest, and that is enough opportunity for the revolutionaries to make good their escape. However, shortly before my arrival, the British government had forced the creation of a rule in Chandernagore, which dictated that the police must be informed about any guests who entered the territory. Similarly, landlords must also inform the police about new tenants. I knew all this, and Mr Shirish confirmed it. I knew that it would be difficult to leave Chandernagore once the police got my address, but, till then, I could roam around the place without fear.

I went out with Mr Shirish in search of a house to rent. We first went to a hotel. The owner of the hotel was an old Anglo-Indian lady. I decided it was not appropriate when

I saw the charges and the ambience there. The place had a wonderful view. There was a broad pathway next to the Ganga in front of the hotel. The French have created such pathways along the ocean front and the river in their colonies in Chandernagore and Pondicherry. You can't find such views in the rest of India. Brick walls have been constructed along the banks of the Ganga, and there are paths on top of them and stairs along the way that lead down to the water. The view from the banks of the Ganga in Kashi is also lovely, but I don't know why there is so much chaos there. There is no organization to the construction of houses, nor have the streets been planned properly. The steps leading down to the river are crumbling and in a terrible condition. The river front in Kashi can be made so beautiful but sheer neglect is ruining it.

Wealthy people from Calcutta come to this hotel on weekends. Liquor flows freely here because the taxes are lower than in Calcutta. How was it possible to stay here with my family? When we told the owner that we would tell her our decision in a couple of days, she insisted that we must have something since we had come all the way—at least a glass of lemonade each. Embarrassed, we ordered a bottle of lemonade and almost had a heart attack when we saw the bill. The price for a bottle of water was eight annas. There was no choice but to pay. Where one had to pay eight annas just to step in, I was never going to step back there!

After lunch and a bath, we stepped out again in search of a house. Chandernagore is not a very small place. We looked far and wide, and found a few houses but didn't like any. I felt that staying in some of those places would mean contracting malaria. But it did not seem right to stay in Mr Shirish Chandra's house, and there wasn't enough space there either. I was anxious about what to do.

There is a small but famous place near Chandernagore called Shri Rampur. Some eminent landlords from Bengal have settled here. My maternal uncle was married into one of these families. And my cousin, my uncle's son, was still living with his maternal grandmother in Shri Rampur. I was very close to my cousin Mr Bhawani Shankar Rai. I did not know for sure if Bhawani Shankar's grandmother would like me to visit them; nonetheless, I thought it opportune to stay with them for a few days. My plan was to leave my wife and children there while I went looking for a house. As far as I remember, I went to Shri Rampur and spoke to Bhawani Bhaiya. Then I went back later with my family. Bhawani's grandmother did not in any way express her displeasure. I had been wary of that. That fear was now gone.

On foot, my cousin and I explored every locality from Chandernagore to Howrah along the Ganga. The railway line from Shri Rampur to Howrah is 12–13 miles long. We looked from morning to evening, finding houses that were vacant, checking to see what kind of neighbours there were, what facilities were available for travel to Calcutta and what the rent would be. I remember with gratitude today the help Bhawani Bhaiya gave me then. I had not informed any member of the Anushilan Samiti that I was coming to Bengal because then the news would probably have spread. I wanted to put all my arrangements in place without their help. On the one hand, the police were trying to find and arrest me, and on the other, I was roaming around looking for a house. There was no place to live, and my family too was displaced along with me. It was only later when I read Trotsky's autobiography in 1930 in Naini Jail and the accounts of Soviet revolutionaries in Siberia in the Lucknow jail in 1934 that I realized my difficulties paled in comparison to theirs. They had to face insurmountable difficulties and extreme sorrows.

But that is why not many people are interested in the revolutionary path. This is true not only for India, but of revolutionaries across the world. History shows that till they achieve success, revolutionaries everywhere are labelled short-sighted, utopian and misguided in their thinking. Most of the so-called intelligent men in the world have not chosen the revolutionary path. Even today, the distinguished and respected leaders of our country consider our views and policies to be childish. To return to my narrative, Bhawani Shankar and I managed to find a reasonably good house in an area called Bali. It took three or four days to figure out which milkman would deliver the milk, where we would get utensils, how far the market, the railway station and the stop for the steamer were, and so on. But we managed to secure the house. Now that there was a roof over my head, I had the opportunity to pay attention to my work.

The monsoon brings illness. Moreover, having lived in the north for so long, we were no longer used to the Calcutta climate. My son soon developed bronchitis. Alone in an unknown place, I was worried about his health. Ultimately, having found no remedy, I decided to move to Calcutta. I settled my family in the house of a cousin, my paternal uncle's son, in Calcutta. My son was treated for his illness there. Then I started looking for a place to stay. We later shifted to another house in Calcutta. Even the people close to me did not know where I lived. I told several of them that I was living in the French territory of Chandernagore. Other than one or two trusted friends, no one in the revolutionary group knew the location of my house.

Meanwhile, I resumed my work. I had always been

attentive to maintaining contact with the distinguished leaders of the country and tried to sensitize them to the revolutionary cause. In view of this policy, I thought it my first duty to meet Deshbandhu Chittaranjan Das, whom I have spoken about earlier. I had an old and deep relationship with C.R. Das's brother-in-law. I had also tried to meet Mahatma Gandhi through him. Gandhi had been aware that I was a fugitive. Mr Das's brother-in-law, Mr S.N. Haldar, had taken a message from me to Mahatma Gandhi. The Mahatma was visiting Deshbandhu Das for some Congress work at the time. I don't know whether it was a meeting of the Congress Working Committee or a meeting of the All India Congress Committee. On the same occasion, I received a message from Mr Hemanta Kumar Sarkar, informing me that Maulana Mohammad Ali wished to meet me. I had last met Mohammad Ali before going to the Andamans. Therefore, I was excited about seeing him. I met him in Deshbandhu's house. Like Maulana Shaukat Ali, he too asked me to change my ways and join the public movement. I did not argue with him.

Mr S.N. Haldar informed me that Mahatma Gandhi would meet me at Mr C.R. Das's house at a particular time on a particular day. Mr Das's house was under surveillance by the secret police, but I knew that they would not recognize me. I reached the house on time. There I met Mr Haldar, who sat me in a room and told me to stay there till he returned. It was the room designated for Mr Das's accountants. Maybe the police thought I was one of the accountants. I was to meet Mahatma Gandhi at eight o'clock. There was a huge clock in the room. I sat there, and from eight, the hour hand moved to nine and then ten and then eleven, but Mr Haldar had not returned. The place was surrounded by the secret police, and I was a fugitive. My mind was plagued by doubts while I waited. I thought that maybe Mahatma Gandhi did not want to meet me, and maybe it was a weakness of character, but I felt insulted. I felt as if the Mahatma was not bothered about me. It is my bad luck that I have never been able to meet Mahatma Gandhi despite trying my best.

Before this, I had tried repeatedly to meet him in Haripur, and every time I was told that he was not well or that it was his free day and he could only spare two minutes, and so on. One day, I went straight to Haripur to see him without taking an appointment, and saw him walking and talking with Mr Manzar Ali Soktha. There was a young lady standing nearby. I hesitatingly asked her if I could approach the Mahatma. She said I could if I wanted to. I went up to Mahatma Gandhi, touched his feet in obeisance, joined my hands and asked him for some time to speak to him. The Mahatma looked at me intently. I told him my name, but he continued to walk and talk to Mr Manzar Ali Sokhta, and did not give me time. Mr Sokhta later told me that they were not having a particularly important conversation at that time. After my release from prison, I had written a letter to Mahatma Gandhi. In reply, his secretary had written to me, asking me to come to the village near Vardha and stay there for a week with them so that I could speak with the Mahatma peacefully. Mr Mahavir Desai had also told me the same thing in Haripur, but I did not have the money to travel to Vardha and meet Mahatma Gandhi in the village. I had also tried to speak to him at the All India Congress Committee meeting in Delhi, but was unsuccessful again.

I left Deshbandhu's house at eleven o'clock. I was agitated and angered by the perceived insult. I felt that I had failed to reach a status that made me worthy of a meeting with Mahatma Gandhi. In Western psychology, this is known as an inferiority complex. I had returned from Mr C.R. Das's house that day with such feelings of unworthiness. I still suffer from this inferiority complex.

When I met Mr Haldar again, I came to know that Mahatma Gandhi had indeed been eager to meet me. He said he had wanted to wait until the other congressmen had left and then to take me on a long drive with the Mahatma so that we could speak with him in the car. But sadly, Mr Haldar had not shared his plan with me beforehand.

Chapter 16

THE STRUGGLE FOR PRINCIPLES

I met Comrade M.N. Roy, whom I had met in Delhi, once again in Calcutta. I have already mentioned Mr Qutbuddin Ahmad. He had houses in Calcutta, and I had hoped that I would get financial support from him. With his contribution, I wanted to send a representative abroad with my message. From the experience of the 1914 revolution, I knew that a revolutionary movement would never be successful unless arms and ammunition were brought in from abroad in huge quantities. I had also realized that we had suffered greatly by not having made contact with the revolutionary groups abroad. Keeping in mind these previous mistakes, I tried my utmost best to send a person abroad, but even with Mr Qutbuddin's help I was not successful.

The police today know of the routes that the revolutionary group used to go abroad and come back. Now it is very difficult to go and return this way. And what the police knows, there is no point in keeping from the public. Mr Qutbuddin told me that they would get their people recruited as Khalasis or to other posts on the ship. These people would disappear as soon as they got off the ship abroad. I had also tried thus to flee to America in 1911, but was unsuccessful.

At the beginning of 1924, some people were arrested under Regulation 3. But after I reached Calcutta, the government had arrested many young men under the new law and jailed them without a trial. Subhas Babu too had been arrested in this manner.

I had met Deshbandhu Das before this, and he had promised to give us some monthly monetary assistance. But unfortunately, before he could start contributing, he got annoyed with me. In a pamphlet titled 'An Appeal to Countrymen', which was published under my name, I had contradicted logically, and in no uncertain terms, the anti-revolutionary arguments used by Deshbandhu in another pamphlet. When I went to meet him at his house after the publication of this pamphlet, he refused to see me. I realized then that I was naïve at political manoeuvring. The Congress leaders could publicly criticize the revolutionary movement whenever they wanted, on various platforms or through newsletters. They are aware that the revolutionaries rarely, if ever, have the opportunity to defend themselves publicly.

Mr C.R. Das had made derogatory remarks about the revolutionary movement as president of the Gaya Congress. He had said that the revolutionary movement could never be successful, and that is why he did not contribute to it. He also claimed that if he felt it had any chance of succeeding, he would join the movement that very instant. It was clear that he did not oppose the revolutionary movement based on the principle of ahimsa. In a rejoinder to his statements, I had written that the day there is an impression that the revolutionary movement is going to be successful, tens of thousands of people will sign up for it, and it will be immaterial if people like Mr Deshbandhu Das participate or not. In the pamphlet, I had written that in a country where a foreign government could make any law that it desired, and where this government ruled by brute force, it is nothing but pretence if you fight for freedom but don't want to retaliate with force. I tried to explain that ours was not a terrorist movement because no revolutionary believed that freedom could be achieved through violence alone. If a couple of people use a revolver against official oppression, it does not mean that the revolutionaries want to achieve freedom only through force and terror. Hence, my pamphlet was a direct answer to the criticism levelled against the revolutionary movement. Printed under my name, copies of this pamphlet had been distributed at all public meetings in Calcutta and caused a lot of agitation at the time. This was the first time that any revolutionary in India had written in favour of the revolution, using his own name and against an established leader of the public movement.

The leaders of the Dhaka Anushilan Samiti were unhappy with me for publishing this pamphlet. I believed then and now that if the revolutionaries express their views to the general public and clearly present their independent thoughts, it is possible for them to make a place for themselves in people's hearts. The leaders of the Samiti did not think so.

After many interactions with the leaders of the Anushilan Samiti, I concluded that they did not have the maturity of European revolutionaries. As I have mentioned before, there were many capable, versatile young men who had immense talent and intellect in this group, but the mode of operation of the organization was such that these young men did not get a chance to use their abilities and skills. In the first wave of the revolutionary movement, many young men of a tender age had left schools and colleges to participate in the movement. The same exodus had happened in Russia, Ireland and Italy, and in those countries, especially in Russia, the revolutionaries had, through their practice, hard work and perseverance, matured and flourished as political activists. When the Russian revolutionaries were not in prison, they would throw themselves into various political activities, and they didn't then have the opportunity to nourish their minds. But while they were behind bars, they would use their time in jail well to sharpen and train their minds. This happened in our country too.

The younger members of the Samiti who favoured direct action were now restive. They wanted a programme that would create a strong impression of the revolutionary movement on the masses. These people had planned their own rebellion against the old leadership of the Anushilan Samiti. They were not satisfied with secret operations any longer. They wanted to do something that would electrify the people and convince them that it was possible to liberate India through revolutionary means. The now deceased Suryakant of Chittagong was the leader of this group. He held complete sway over Chittagong and had many supporters in the surrounding villages also.

I, too, was dissatisfied with the policies of the leaders of the Anushilan Samiti. From my experience of the earlier phases of the movement, I had understood that to win over more people, it was imperative to produce a literature of the revolution. We had not made any efforts in that direction. Moreover, we had no methods to inspire the general public to take to the revolutionary path. How could the whole country be liberated by putting together a few pistols and rigging up some bombs? Italy's famous revolutionary Giuseppe Mazzini has said that one revolutionary uprising is a thousand times more work than tens of thousands of public meetings and pamphlets. Maybe these aren't the exact words, but this is exactly what he meant. It is also certain that the literary quality and revolutionary effect of the newsletter called *Young Italy* that Mazzini published will be recorded in golden words in history. These pamphlets came into Italy from other countries as Mazzini edited these pamphlets from outside his homeland. In Italy, at that time, any person who was caught with this newsletter was sentenced to death by hanging. A collection of the essays from *Young Italy* is today available in English; all educated people enjoy reading it and learn from it. Its literary and moral value remains unabated.

We have nothing comparable to show in reference to the national movement or the revolutionary movement. If we look at the Russian revolution, we realize yet again how backward our own revolutionary movement was and is in terms of literature. The revolutionary leaders in Russia also brought about a revolution in the world of thought and philosophy. In China, too, innumerable pamphlets and booklets have been distributed in connection with the national revolutionary movement. In that country, a new movement gave rise to a new literature. Moreover, the writings of prominent leaders like Dr Sun Yat-Sen and others enriched Chinese philosophy too. In India, brilliant and distinguished leaders like Mr Aurobindo, the late Swami Vivekananda, Ram Tirth, Dayanand Saraswati and Lokmanya Tilak also created a new awareness in Indian thought and started a new philosophical movement.

What I want to emphasize here is that I had not found the leaders of the Dhaka Anushilan Samiti to be intellectually sharp. I also did not care for their modus operandi and that is why they did not get along with me. The leaders of the Samiti did not give any importance to the programme and manifesto that I had written and printed. They laughed at rules and regulations on paper. Most of these leaders were unaware of modern thought. I tried to explain to them the importance of the manifesto by saying, 'What if we had to go to an intelligent and learned person like Pandit Jawaharlal Nehru with a programme? What would we go to him with?' The manifesto of the Hindustan Republican Association is such a programme, outlined and organized in a way that can be proudly presented to any thinking person. But the leaders of the Anushilan Samiti only laughed and brushed it aside. I realized that their understanding had simply not reached the level of the thought that went into the manifesto of the above-mentioned Association.

These leaders did not have any programme or manifesto to place before the people. I wanted to organize something that would ensure that the revolutionary movement had a positive impact on the general public. The leaders of the Anushilan Samiti were opposed to it. They did not want to do anything to attract the attention of the public towards revolutionary activities. This was because their main goal was to avoid police attention at all costs. They wanted to have their cake and eat it too, but that is not possible in the current political scenario.

As I have already mentioned, after my conversation with Deshbandhu, he had realized that the revolutionary movement was making great strides in North India. Around that time, Mr Das had warned the government in a speech that there would be dire consequences if the demands of Indians were not met soon. If the government thought that the Indian revolutionary movement had been quashed, he pointed out, it was making a huge mistake. The movement was in fact thriving, and the government had no idea how aggressive it was going to be. I have also mentioned earlier that after Mr Das had made these statements publicly, the superintendent of the secret service, Mr Bhupendra Chatterjee, was sent by the government to meet him. I spoke to Mr Das a few days after the incident. According to his analysis, the government was scared that the revolutionary movement would revert to the aggressive mode that it had adopted during the World War. Mr Chatterjee wanted to know from Mr Das if he thought that there would soon be a mutiny in India and to what extent he was involved with the revolutionaries.

The leaders of the Anushilan Samiti were unhappy with me because of Mr Das's statement. They believed that it would harm the revolutionary movement. I, on the other hand, felt that the statement would help promote revolutionary sentiments and make it easier for us to work for our cause.

Many days before this statement, soon after the special session of the Congress in Delhi, some people had been arrested in Bengal under Regulation 3.[38] I used to tell my companions in the Anushilan Samiti that they would all be arrested under some special law or the other, no work would take place, and the revolutionary movement would collapse, or at least come to a standstill for some time. Before that, it was necessary to do something that would prove to the people that even in the face of the martial power of the British, the people of India had the capability to come together and do something formidable—something that revolutionizes the perception and thoughts of our society. The Congress leaders had been saying day and night that it is not possible to liberate India through the revolutionary path. Most Indians also believed that they did not have the power to combat the military might of the British. If this was true, then India was unlikely to ever gain independence. How was a revolution possible with such a mindset? We would have to change our mindset to combat this mental weakness. What good will planning secret conspiracies do?

But the leaders of the Anushilan Samiti did not like this. They wanted to enlarge the network of the organization and secretly import arms and ammunitions before turning our attention to other tasks. But I knew that it was not easy to keep the organization working under these circumstances. It would soon be impossible to run the organization without resorting to other operations. An organization cannot progress if all the members are not assigned appropriate tasks. All organizations need financial support. It was increasingly difficult to collect funds for revolutionary organizations in India, and no work is possible without money. It is not possible to run a revolutionary movement with people other than those who would give up home and hearth, and are selfless, brave and completely dedicated to the cause. But the question was: how to sustain all these people? On top of that, their travel expenses were heavy, for these workers had to go all over the country, to every province. To promote the revolutionary literature, to distribute pamphlets and run monthly newsletters—all these activities require money. Then there are trips abroad, getting arms and ammunition from foreign countries in large quantities. Where would all this money come from?

It is easier for the Congress and other such organizations. They can publicly collect funds. People are not scared of making contributions to these parties either. However, there is a danger in donating to the revolutionary movement, and many Indians are still not willing to take that risk. How can the revolutionary movement succeed in such circumstances?

There is no resolution to this problem, if we look at the history of revolutions in other countries. Mazzini had also faced a similar crisis and he couldn't get a penny from his countrymen. The Bolshevik Party of Russia did not consider dacoity as a legitimate mode of collecting funds, but Stalin's group had had to resort to dacoity with Lenin's permission and approval. As for the Sinn Féin Party in Ireland, all the members would contribute to the party fund and that is how they sustained the party.

Had we participated in the movement of the farmers and workers in our country, it is possible that our economic difficulties would have been reduced. But we did not have the kind of people required for such a movement. We had many volunteers and party workers, but we did not have people who could lead and organize. In any case, we had already incorporated all the people we had in various tasks of the revolutionary organization. Had I not become a fugitive, I could have continued my work with the labourers' unions that I had begun in Jamshedpur. But now that I was on the run, it was impossible. Nonetheless, I started sending my men to campaign among the workers—to the factories near Calcutta, for instance, with the help of Mr M.N. Roy's assistant whom I had met in Delhi. The expenditure for going to places like Kanchrapara from Calcutta was borne by Mr Qutbuddin Ahmad. We even published a weekly newsletter to educate the workers. Our people would circulate them among the workers in the factories. But Mr Qutbuddin was not willing to contribute to the revolutionary movement. Had my arrest been delayed by just a few days, it is even possible that the workers' movement led by our group too would have gained strength.

The Anushilan Samiti leaders were against dacoity as a means of collecting funds. They believed that doing so would alert the police, harming the movement and making it difficult to work quietly. At that time, I did not agree with them. I believed that forcibly collecting money would train us in guerilla warfare, get us money and serve as practice for teamwork in dangerous situations. It would also reveal to us the members of our group who were the most courageous and capable of selfless sacrifice for the cause. But I was not in favour of robbing the villagers' houses. Ignoring the opinion and policy of the leaders of the Anushilan Samiti, I started making plans for robbing the British owners of big factories near Calcutta. They were aware of my intentions. I was also preparing to raid the mail compartments of the Bombay and Punjab mail trains. Meanwhile, I was writing an essay on revolutionary policies. I wanted to put across to the people, in clear words, the manifesto and the programme of the revolutionary movement. If we didn't have the opportunity to publish a public newsletter regularly, we could at least try and secretly distribute pamphlets. The leaders of the Anushilan Samiti were strongly opposed to all my plans and actions at this time.

When I got back from Calcutta, I got busy with public work that was independent of the Anushilan Samiti. I managed to collect a few people who were undergoing martial training at the University Training Corps. They were all college boys and a couple of them were from the Engineering College. Through these young men, I met a very good and useful worker by the name of Sushil Kumar Banerjee. He was already a member of the Anushilan Samiti. One day, while walking with Sushil Kumar, I saw some young men involved in carrying out the work of the Congress. I was particularly interested in one of them. He must have been about 20 years of age, and I told Sushil Kumar that I wanted to get to know this young man. Sushil Kumar said that he, too, had his eyes on that young man, but none of his friends were members of our Samiti. I said that there was no cause to delay any further. Sushil Kumar wanted to wait a couple of days, but I said that I wanted to meet him that very day. I was introduced to the young man within a couple of days. His name was Jatindra

Nath Das. This young man was later arrested along with Sardar Bhagat Singh in the Lahore Conspiracy Case, and he was the first person in India who sacrificed his life by going on a hunger strike for the fulfilment of the demands of political prisoners. It was principally thanks to his sacrifice that many political prisoners and especially those of the revolutionary movement received better treatment in jail. Today, when I think of it, I feel proud for having spotted the young man. Is it not a matter of pride that my attention was riveted on a young man while walking along the road and that young man turned out to be Jatindra Nath Das?

I needed some weapons for my fund collection activities. I had some arms in the United Provinces and Punjab, but I didn't want to have them brought to Bengal. The Anushilan Samiti did not wish to help me in this matter. I realized that I was not getting along with the leaders of the Samiti. They, too, realized that I was not going to change my views and beliefs. It was suggested that I keep my plans on hold for a couple of months and they would meanwhile work on their futile scheme of printing counterfeit currency. I had agreed to keep quiet, but I did not stop my preparations. I sent my men on a reconnaissance foray to the factory that we were planning to raid and then I made a visit myself to verify their reports. All questions related to the raid were researched—which way do we go in, how to return, when is a house to be rented, where are the arms to be dumped after the dacoity, till what point the car could go, where is the money to be kept safely, how many people will be needed, where will the Bombay and Punjab Mail trains be stopped, how will we escape after the raid, and so on.

Meanwhile, there was a meeting to broker an understanding between the Anushilan Samiti leaders and me, and to find a middle path between our policies. I was to go to Berhampur from Calcutta for this purpose. Berhampur is a well-known district in Bengal. During Mughal times, it was known as Murshidabad. Murshidabad and Berhampur are right next to each other, just like Patna and Bankipur. There was a strict police vigil at the Howrah and Sealdah stations, but it was imperative for me to make the journey. I got on to the train at a small station about 12–14 miles from Calcutta and got off at the station before Berhampur. Arrest was highly probable when you made small mistakes while travelling. A lot of my companions had been arrested in this way. The fight against a mighty empire is difficult and full of danger, and our countrymen are yet to be inspired by examples from history—the successful rebellion of the German revolutionaries against the Kaiser, or that of Ireland against England. Russia has seen a successful revolution too. But most Indians continue to believe that a revolution against the mighty British Empire is just an illusion and a dream. I can't understand how we came to think like this.

We could not reach any compromise in Berhampur. After a lot of quibbling, I made it clear to the leaders of the Anushilan Samiti that if they did not agree to a policy of aggressive attack, I would start working in the United Provinces and Punjab of my own accord, and I could not help it if they opposed it. The ordinance was going to be issued. We were all going to go to jail. Why not do something worthwhile before that? Much before Mr C.R. Das's statement, there had been strong rumours in Calcutta that a new draconian ordinance, much like the Defence of India Act, was going to be issued. It came into force soon after Mr Das's statement. There is no doubt that this ordinance would have come about even if Mr Das had not made the statement as preparations for the same had been on for some time. I knew this for a fact. The Anushilan Samiti leaders were agitated with my attitude and continued to insist that I should put the dacoity on hold for some time and publish and distribute the pamphlets while they printed counterfeit currency. The only thing to keep in mind was to avoid distributing the pamphlets near the hideout of the leaders so as not to attract the attention of the police. I accepted the proposal.

A meeting of the leaders of our group was held in a village of the Mymensingh district. There were about eight leaders in the Mymensingh meeting, but only two or three from Berhampur. On this occasion, I put forth the manifesto of the Hindustan Republican Association. But the leaders had contrary thoughts. They praised the manifesto but said that there was no need for written guidelines at all. I believe none of them understood the principles on which the manifesto was based. They were unfamiliar with the ideology of communism. They had so far only given importance to anarchist terrorism; the thought of organizing a mass revolution was alien to them. Today, in 1938, the Bengal Anushilan Samiti has declared that it will merge with the Congress Socialist Party. Ironically, the group that now wants to incorporate the principles of communism does not wish to be part of the Communist Party. It is natural to assume that either the Anushilan Samiti has not understood the principles of communism at all or that they reject them deliberately. I am merely pointing out that today the leaders of the Anushilan Samiti are accepting the tenets of socialism to a certain extent. But they had rejected all the socialist principles that had been proposed in the Mymensingh meeting of the Hindustan Republican Association.

The Mymensingh meeting had carried on for an entire night, but as far as I was concerned, no important decision was taken. For some time, I participated in their discussions, but when I saw that it only lengthened the debate, I decided to keep quiet. It was apparent that the leaders of the Anushilan Samiti could not provide the answers to many vital questions—*that is,* how to take advantage of the political situation, what are the forces at work in these circumstances, how can these circumstances be changed in the future, how to present our policy to the masses so as to change the course of the Indian national movement and how to ensure that the revolutionary leaders had more influence on the general public than the leaders of the other public movements.

Nonetheless, I was given the entire responsibility of the organization in the United Provinces, Punjab and Bengal at the Mymensingh meeting.

The monsoon had not yet ended. The extreme humidity was causing people to be despondent. Just as one looks forward to clouds in the sky during summer, the monsoons bring to North Indians a yearning for a glimpse of the sun in a clear blue sky. But in Bengal, the brooding atmosphere and constantly crossing clouds over the water bodies at the end of the monsoons dismay and perturb people who have lived much of their lives in North India. The number of rivers in East Bengal are more than you find in the rest of India. It is as if there is a net of rivers spread out over the land. More steamers run on the waterways of East Bengal than anywhere else in the country. During the monsoons, one can travel in this region only on steamers and boats. The beauty of these boat rides and the dangers they present cannot be described in mere words. The use of language can give wings to imagination, but there is a vast difference between imagination and reality. A small boat floats near the riverbank and a couple of steamers pass by. The boat is endangered if the steamers are too close, and even when they are farther away, because they cause high waves. The waves must be negotiated. The boatmen of East Bengal are very alert because the boats are in constant danger of overturning with the onslaught of these waves. They turn their boats to face the oncoming waves and ride them, to avoid being overturned.

There are so many storms in the month of Vaisakha[39] that travelling by boat is very frightening. These are sailboats that can overturn in the blink of an eye with just a small mistake, but the boatmen of East Bengal are very experienced in using sails. Besides, just as there is a chance of accidents on the road, the boats in the river too can collide. And just as there are crossings on the roads, there are similar crossings in the rivers of East Bengal. They are known as *mohana* (the widest part of the river where it merges with other rivers or the sea). In Bengal, it is at these confluences that the boats face the greatest danger. There are myths about certain mohanas—points where boats overturn regularly—and it is said that when even Muslim boatmen cross these points they pray to the goddess of the rivers. Most of the boatmen in East Bengal are Muslims, but when faced with danger they turn to local deities and jinns. According to an English historian, the boatmen of this region are highly suspicious in nature, as nature is cruel and erratic in their land. It seems logical.

I had come to Mymensingh at the end of the monsoons. However, I had been to East Bengal a couple of times earlier and had seen first-hand the secret skills of boating in this region. Sometimes seeing the boatman's anxiety would worry us too, making us wonder if we had escaped the clutches of the British police only to be executed by the gods and goddesses of the river. Often the conversation on these boats was about which boatman had disappeared with his passengers into the river and when. In such a situation, superstition can make a home in even the most logical person's head. The most hard-headed, in such a situation, will keep a smile on their face and make fun of the local superstitions, but also in his heart be tormented by the fear of drowning. The dark clouds hovering in the sky also cast a pall of fear. Naturally the boatmen were not as frightened of all this as I was.

The inhabitants of the northern and western parts of the country cannot even imagine how, during the rains, entire villages in East Bengal float in water like islands. Thousands of acres of land are submerged in water, but the paddy on that land rises at least two feet above that water. The boats manoeuvre through these paddy fields. How they find the way through the fields is a mystery. The boats in East Bengal often have thatched roofs, and there is enough place to sit and lie down beneath them. We were peacefully lying under the roof of our boat and didn't realize it when we left the river and sailed towards a village. When I heard the sound of the paddy rubbing against the thatch and looked around, I saw that we were hidden somewhere in the fields. The boatman was pushing forward by using a long pole. I got out from under the roof and stood in the open boat, and all I saw were immense paddy fields interspersed by some huge trees. Maybe the boatman decided his course by these trees. Sometimes we would see a boat or two coming or going. Sailing through the paddy fields we reached a creek. This seemed to be a place straight out of heaven. The creek was surrounded by trees and even with the sun shining all around, it appeared to be dark inside the grove of trees. No writer's imagination can match this scene. And here we were, revolutionaries who had set out to challenge the might of the British Empire, escaping detection by the police and roaming among these dreamy creeks in boats—reaching a village near Mymensingh where our meeting was to take place.

The house in Mymensingh where we stayed had many rooms that were raised on bamboo stilts. The waters had receded but there was sludge all around. It was a sight that would cause anxiety to any man. We had to stay in this house for an extra night after the secret meeting. Mr Pratul Ganguli of the Anushilan Samiti and I shared a room, and after having been awake the previous night, we slept soundly. The police were looking for us and we could be arrested any moment under the Bengal ordinance. Warrants had been issued for us. Mr Ganguli had organized a guard where two people at a time would take turns to keep watch through the night.

Mr Ganguli and I went back to Calcutta after the meeting. I had with me some issues of the famous Bengali monthly *Vangvaani*. Excerpts of the second part of *Bandi Jeevan: A Life in Chains* had been published in this magazine. On the way, I read the excerpts out to my companion. Mr Ganguli wanted me to visit some of the districts of Bengal with him, but I knew that the secret police in Bengal recognized him although they did not yet know me. Therefore, I did not want to go with him. Although he requested me several times to accompany him on his journey, I declined. In the end, what I had feared came true. He was arrested while I managed to get back safely to Calcutta.

Once I reached Calcutta, I tried to tell the other members of the Anushilan Samiti that each one of us would be captured like Mr Pratul Ganguli and not have accomplished anything. That is why we needed to make immediate changes in our programme—to be able to make progress in the fight for India's independence before we were arrested.

In my conversations with Pratul Babu on our way back

from Mymensingh, I realized that he was not familiar with the principles of communism. When the awakening in society is transferred to the consciousness of the political sphere, there will be landmark changes in literature, art, historical research, philosophical concepts and religious sentiments. And because they were unaware of these new ideologies, Mr Ganguli and his companions were working within the confines of a narrow political programme. As I have already mentioned, I had read out some excerpts from *Bandi Jeevan: Life in Chains* to Pratul Babu on our way back from Mymensingh. There were philosophical concepts also in these writings. Mr Ganguli responded disparagingly to these ideas. The communist leaders have understood that principles that are not established on a philosophical foundation are useless and doubtful. An all-around development of society is possible only if it is based on well-thought-out and well-organized ideology. The youth in India today lack this kind of intellectual rigour.

When I came back to Calcutta, I summoned my workers from all the districts. Most of them were in favour of an aggressive approach. The problem we faced was that on the one hand, the government had started arresting us and sending us off to jail without so much as a trial, and on the other hand, the leaders of the Anushilan Samiti did not want us to undertake any programme that revealed our revolutionary sentiments to the public. I believed that it was imperative at this stage to promote good literature about the revolutionary movement in a structured and organized manner amongst the public. I also believed that we would soon have to work on the idea of looting government property instead of approaching rich foreigners for our funds. Needless to say, the other leaders of the Samiti did not agree with me, but I started planning a course of action independently.

According to the decision taken in Mymensingh, the older workers of the Anushilan Samiti had introduced me to the members of their teams. I also started meeting leaders of other revolutionary groups independently. Consequently, I met senior members of a group from Chittagong. Suryakant Sen was their leader. This group was a branch of the Anushilan Samiti that had outgrown the policy of the Samiti and separated from it. Their beliefs were the same as mine. After speaking to a couple of trusted members of this group, I had a feeling that I would get along with them. Eventually, I had many conversations with Mr Sen's men. Some people from other groups in Calcutta had also started working with the Chittagong group and I spoke to them as well.

As a result of all these conversations, the Chittagong revolutionaries met our group in North India. And when a bomb factory was discovered in Dakshineswar, a prominent member of our group, Rajendra Nath Lahiri, was also arrested. I wanted to include the other revolutionary units in Calcutta and create a huge group. In this context, I met many workers from other groups, and I decided that we would jointly distribute a series of pamphlets. I wanted to outline the manifesto of the revolutionary movement in the first pamphlet. I was constantly thinking of how best I could write the pamphlet to make it impressive. One day, I was at a friend's place, sitting with my friend's brother who was a professor of history at a college in Calcutta. He knew that I was a revolutionary. During our conversation, we spoke of violence and non-violence. In this context, the professor told me something interesting about the history of Ireland. In a book on English history written by Grant Robertson, he showed me a sentence: 'English statesmen have taught the Irish politicians that England can be bullied but not argued into justice and generosity.' I noted the title of the book, *England under the Hanoverians*, in my notebook. I had also studied the history of the Italian freedom struggle. There were many things in the history of Italy that pricked my conscience constantly. One day, I read an article by Lala Har Dayal. He had quoted lines from the Bible that I liked. I made a note of those sentences too. In those days, I was also reading Nietzsche. I liked tremendously one thing that he said: 'Chaos is necessary to the birth of a new star.' I noted this down as well. I was, as you can see, constantly thinking of what to write in my pamphlet. Even while reading, meeting people and travelling, that is all I thought about.

While I was in talks with workers of other revolutionary groups and working on publishing the pamphlet, I was also planning to secretly send workers to Japan, France and the United States of America. This was for two reasons. I was keen that our workers should go abroad and train scientifically in martial matters and also learn to set up factories to make bombs and ammunition. If we did not have the capability to manufacture arms and ammunition, it would not be possible to sustain a rebellion for very long. The other reason was that I wanted our people to reach out and establish contact with all Indian revolutionaries and their organizations abroad. I was also making plans to loot British property near Calcutta.

There were many jute factories near Calcutta which were managed by the British. They used to receive 8,000–10,000 rupees every week for the salary of their coolies. The security arrangements that had been made for this money were inadequate. We started to investigate the best way to get to these factories, whether to go by car or by train, where arrangements could be made for staying en route and how the money and the arms could be transported, maybe separately so as not to arouse the suspicion of the people or police. I researched every detail along with a couple of my trusted associates.

We also had in mind another simple task of extreme bravery. A member of our group worked in the railway mail van. We decided that we would stop the Bombay Mail and loot the insurance money. It would be easy for us find out, through our man in the mail van, where the money was kept. While pretending to resist, our man would give us the necessary signal. We were researching the logistics for this operation as well. Meanwhile, the older leaders of the Anushilan Samiti had started to vehemently oppose our plans. I became even more adamant in response to their attitude. As a result of this confrontation, another secret meeting was held in Berhampur shortly after Mr Pratul Ganguli's arrest. Senior leaders like Mr Narendra Nath Sen and Ramesh Chandra Acharya were present in the meeting.

The police are very vigilant at the Howrah and Sealdah stations of Calcutta, and even at the small stations in between and nearby. I had to avoid detection and reach Berhampur. By then, I was suspicious that the police had begun an intensive hunt for me in Calcutta. However, I will not give a detailed account here of how I managed to get out of Calcutta and safely made my way back. I came back from Berhampur and plunged again into my projects.

I have mentioned earlier my companion Mr Jitendra Mukherjee's younger brother, Dhirendra Mukherjee. I was constantly trying to get him to join my group. The reason I was spending so much time on trying to recruit Dhirendra, despite having so many workers already, was that Dhirendra was a very bright scholar and student of science. There were very few amongst us who were self-sacrificing and brave as well as intelligent, educated and knowledgeable about science. If I could bring Dhirendra into the revolutionary group, we would have a person who was an amalgamation of all these qualities. Second, he was somebody we knew. When we met in Allahabad, he had expressed his desire to get into politics. The entire police force of the British empire was looking for me at the time. In such a scenario, the fact that Dhirendra was not averse to my contact spoke volumes of his character. I believed that a man like him was bound to succeed in any task he devoted himself to. And that is why I kept going back to him again and again, in the hope of recruiting him to our group.

Like many others, Dhirendra too believed that there were no intelligent and thinking people amongst the revolutionaries. He was of the opinion that some brave but thoughtless young men, having lost their way, had merely taken to terrorism in a disorganized manner; in reality, there was no real impulse or organized effort to rebel against the British Empire. Even after the publication of several books, including *Bandi Jeevan: A Life in Chains*, the general public was not very aware of the scale and intensity of our work against the government. However, Dhirendra also eventually realized how mistaken he was in thinking that the revolutionary movement was just a child's game. But his fascination for Gandhi's principles prevented him from joining our group. If some day after a lot of debate and discussion, I would find him a bit flexible, the very next day it was the same logic and argument once again. Dhirendra constantly insisted that a mass movement could only be based on a policy of ahimsa like Mahatma Gandhi's. I could not comprehend, despite his many explanations, the need to stress the principle of ahimsa so much.

According to Mahatma Gandhi, it is not true that the

victory of non-violence over violence in personal life, achieved through strife, sacrifice and devotion, could be replicated at a mass level. This was the reason we could not use ahimsa in politics as an ideological base. This did not mean, however, that we were equipped to carry out a mass movement based on violence; we did not have the necessary supply of arms and we would soon be forced to turn the movement to a path that does not require weapons. To return to the concept of ahimsa, Mahatma Gandhi wishes to make his life significant by gifting this 'religion' to the world. The question of India's freedom has lost value next to the promotion of this new religion of ahimsa. But it is only fair to ask how Mahatma Gandhi had followed the principle of ahimsa when he had contributed money and manpower to the British during the World War.

For a revolutionary like me, ahimsa is akin to an able doctor operating on his patient to cure him. That is not violence. It is not violence when a revolutionary who wishes to serve his country with a true heart and for the betterment of his fellow beings plans an armed revolt. The question of violence and non-violence does not determine whether the armed revolution is morally right or wrong. In Indian philosophy, when a person has transcended attachment, violence for them *is* attachment. A person who is truly detached and whose purpose in life is to serve humanity is also part of society. We must always ask which aims are propitious to the well-being of humankind; it is a question that deserves to be asked. Violence and non-violence have nothing to do with this question. The concepts of human welfare and suffering are not related to them. Therefore, if we choose a path that deals out certain forms of punishment for the betterment of society, then we are not violent. A country or a society can be governed properly only when we use modes of punishment to establish rules as and when necessary. It would not be right to infer from this that the punishers believe strife is preferable to peace. Everyone in the world wants peace. But this peace is possible only when human behaviour is just. A selfish mind is the root of all problems. As long as this self-centredness exists, there will be no peace. Therefore, only preaching ahimsa without changing basic human nature cannot bring peace into the world. Till we do not mature spiritually, peace is not possible in the world.

There have been massive revolutions in Korea, China, Greece, Ireland and Russia. Unlike in India, they did not have a needless debate on violence and non-violence. To stress unduly on the principle of ahimsa for the success of a mass movement seems to be a sign of cowardice. I kept up my debate with Dhirendra, and in the end, he offered to become a part of our group. Preparations for his trip to America began. I had sensed that Dhirendra was still hesitant to participate in the revolutionary movement in India. I think he felt that by doing so he wouldn't achieve much and would unnecessarily find himself punished. Going abroad, on the contrary, seems hopeful and romantic. It signals a certain kind of success. I was hoping that this temptation would entice Dhirendra to join us, and my hope was fulfilled.

Today, the very same Dhirendra Nath Mukherjee, once a staunch follower of Gandhi, is an atheist and a zealous communist. I have spoken so much about Dhirendra for a special reason.

For his voyage to America, arrangements had been made for him to work as a 'boy' on the ship. The day of departure was decided. With great difficulty, I had managed to raise 500 rupees and gave them to him. As the date approached, I noticed that Dhirendra became sadder. One day, I found a petrified Dhirendra standing next to me. He told me that he had gone to the exchange office to convert the rupees into dollars, and when he got off the tram, he realized that his pocket had been picked.

I felt disappointed, angry and disgusted. What should I say and what should I not say? Should I scream at him, curse him, beat him or just shake him? I could only stare at him. Thankfully, by the grace of God, I got a hold on myself. Quietly and calmly, I told him, 'Never mind. If you are still interested in going, I will arrange the money again. What has gone, is gone. But you should be more responsible and not keep such a large sum so carelessly in a pocket.' The latest studies in psychology say that a man's behaviour is strange when he is besieged by doubts. Had Dhirendra joined us with a clear conscience and put his heart into the work, he would not have been so careless with this money.

NOTES

1. Haldane, J.S., *Materialism*, Hodder and Stoughton, 1932, p. 39.
2. Carrel, Alexis, *Man, the Unknown*, 1935.
3. Russell, Bertrand, 'Introduction', in Friedrich Albert Lange, *The History of Materialism*, Kegan Paul, Trench, Trubner & Co Ltd, 1925.
4. Rashbehari Bose
5. Sir Reginald Craddock
6. I would like to clarify a couple of things about the police here. The statement about the police fabricating stories and myths to construct a case and embroil innocent people in them is true. Among those who were tried for the Kashi Conspiracy and sentenced, many were innocent. I know of many political cases in which the accused were innocent. Sushil Lahidi was hanged to death in the Lucknow political killing case, but he was not guilty according to many people.
7. In 1907, Khagendra Chandradas, Pandurang Khankhoje, Taraknath Das, Adharchandra Lasgar and other Indian students established the Bhartiya Swatantrata Sangh in California, America. The headquarters of the Sangh was set up in Portland in 1908. Lala Har Dayal and Bhai Parmanand came to California in 1913. That is when the organization was renamed as the 'Ghadar' party. In 1916, the Ghadar Party bought two plots of land in San Francisco, USA, for its offices which were constructed there. On 22 January 1917, the Ghadar Party was officially constituted. Members of the party came to India regularly to participate in the Indian independence movement.
8. Kartar Singh Saraba, at 19, was the youngest in age amongst the revolutionaries of the mutiny. He was born on 24 May 1896 in Saraba, Ludhiana, to Mangal Singh and Sahib Kaur. In 1912, he went to study in America. There, he met Lala Har Dayal who was in the process of forming the Ghadar Party. The Party published a newspaper called *Ghadar* on 1 November 1913. He came back to India in 1914 to participate in the revolutionary movement for India's freedom and was recruited by Shree Sachindra Nath Sanyal and Rashbehari Bose who were banding together youngsters for the Punjab chapter of an armed uprising. Kartar Singh

worked with all his heart and soul for the rebellion, but, unfortunately, the plan failed, and a cavalryman who was an informant, Ganda Singh, had him deceitfully arrested on 18 March 1915 in Sargodha. On 26 April 1915, the case against him for treason began, and on 13 September 1915, he was sentenced to death. This martyr was hanged on 16 November 1915 in Lahore jail. Bhagat Singh was particularly inspired by the example of Kartar Singh Saraba and always carried a picture of the young revolutionary in his pocket.

9. S.N. Banerjee was a senior leader of the Indian National Congress and an early nationalist. Although he is usually placed in the 'moderate' faction of the party, he was sympathetic to some of the demands of the 'extremist' faction and of the revolutionaries.
10. Referring to Rashbehari Bose. In Bengali, the elder brother is respectfully called dada. The suffix 'Da' is the shorter form of that. This is added to the abbreviated name 'Rashu'.
11. This relates to the 1915 uprising, which has been discussed later.
12 This refers to Sanyal's organization.
13 A large multi-component cluster of castes, kin bodies and local groups, sharing social status and ideology of genealogical descent originating from the Indian subcontinent. The term 'Rajput' covers various patrilineal clans historically associated with warriorhood.
14. His full name was Vishnu Ganesh Pingle. He was born in 1888, in the mountainous region of Pune, to a poor family. He went to the USA to study engineering after finishing school in Pune. There he came in contact with the Ghadar Party and became a revolutionary. He joined Rashbehari Bose and Sachindra Nath Sanyal for an armed revolution in 1914 after he came back to India. He was attached to the Punjab revolutionary organization because he spoke good Punjabi. When he was later given charge of the Meerut cantonment in Uttar Pradesh, he shifted to Meerut from Banaras. Once, he transported 10 powerful bombs into the city with an associate, a sergeant in the British Army named Nadar Khan. Khan betrayed him, and Pingle was arrested the moment they reached Meerut on 23 March 1915. He was charged with sedition on 26 April 1915 and sentenced to death on 13 September 1915. He was hanged in Lahore jail on 16 November 1915.
15. Madr is the name of an ancient region and its inhabitants, located in the northwest of the Indian subcontinent. The kingdom's boundaries are believed to have extended from portions of the Hindu Kush (possibly as far as northeastern Iran) to the present-day Punjab and Haryana provinces of India.

16. Khalsa refers to both a community that considers Sikhism as its faith, as well as a special group of initiated Sikhs.
17. Thakur is a historical feudal title of the Indian subcontinent. It is also used as a surname in the present times.
18. Prabhu Jagadbandhu was a Hindu saint of Bengal who belonged to the Pancha Tattva tradition of Vaishnavism. He spent much of his life meditating and preaching in the Sri Angan ashram in Faridpur, British India (present-day Bangladesh).
19. A deputy superintendent of the secret police had got 'Kripal Singh' to join the revolutionary group to spy on them. A cousin of Kripal Singh's was a soldier in the British Army and a member of the revolutionary group. He did not know that Kripal Singh was a spy for the secret police. Kripal Singh would pass on the information obtained from his cousin to the secret police. It was he who informed the police about the change in the date for the revolt. As a result, the revolution failed. Baba Harnam Singh, a member of the Ghadar Party, and two of his companions, Lala Ramsaran Das and Amar Singh, had planned to assassinate the traitor, but their plan failed.

    The snitch Kripal Singh had police protection and was saved. In 1931, one day while he was asleep at home he was killed by unknown assailants; till date we do not know who these bravehearts were.
20. The name 'Chandannagar' has also been used in the original.
21. Thakur Keshari Singh claimed that the bomb aimed at Lord Harding on 23 December 1912 in Chandni Chowk was thrown not by Basant Kumar but by Thakur Jorawar Singh.
22. He was later released in July 1919 but the warrant for his brother continues to be in force.
23. In 1720, a saint by the name of Wali Ulla Khan appeared in Delhi. He was philosophical and political. He wrote many books on Muslim philosophy and his writings are taught even today in many Muslim countries. He was a savant in Arabic, Persian and Urdu. His book *Hujjat-ul-Baaliga*, written in Arabic, is famous the world over for establishing social, economic and political norms. He inspired people to strive for their morals and principles. His son Abdul Azeez succeeded him after his death. Slowly, his organization turned into a military one.

    This military organization confronted Maharaja Ranjit Singh of Punjab, who was a strong supporter of the British. A disciple of Shah Abdul Azeez, Sayyed Ahmed Barelavi, managed to reach Afghanistan via Karachi with thousands of his companions. From the Peshawar frontier, they fought the forces of Raja Ranjit Singh. They were helped by Pathans settled across the border, but unfortunately Sayyed Ahmed was not successful. He was martyred in 1831, fighting the Sikh forces. His companions who survived settled there and intermittently engaged the British forces in battle ever since.

In 1857, they made immense contributions to the fight for independence from British rule. They went to Mecca after the failure of the revolution to avoid persecution by the British. They opened many madrasas, wherever they went. The madrasa in Saharanpur, Uttar Pradesh, is famous throughout the world. The first principal of this school had participated in the revolution of 1857. The followers of Shah Abdul Azeez continuously fought the British at the Afghanistan border. Many Muslims sacrificed their lives fighting the Raj in 1860, 1862 and 1865.

24. In Hinduism, Satya Yuga is the first of the four Yugas, the 'Yuga (Age or Era) of Truth', during which humanity is governed by the gods, every manifestation or work is close to the purest ideal and human beings allow their intrinsic goodness to rule supreme. It is sometimes referred to as the 'Golden Age'.

25. Rashbehari Bose left India on 12 May 1915. He travelled on a Japanese ship under the name of P.N. Tagore because the poet Rabindranath Tagore was to travel to Japan soon. Rashbehari fooled the British government into believing that he was a relative of Tagore's and was going to Japan to make arrangements for his trip. The government had announced a reward of one lakh rupees for his capture. Had he been captured, he was sure to be hanged. When the government got wind of Rashbehari's presence in Japan, it tried to pressurize the Japanese government into handing him over. The Japanese agreed. Rashbehari immediately went into hiding, and had to stay underground for even longer than he was in India. Later, with help from Japanese friends, he managed to get citizenship in Japan. His friends in Japan provided extraordinary help and support.

    Rashbehari reappeared on the revolutionary scene during the Second World War. As soon as the Japanese declared war on the British, Rashbehari set up an organization of Indians living in Japan and once again started working for India's independence. He set up the Azad Hind Fauj and handed over its reins to Subhas Chandra Bose when the latter came to Japan. Rashbehari died in January 1945 in Tokyo.

26. The Dhaka Anushilan Samiti was a branch of the Anushilan Samiti founded in the city of Dhaka in November 1905. Initially a group of 80 under the leadership of Pulin Behari Das, it 'spread like wildfire' throughout the province of East Bengal. More than 500 branches were opened, linked by a 'close and detailed organization' to Pulin's headquarters at Dhaka. It

absorbed smaller groups in the province and soon overshadowed its parent organization in Calcutta. Estimates of Dhaka Anushilan Samiti's reach show a membership of between 15,000 and 20,000 members.

27. Her name is Agnes Smedley. Her articles are regularly published in Indian magazines.
28. This traitor was probably Kumud Nath Mukherjee. The Indians abroad had sent financial aid for the revolutionaries in Calcutta through the German counsel, but Mukherjee got greedy. He ate up the money and snitched to the British government about the plans for the revolt.
29. A saheb of high status/rank, a very important and imposing personage. '*Laat*' may be an Indian corruption of 'Lord'; the phrase was most often used for Englishmen.
30. It is mentioned in the foreword that he passed away in the mental asylum in Berhampur.
31. The mahant of Nimej was assassinated in 1913. It is mentioned in the Bihar–Orissa chapter (Chapter 8) of the Rowlatt Committee Report.
32. Some excerpts of this chapter have been taken from Nalin Babu's *Viplavvaad*, an article by Gopendra Lal published in *Aatmshakti* and Nalin Vukich's story published in *Shankh*.
33. A Sanskrit astrological treatise attributed in its introduction to Maharishi Bhrigu, one of the seven sages of the Vedic period, but likely compiled in a later period by a descendant of the same lineage.
34. Ullaskar Dutta (16 April 1885–17 May 1965) was an Indian revolutionary associated with the Dhaka Anushilan Samiti and the *Jugantar.*
35. The ritual of Upanayan or the sacred thread ceremony is performed after a Hindu boy turns seven years old. The ritual symbolizes the end of an era in a child's life and the initiation into that of a student.
36. This was the original revolutionary network set up by Aurobindo Ghosh and his brother Barin c. 1905. It was a network of akhadas or quasi-religious gymnasiums.
37. Now called Azad Park, located behind the Town Hall in Chandni Chowk.
38. This law allowed arrest on mere suspicion and did not require authorities bring the matter to trial.
39. The month of the Hindu calendar that corresponds to April/May in the Gregorian Calendar.

INDEX

www.ingramcontent.com/pod-product-compliance
Lightning Source LLC
Chambersburg PA
CBHW030906070526
44654CB00030B/389/J
9789357025638